The Gardens and Parks at Hampton Court Palace

The Gardens and Parks at Hampton Court Palace

Todd Longstaffe-Gowan

Photographs by Vivian Russell

Frances Lincoln Ltd
4 Torriano Mews
Torriano Avenue
London NW5 2RZ
www.franceslincoln.com

Set in Adobe Caslon and GillSans

Printed and bound in Singapore by Tien Wah Press

First Frances Lincoln edition 2005

Dedication
To the gardeners of Hampton Court past and present

Contents

Preface

A great many writings from the sixteenth century onwards
have described the parks and gardens at Hampton Court Palace.
The aim of these accounts – whether in the form of pocket
companions, diary entries, topographical surveys or gazetteers –
has been to proclaim the virtues or condemn the deficiencies of the
setting of a palace so immense and so varied as to appear, as the
topographer William Howitt remarked in 1882, 'like a little town
in its extent'.

Few British landscapes are so rich in historic associations,
or have been so celebrated, so visited and the subject of so many
panegyrics as Hampton Court; fewer still retain attractions so
uncommon and yet so varied and numerous – from ranges
of humble Tudor courtyards to miles of grand and venerable
avenues – which chart comprehensively almost five centuries
of landscape change.

Although a royal demesne, Hampton Court was only a royal
residence for two centuries (1528–1737); for much of its long life
it has served as a residence for courtiers and grace-and-favour
inhabitants and their scores of retainers, and latterly as a public
garden. Therefore, while significant landscape changes were made
by a handful of improving monarchs, much of what we see today
has been wrought by a more diverse cast of characters – from
Knights Hospitallers and a prince of the church to royal gardeners,
rangers, keepers, surveyors and garden superintendents.

The impulse for improvement has also been determined by
changing circumstances: whereas in the early sixteenth century
Hampton Court was fashioned as a country house for sumptuous
private displays of regal hospitality, by the mid-eighteenth century
it had assumed the guise of a stately asylum for decayed gentlefolk
– people with little means but courtly pretensions; and by the
mid-nineteenth century large parts of the estate had been opened
to the public, serving annually a constituency of several hundred
thousand excursionists. The embellishments made by and for the
royals and their courtiers, the grace-and-favour inhabitants and
the day-trippers can still be seen today.

The common perception of the royal estate since it was
opened to the public in the early nineteenth century has been that
it is a curious relic of a bygone age; it has also been portrayed as
a landscape in gentle decline – as Nathan Cole remarked in *The
Royal Parks and Gardens of London* (1876): what was originally
beautiful was now picturesque, and the 'specimens of ancient
gardening' at the palace were esteemed by those with a taste for
'natural scenery' as 'remains of antiquity'. While Hampton Court
has an extensive and remarkable legacy of historic fabric, the
landscape over the last two centuries has nonetheless undergone
numerous dramatic reorderings and has fostered and indeed
initiated a range of new and bold gardening traditions, such as
herbaceous flower gardening and carpet bedding. These and other
innovations continue to this day as the palace repairs and enhances
its setting for the benefit of the one million visitors who pass
through its gates annually.

This book – the first official guide to the parks and gardens
in several decades – purports neither to be a complete history of
the royal landscape, nor a royal biography. This is a handbook –
in the traditional sense – and my narrative is intended above all
to consider the reception of Hampton Court over the centuries:
to acquaint the reader with a range of curious and sometimes
contradictory accounts of the royal estate, written by those who
viewed it and reflected upon it. The introduction sets the stage and
presents a concise chronological survey of the royal estate.
Subsequent chapters deal with distinctive areas of the parks and
gardens – such as the Privy and Pond Gardens, the courts and the
Wilderness: here, too, the material is presented in a roughly
chronological format, although greater attention is paid to factors
and features which have played an important part in defining the
distinctive character of the areas in question. The book concludes
with a discussion of the influence that Hampton Court has exerted
on landscapes beyond its own pale.

Many persons have kindly offered observations and
information during the course of compiling this book, including
Brian Allen, John Fisher, Eileen Harris, John Harris, Annie
Heron, Malcolm Holmes, Edward Impey, Geraldine Kenny, Tim
Knox, Marcus Köhler, Amy Meyers, Sarah Randall, Lord
Rothschild, Frank Salmon, David Souden, Bill Swan, Liz Whittle,
Sally Williams and Giles Worsley. I have benefited immensely
from access to a range of unpublished research: reports compiled
over the past two decades by Land Use Consultants and Elizabeth
Banks Associates, and scholarly histories of diverse aspects of the
landscape by Graham Dillamore (Palace Gardens Operations
Manager), Marylla Hunt, David Jacques, David Lambert,

Jan Woudstra and Tom Wright. Paul Christianson has been unfailingly generous in reading extracts of the text – specifically as they relate to the early gardens – and has made many useful and constructive comments; our mutual enthusiasm for the subject has been invigorated by Jonathan Foyle's ground-breaking work on the development of Wolsey's palace and its surroundings. Brent Elliot generously shared the contents of his Hampton Court file cards – an impressive bibliography of articles published in the nineteenth-century horticultural press relating to the palace gardens.

I owe a debt of gratitude to a variety of persons at Historic Royal Palaces (HRP): Susanne Groom (Curator of Collections) supplied me with transcripts of the fruits of her detailed and protracted research into the palace's rich collection of garden statuary and ornament; Clare Murphy (Publications Manager) helped me with picture research, painstakingly edited my text, and provided advice and assistance during all stages of the book's development; and Anne Young (Retail Business Development Manager) showed unruffled skill and tact in dealing with various matters and authorities which at times conspired to distract me from enjoying the process of compiling my narrative. Anthony Boulding (Palace Gardens Horticultural Manager) and Martin Einchcomb (Palace Glasshouse Nursery Supervisor) have supplied valuable information on plant cultivation at the palace.

A generous grant from the Paul Mellon Centre for Studies in British Art enabled me to research at first hand in St Petersburg, John Spyers's extraordinary late eighteenth-century topographical record of the Hampton Court estate. Catherine Phillips proved an amusing and invaluable agent in all matters pertaining to my Russian excursion. John Phibbs encouraged me to travel to St Petersburg, and his informed insights into Spyers's and 'Capability' Brown's work and their working practices have been enormously helpful in interpreting the views in the Hermitage albums.

It would have been unthinkable to have considered writing this book without the full co-operation and assistance of Simon Thurley (former Curator of Historic Royal Palaces), who very generously made available his draft manuscript of his book *Hampton Court: A Social and Architectural History* (2003) – and who entrusted me with dozens of box files brimming with material on every aspect of the estate's development compiled by Esther Godfrey, Anna Keay, Daphne Ford and others at Historic Royal Palaces.

Anne Fraser, Michael Brunström, John Nicoll and Jo Christian at Frances Lincoln have always shown keen support for this project. Many lively and informal conversations with Chloe Chard, and a series of regular 'tutorials', have clarified in my mind a range of matters relating to the content of the book and its presentation. Mette Heinz skilfully designed the book and Judith Menes compiled the index.

Vivian Russell – who is both a photographer and a writer – has been a most sympathetic collaborator. She has scoured the estate with an informed eye and has produced an excellent record – possibly the most comprehensive visual survey undertaken since the late eighteenth century.

Finally, I extend my deepest gratitude to Terry Gough – Gardens and Estate Manager at Hampton Court. Our collaboration began in 1995 with my appointment as Gardens Adviser, when he and his team of thirty-eight gardeners and a rash of external consultants were in the throes of restoring the Privy Garden. This project launched the palace's 'Landscape Conservation Management Plan' – a document which outlines a framework for future care and restoration of the historic estate. Terry has been at the forefront of this initiative and continues to implement its aims and objectives; he blithely takes on these responsibilities and those of the day-to-day running of the gardens with dignity and gusto. That Terry is able to carry out such work is largely due to the fact that Hampton Court – very unusually – retains its own directly employed labour force: this ensures that there is the continuity of skill and experience to undertake specialist work in such an outstanding setting.

Over the past twelve years Terry has been at the helm of dozens of garden projects – from the replanting of the Cross Avenue in the Home Park and the avenues in the Great Fountain Garden to the temporary display of floral arrangements in the palace's state apartments. None, however, has he championed more vigorously than the re-display of Queen Mary's late seventeenth-century collection of tender exotic plants and citrus trees in the Glass Case Garden. He, like 'that excellent Princess', is obsessed with this 'innocent diversion' and nurtures the hope that some day the palace will once again boast the finest collection of 'curious Exoticks' in England.

Introduction

Hampton Court is a site of great antiquity. Archaeological remains suggest that there were settlements in the park from at least the Early Bronze Age (2200–1200 BC) and that the Romans and later the Saxons cultivated and grazed the land. The estate began to take its present shape some time after the Norman Conquest when the Manor of Hampton was granted to Walter St Valery in c.1086, and the demesne – or what now comprises the Home Park, Bushy Park and the palace and its gardens – was established at roughly 2,000 acres. By the mid-twelfth century the Knights Hospitallers of St John of Jerusalem became established at Hampton and by 1338 their Surrey estate had become one of the largest and best appointed Hospitaller manors in England. It was about this time, too, that Hampton Court began to assume its role as a guesthouse and a place of hospitality.

On Midsummer Day in 1514 the manor of Hampton Court was leased by the prior, Sir Thomas Docwra, and his brethren Knights Hospitallers to the Most Reverend Father in God Thomas Wolsey, Archbishop of York, for a term of ninety-nine years. The lease describes the presence of a small manor house on the site of the present palace. This brick-built, moated courtyard house had been raised by Lord Daubeney between 1495 and 1500, who had leased the property from the Knights Hospitallers from 1494. The new house faced the river and stood in the midst of extensive pastureland. The estate also boasted a large rabbit warren.

Cardinal Wolsey was an energetic improver and in the course of fourteen years he overhauled the manor house and its setting, and transformed it into one of the greatest episcopal, archiepiscopal and conventual establishments of the age – a setting worthy of a prince of the church and the reception of royalty and foreign dignitaries. Wolsey's interest in gardening appears to have played an important role in determining the redevelopment of the house, and his improvements established the basis for the future development of the estate: the principal land access to the house was changed from the south to the west and a great court (Base Court) was built west of the early house. The westward thrust of the new development freed up the area south of the house for the creation of gardens between the mansion and the Thames. Wolsey's most important garden innovation was the erection of a 'long gallery' on the south side of the mansion; the gallery was glazed on both sides – giving views to the south over what is now known as the Pond Gardens and the Privy Garden, and to the north over what was at the time a knot garden (now Clock and Fountain Courts). Wolsey also made other lasting improvements to the estate: fishponds were dug south of the house (the present-day Pond Gardens), a Privy (private) Orchard was planted north of the mansion (the site of the present nursery), and Home and Bushy Parks were enclosed with timber pales to form hunting parks.

The Royal Demesne

In 1528 Wolsey fell from royal favour and was forced by Henry VIII to vacate Hampton Court. Thus began two centuries of almost continuous royal occupation of the palace and estate, during which time various sovereigns would leave their mark. As soon as the King had requisitioned the estate he embarked upon twenty years of royal building on a scale never to be repeated in the history of the Crown.

The royal kitchens were rebuilt and extended, Wolsey's chapel was recast and new suites of royal lodgings, the Great Hall and the Tennis Court were also raised. Much of the extension of the palace took place through the addition of new courtyards, some of which were gardens: Cloister Green Court (now Fountain Court) was built to provide royal lodgings and to complete the eastern flank of the palace, Outer Green Court (now the West Front) was raised west of Wolsey's Base Court to form a magnificent forecourt; Chapel Court was enclosed and the Privy Garden, the Mount Garden and the Pond Gardens – which at the time were also considered courtyards – were formed on the south side of the house. Further landscape improvements took place beyond the immediate surroundings of the palace – a tiltyard for jousting was built north of Outer Green Court and the King's Great Orchard was formed north of the Privy Orchard. Henry VIII also replaced Wolsey's park pales with brick walls, subdivided the parks into divisions for different sports, stocked them with deer, pheasant and partridge, and developed a large hare warren in Bushy Park.

The model for the King's gardens was the fifteenth-century court of the Dukes of Burgundy, where the garden was 'cultivated as part of the life and symbolic pageantry of the late medieval

Introduction **9**

2. Bird's-eye view of the
Great Fountain Garden
and the Long Water in
Home Park.

3. *Charles II Leaving Hampton Court*, English School, seventeenth century. This painted view shows the East Front of the palace before the Great Fountain was created in the late seventeenth century.

palace-castle and as a symbol of political power'. Under Henry VIII the gardens at Hampton Court became 'an essential attribute of the palace-castle of the reigning dynasty'.[1] The pleasure gardens were seen to pertain to the King and to the court as outward signs of regal magnificence.

After the death of Henry VIII in 1547 Hampton Court appears to have remained the royal house of choice for entertainment. There is, nevertheless, little evidence to suggest what use Edward VI and Mary I made of the palace. Although ostensibly fond of gardening, Elizabeth I left few records to indicate the level of her direct involvement at Hampton Court; one notable exception is a splendid fountain built in Clock Court. The Queen had an 'ardent love of stag-hunting' and she often shared in the sports provided for the entertainment of her guests at Hampton Court. It is presumed that during her reign a great

many oak trees were planted in the parks, very few of which remain today (fig. 1).

James I, like Elizabeth, was fond of hunting: it was, in his view, essential to his royal dignity to maintain the noble sport. He made numerous improvements to the parks, including erecting a new pale in Bushy Park and stables at the royal stud. The King also had an interest in the medicinal properties of plants and formed an apothecary garden adjacent to the Privy Garden.

Like his precursors, Charles I enjoyed the pleasures of the chase and was determined to enlarge the park. In this aim he was frustrated by landowners who obstinately refused to part with their lands. He did, however, succeed in forming a long artificial river – the Longford – to supply water for the purposes of decorative display in the palace gardens and parks. The river flows to this day, remains the property of the Crown and is maintained by the Royal Parks Agency.

4. Leonard Knyff's view
of Hampton Court
from the south, c.1702.

After the execution of Charles I in 1649, Parliament at once made preparations to dismantle the royal estate: it was decreed that Hampton Court should be surveyed, valued and sold for the benefit of the Commonwealth. Parliament, however, showed bewildering vacillation in deciding the fate of the estate and in the event it was not sold but given in 1653 to Lord Protector Cromwell, who used it occasionally as an out-of-town residence until his death in 1658. The Commonwealth years have usually been portrayed as destructive for Hampton Court: large numbers of ancient parkland trees were in fact felled and sold for timber; Cromwell himself, however, may be credited with recasting the Privy Garden in the 'modern taste' and admitting statuary plundered from Whitehall, St James's Palace and Somerset House into the palace grounds.

Charles II had an informed interest in garden planning, which he developed during his exile in France and refined through his close friendship with John Evelyn.[2] His zestful patronage transformed the parks and gardens at Hampton Court. The garden writer Stephen Switzer remarked in *The Nobleman, Gentleman, and Gardener's Recreation* (1715) that during his reign the King laid the 'preliminary Foundations of Gardening', and under his enlightened stewardship 'planting began again to raise its dejected Head'.[3] He was fortunate to have André Mollet at his side – a gifted garden planner who came from a long and distinguished family of French royal gardeners – whom he appointed 'Master of His Majesty of England's Gardens'.

Charles embellished the Home Park with a long, broad canal flanked by double rows of lime trees (fig. 2). This regal gesture was contrived to thrust the east–west axis of the palace beyond Fountain Court and paved the way for future improvements to the East Front – the most notable of which was the Balcony Garden below the Queen's lodgings, which was subsequently expanded and formalized by William and Mary to create the Great Fountain Garden. Changes were also made to the Mount and Privy Gardens, and a vineyard was planted on the Thames foreshore. On the north side of the palace the King laid out the area known as the Wilderness, which contained four mazes – the largest of which survives, and is the most enduringly popular and celebrated feature of the royal gardens. Charles's love of physical exercise also galvanized a range of changes to the layout of the parks.

The next significant round of improvements to the royal estate took place under William III and Mary II. Switzer informs us that this royal couple made Hampton Court their chief summer residence, and that during their reign they raised gardening to 'its highest Meridian' (fig. 4).[4] The King took every opportunity 'in the least Interval of Ease' to garden, and he and the Queen possessed a great enthusiasm and informed judgement in all matters pertaining to gardening and landscape planning. Like their predecessors, they benefited from the advice of a cast of distinguished nurserymen, designers and garden builders from England and abroad: the nurserymen John Rose and George London were called upon to assist with remodelling and building the parks and gardens; the architects Sir Christopher Wren, Nicholas Hawksmoor and William Talman were involved in landscape planning; the Dutch gardeners Hendrick Quellingburgh, Samuel van Staden, Casper Gamperle and Hendrick Floris assisted with the management of the gardens and the Queen's collection of exotic plants; and William Bentinck – William's principal adviser for the construction of his Dutch gardens – was appointed Superintendent of the Royal Gardens.

Between 1689 and 1702 the Privy Garden and the Tiltyard were recast 'with great dispatch'; the Lower Wilderness and the Great Terrace (now the Pavilion Terrace) and the Bowling Green were laid out (fig. 5); the Mount Garden was levelled, the Banqueting House built, the West Front was reconfigured and Queen Mary's botanical collection was formed. The sovereigns' greatest contribution to the layout of Hampton Court was the rebuilding of the East Front of the palace and its associated landscape embellishments, including the Great Fountain Garden and the Broad Walk – features which still dominate the palace gardens. Three long avenues were planted in Home Park and stately lime-tree groves and a quadruple lime and chestnut avenue were projected in Bushy Park, north of the palace. By the close of William's reign in 1702 the royal estate had taken on the basic layout that it still possesses today.

Upon her accession to the throne, Queen Anne – 'whose love to Gard'ning was not a little'[5] – announced her intention to restrain the expense of the gardens. She nonetheless undertook some improvements of her own. There also ensued a shake-up in the Royal Gardens Administration: various senior officers were

dismissed, with the exception of George London. He, too, however, soon fell from favour and was replaced by his former business associate Henry Wise. Wise had been Superintendent of the Royal Gardens since *c.*1689 and had been London's sole partner at their Brompton nursery. Among Wise's first duties was to prepare a 'Scheme of Her Majestys Severall Gardens and Plantacions' to guide the future management of the estate.

The effect of Queen Anne's refurbishment of the Great Fountain Garden can still be seen today: the yews which she planted in 1707 have become topiary giants and are among the greatest horticultural curiosities at Hampton Court (fig. 8); and the north and south canals she had dug continue to flow on either side of the garden. The Queen also established a network of 'chaise ridings' in Home Park and laid out the round basin and its attendant figure of Arethusa in the centre of the Chestnut Avenue in Bushy Park. When the Queen died in 1714, her improvements to the north approach to the palace were unfinished: only the piers of the Lion Gates in Hampton Court Road had been erected. These two projects were hastily completed in time for the first visit to the palace of her successor George I. While Queen Anne did not wish to lavish great sums on new building works, she was well disposed to keeping the gardens to a high standard – the marble statues were periodically cleaned, paths were mended, pots and tubs were repainted, evergreens were clipped, other plants were staked and the collection of exotic plants in the Pond Gardens was kept in good order.

There were few notable alterations to the gardens under George I and George II. Although the first George was reputed to like Hampton Court, he preferred to lavish money on his gardens at Herrenhausen in his native Germany. He did, nonetheless, maintain the gardens to a high standard, replant the Lower Wilderness in Home Park that had been damaged by flooding, and replace the decayed bower in the Privy Garden. George II enjoyed Hampton Court as a summer residence and Queen Caroline simplified the layout of the Privy Garden, replacing the *gazon coupé* with a garden of grass and evergreens.

After 1737, however, the court stopped visiting the palace on a regular basis. Henceforth the reigning sovereigns played an ever-diminishing role in the management and improvement of the parks and gardens, and the royal gardeners, palace administrators

and courtly lodgers were given greater latitude to indulge their own interests.

The End of the 'regal splendours of the Palace'
The accession to the throne of George III in October 1760 marked the end of what Ernest Law – author of the magisterial three-volume *History of Hampton Court Palace* (1890–1) – referred to as the 'regal splendours of the Palace'. Hampton Court ceased to be an inhabited royal residence and the whole building, with the exception of the state apartments, was apportioned into suites allotted by the grace and favour of the reigning monarch to private individuals.[6] Lodgings were conferred, almost invariably, in recognition of distinguished service rendered to the Crown and country by the husbands or near relatives of the recipients. It was observed in 1834 that the number of persons lodged in the palace – including servants – 'is not less than 700; but, judging by the deserted appearance of the place, it is difficult to believe that it can be the nest of so large a population'.[7]

During this period the palace suffered what Ernest Law described as a rash of 'reckless defacements of its ancient structure by additions and excrescences, to afford various offices . . . for the inhabitants'.[8] The gardens, too, are said to have suffered, though not from defacements, but neglect. In 1770 the Board of Works reprimanded the Royal Gardener, Lancelot 'Capability' Brown, for failing to keep the gardens in good order – a charge which he robustly denied, replying that it was his 'wish and intention' to keep the gardens 'better and to put them in better order than ever I saw them in'. Brown was appointed Royal Gardener at Hampton Court in 1764 and held the post until his death in 1783.

Dorothy Stroud asserts in *'Capability' Brown* (1984) that the Royal Gardener made 'few perceptible changes' to the landscape, although George III is said to have suggested that he should improve the formal layout.[9] New evidence suggests, however, that Brown exercised his characteristic playful ingenuity in maintaining and improving the royal landscape: while he retained many of the elements of the late seventeenth-century parks and gardens, he made several bold innovations. Brown's most lasting contribution to Hampton Court was the Great Vine which he planted in 1768, and which flourishes to this day (fig. 7).

6. (far left) Detail of
one of Jean Tijou's late
seventeenth-century
screens in the Privy
Garden.

7. (left) The Great
Vine was planted
by 'Capability' Brown
in 1768.

8. Yews planted in
1707 in the Great
Fountain Garden.

9. View of the East Front, published in William Henry Pyne's *History of the Royal Residences* (1818). Note the overgrown early eighteenth-century yews and the flowerbeds beneath their canopies.

10. (right) 'Holiday Group – Hampton Court Gardens', 1843.

11. (far right) 'Pleasure Vans – School Children's Hampton-Court Holiday', 1849.

Throughout George III's reign, Hampton Court continued to be a 'show place', to which excursions were frequently made by those interested in archaeology or the fine arts. Horace Walpole, for instance, who knew Hampton Court well, began to show an interest in the antiquarian aspects of the estate from the early 1760s. The antiquarian Daines Barrington referred to Hampton Court in a paper given to the Society of Antiquaries in 1782: he found much to admire in the gardens, including the 'elegant and most capitally executed' ironwork screens by Jean Tijou – at that time arranged along the Pavilion Terrace (fig. 6).[10]

According to Ernest Law, under George IV 'an air of stately desolateness' attached itself to the palace surroundings. The King depopulated the gardens of their statuary and his brother, the Duke of Clarence, felled hundreds of ancient trees in Bushy Park which had survived the vagaries of the Commonwealth, and put most of the park under the plough. John Loudon remarked in the *Gardener's Magazine* (1833) that the gardens were 'excellent of their kind', but it was to be regretted that they were

> not kept up, either with sufficient care in point of order and neatness, or due attention to their original form. The walks are harrowed, instead of being rolled, and look more like newly sown ridges of corn land in a gravelly soil, than walks. The flowers and shrubs are straggling and tawdry, neglected or badly pruned, and either overgrown or deformed. The fountains, too, are in bad order.[11]

'That Well-loved Resort of Cockneydom'

The character and management of the palace and its gardens changed dramatically in 1838 when Queen Victoria ordered that the palace 'should be thrown open to all her subjects without restriction, and without fee or gratuity of any kind'.

The monarch's act of queenly beneficence was not greeted with universal enthusiasm. Ernest Law reported that 'so great a change, we can well understand, was not carried out without the gloomiest forebodings on the part of many, as to the disastrous results, which they alleged would infallibly ensue'. Some declared that if the general public were admitted without restriction neither the palace nor its contents would be safe:

> Visions of an insulting rabble, such as that which invaded the Tuileries in the time of Louis XVI, marching through the State Apartments, tearing down the tapestries, wrecking the furniture, and carrying off the pictures, seemed to arise in the terrified imaginations of some; while there were others who, though taking a calmer view of the situation, yet affirmed that it would be impossible to safeguard the contents of the Palace from mischievous injury and depredation, without an army of warders and guardians.[12]

Giving up the palace 'to the use and refreshment of the people' had a considerable impact on Hampton Court's population of 'decayed nobles and court pensioners' who, according to Law, 'valued the seclusion and quiet of Hampton Court, and appreciated the immunity they had hitherto enjoyed from the more objectionable accompaniments, inseparable from crowds of noisy excursionists and trippers'. In *Little Dorrit* (1857), Charles Dickens paints a vivid picture of these 'venerable inhabitants of that venerable pile' as they appeared to the throngs of Victorian holiday-makers: they seemed, in those times, to be 'encamped there like a sort of civilised gypsies', and there was a 'temporary air about their establishments, as if they were going away the moment they could get anything better; there was also a dissatisfied air about themselves, as if they took it very ill that they had not already got something much better.'[13]

The commingling of the palace inmates and the crowds of 'trippers' resulted, inevitably, in some social friction and, indeed, social comedy. Law, however, assures us that what Hampton Court lost in repose and dignity it gained in cheerfulness; and that what was sacrificed by its popularization was compensated for by the greater interest taken in the palace, and the care devoted to it.[14]

As soon as the palace opened free to the public it became extremely popular as a holiday resort: visitor numbers shot up from scores in the late 1830s to hundreds of thousands in the 1850s. Hampton Court became, according to Anthony Trollope, 'that well-loved resort of Cockneydom' (figs 10, 11). The topographer John Fisher Murray remarked that the roads to the palace were 'crowded with numbers of holiday-makers on their delighted way to Hampton Court, emancipating themselves, their wives and children, for the day, from the contagion of the town, or the sensual gratifications of suburban pot-houses' to relax in the palace's refined surroundings; and William Howitt, writing in 1840, remarked that the palace was 'one of the bravest pleasures that a party of happy friends can promise themselves. Especially as it is

calculated to charm the thousands of pleasure-seekers from the dense and dusty vastness of London'.[15]

At thirteen miles from Central London, Hampton Court was considered a delightful day excursion – indeed, 'one of the prettiest excursions near London'.[16] The journey was, in fact, generally considered to be no less pleasurable than the ultimate destination: the routes to the palace were various, and all agreeably diversified. The tourist from town could travel by a great range of conveyances: steam launch, omnibus, van, charabanc, 'wagonette', cab, dog-cart, carriage – and, from 1849, by railway. Throughout the nineteenth century the greatest numbers of holiday-makers arrived in the height of summer, and primarily on Sundays.

The palace's so-called 'free Sundays' – whether dedicated to the seasonal displays of chestnut, rhododendron or daffodil – greatly inconvenienced the grace-and-favour inhabitants. This 'much dreaded "Continental Sunday"', moreover, galvanized 'the whole artillery of Puritan invective' of defenders of that fine old British institution, the British Sabbath. Sabbatarians such as the Rev. D. Wilson denounced Hampton Court on Sunday in *The Times* in 1852 as '*a hell on earth*; the people come intoxicated, and the scenes in these gardens on the Lord's day are beyond description'.[17] Such imputations were generally denied in the popular press, which praised the 'good and quiet behaviour of the multitude'. Ernest Law asserted that Sunday sightseers arrived 'full of high spirits, intent on enjoying themselves', and there was nothing more cheering than the sight of throngs of young men and women

> not perked out in 'Sunday-go-to-meeting best', but men rationally dressed in easy shooting suits or flannels, and girls in neat and pretty lawn-tennis or boating costumes . . . treading the velvet turf and scenting the flowers, in the gardens; strolling in the lime walks; roaming beneath the broad-boughed avenues, or picnicking among the ferns, in Bushey Park; rollicking in the maze; or rowing on the river.[18]

The grace-and-favour inhabitants sometimes found the officials 'rather difficult to deal with; especially owing to the subdivision of the departments, distinct and even antagonistic authorities claim control.' There were four principal authorities. All matters pertaining to the 'shell' of the building fell under the jurisdiction of the Board of Works, as did the areas of the palace open to the public. The regulation of the interior was, however, the province of the Lord Chamberlain. Both the Board of Works and the Lord Chamberlain were accountable to the 'indefinable authority' of the Lord Steward, or the Board of the Green Cloth, which dealt with the most 'recondite legal arguments, and involving points of the subtlest metaphysics'. The fourth department – the Office of Woods and Forests – had a 'roving commission over everything in the nature of parks, gardens and open spaces'. Further to complicate matters, there were other smaller departments which occasionally entered the fray, including the Master of the Horse, the War Office and the Metropolitan Police.[19]

The palace inmates were expected to abide by a strict, if bewildering, code of conduct. Not surprisingly, they often found themselves infringing one regulation or another, and official records abound with proceedings against improper conduct in the palace precincts. In the mid-1850s proceedings were taken against Mrs L'Estange 'for destroying and taking away flowers from the Palace Gardens', and Mrs Henry Brownrigg was 'prosecuted for plucking a pink in the gardens'. In August 1857 Lady Henry Gordon was reprimanded for 'having a picnic party in Home Park and lighting a fire near three elm trees'; in September of the same year Mr Gordon was 'obstructed by the Park Superintendent while gathering mushrooms in Home Park'. Inhabitants were similarly reproached for violations of taste: Mr C. Rigby was ordered 'to remove Birds and Vases etc. which have been placed on the coping of the wall of Hampton Court Gardens'.[20] Failure to comply with the official line inevitably resulted in the withdrawal of the use of the garden key, which gave privileged key-holders unfettered access to the royal gardens. Bath chairs were admitted to the gardens, but 'Children's Chaises' were not; lawn billiards, archery and boating were forbidden in the parks and gardens, but 'playing with hoops, India rubber balls, etc. in the pleasure grounds' was allowed. Dogs were not permitted to run around free in the gardens.

The inmates were not the only persons subject to behavioural control. From the early 1840s Edward Jesse (1780–1865) – one time Surveyor of the Royal Parks and Palace – laid down and vigorously enforced regulations to control visitors, who were 'in the habit of committing depredations on the gardens'. The ordinances were calculated to educate the popular conscience to 'an adequate

14. The Long Border
and the Broad Walk
flank the east side of the
palace. The flowerbeds
were recently replanted
to Ernest Law's designs
of the early 1920s.

15. A grace-and-favour
inhabitant gardening
in the Flower Quarter
of the Pond Gardens
in 1904.

16. (overleaf)
The Auricula Quarter
in the Pond Gardens.

appreciation of Hampton Court and its attractions'. Ernest Law
was able to announce that by the late nineteenth century there had
been a 'great improvement in the manners of the populace', and
that scenes of rowdy behaviour on the part of holiday-makers –
especially on Bank Holidays – were exceedingly rare.[21]

From the second half of the eighteenth century many visitors
armed themselves with handbook guides.[22] These booklets appeared
in greater numbers from the early nineteenth century, and were
generally inexpensively produced and provided modest accounts of
the palace's social and topographical curiosities. Few were as specific
to the palace and successful as those of Edward Jesse, who was
among the first nineteenth-century writers to promote Hampton
Court as a popular tourist attraction and to make the free opening to
the public a success. *Gleanings in Natural History* (1832–5) and *A
Summer's Day at Hampton Court* (1839) instantly captured the public
imagination. In *Gleanings*, Jesse explored such diverse subjects as the
habits of the giant spiders – called 'Cardinals' – that infested the
palace and the parks' ancient trees. *A Summer's Day* contained
descriptive itineraries to and from the palace from Central London,
and accounts of the chief attractions at Hampton Court. The
gardens, parks, the Great Vine and the Maze were singled out for
particular attention. John Grundy's *The Stranger's Guide* (1843) was
the earliest guidebook to refer to the remains of Queen Mary's
collection of exotics in the Lower Orangery and the orange trees
and myrtles in the Upper Orangery.

Excursionists were fascinated by the archaic aspect of the
palace grounds and their antique and picturesque surroundings.
For instance, Charles Dickens Jr. remarked in 1879 that the
principal attractions to the general public are the gardens, with
'quaint old-world arrangement'.[23] And Ernest Law, writing two
decades later, praised the 'original formal trimness' and 'old-
fashioned air of the gardens'.[24] The topographer William Holden
Hutton remarked in 1897 that the palace appealed to the visitor
in two different aspects: it was a 'holiday-ground for thousands
of Londoners . . . orderly folk, merry, and not very attentive to
historical association or even natural beauty, [who] make sport
and play here', as well as an object of interest for those who were
attracted to the history of the 'mighty palace' and a 'world invisible
or half known . . . [where] imagination and tradition vie in
bringing forth tales of strange noises and mysterious presences'.[25]

17. The Herbaceous Garden was formed in one of the six 'divisions' of the Tiltyard in the 1930s. All six divisions of the former Tiltyard were cultivated as kitchen gardens from the late seventeenth century to the early twentieth century.

In the early twentieth century the palace gardens were vaunted by many commentators as retaining 'more of the form and spirit of former days than any others in England'. This did not mean that the gardens were old-fashioned, nor did it preclude the practice of modern garden design; indeed, the floral alleys in the Privy Garden and the mixed flower and herbaceous borders on the west side of the Broad Walk were all recent introductions to the pleasure grounds (fig. 14). Visitors enjoyed the gardens because they possessed such 'varied, thrilling, and artistic bedding'. An editorial in the *Journal of Horticulture* (1910) proposed that the superintendent of the grounds deserved the warmest thanks of the public, and the gardening public in particular, for 'having been courageous enough in these days of the craze for "wild gardening" and all the varieties of free informal gardening, to provide those of us who are catholic enough to love all styles of gardening, so long as it is good, with a fine "carpet-bed".'[26]

The interest in planting styles was, however, less noteworthy than what contemporary journalists called 'the irresistible influence of flowers': flowers were credited by a correspondent to the *Daily Telegraph* in 1908 with engendering a 'subdued and absorbed demeanour' in garden visitors. The same correspondent observed that at Hampton Court one could witness 'practical proof' that 'the influence of flowers is something more than a poetical fancy': the prim formality and the 'gay borders' of the Pond Gardens were remarked to convey the sentiment of the past, and some of the 'old-world plants' awaken 'a latent poetry even in the holiday-maker's breast . . . reducing him to a proper frame of mind for appreciating the charming bit of Tudor architecture that is passed on the way to the Dutch garden'. Other contemporary accounts also note that the profusion of old-world plants evoked 'astonished admiration' and that the planting heightened the appreciation of the setting and 'fine old Tudor brick-work' of the palace in particular.

According to the *Morning Post* in 1910, the gardens also inspired a 'modest spirit of emulation'. Gardening was carried nearer to perfection at Hampton Court than in any easily accessible ground; the resources of the establishment with its vast greenhouses, its command of scientific skill, and, 'not least, its superiority to small economies', were said to place its achievements 'so far beyond the scope of the average amateur that he can only look on in wonder and pick up a hint here and there'.

During the First World War the palace gardens were sadly neglected: vegetables were grown in some of the flowerbeds, others were turfed over, and the lawns ran riot. The contemporary press observed that the limitation of the spring and summer bedding displays in the palace gardens led to considerable dissatisfaction among the general public; ordinary visitors who once thronged the gardens were denied their 'manifold and simple pleasures', and the local economy was deprived of the profits generated through popular tourism. By 1915 some of the attractions were, in fact, restored, but only after the palace began to levy an admission charge to cover the increased running costs of the gardens.

In 1919 the Office of Works finally rescinded the war-time austerity measures and agreed to restore the gardens to something approaching their original pre-war condition; the improvements were not, however, devised by the palace officials but by a small committee of horticultural and landscape garden experts. The *Surrey Comet* played an important role in arresting the 'vandalistic hands' which were despoiling the gardens; Hampton Court was, it exclaimed, 'a tradition, of which its famous gardens form as much a part, as the historic pile itself, and their beauty is of fame all over the world'.

Two aims guided the refurbishment of the gardens. The first was to promote a vague sense of English history and a generalized evocation of old English vernacular gardening. This was championed by Ernest Law who, through his publications and practical example, sought to cultivate in the ordinary visitor the 'desire to explore at leisure many an alluring corner in these gardens, which owe much of their attractiveness to surroundings and accessories until recently too often despised'. In his book *Hampton Court Gardens: Old and New; A Survey, Historical, Descriptive and Horticultural* (1926) he cited the newly laid-out Elizabethan Knot Garden (1925) and the recently replanted Henry VIII's Pond Garden as outstanding examples of the revival of Tudor gardening. It was, he observed, the palace setting that rendered these spots 'particularly interesting'. He described the Pond Garden as remaining 'very much as it did, when Henry VIII strolled therein with Anne Boleyn . . . a spot of the daintiest and rarest beauty, the product of nigh four centuries of care and time, which no expenditure of money or art could possibly create'.[27]

The second aim was to exploit the commercial potential of the gardens through the introduction of new visitor facilities for refreshment and recreation. During the period 1923–38 the Tiltyard (fig. 17) – which had been let as a private kitchen garden since the 1850s – reverted to the palace and was transformed into public pleasure grounds: public lavatories were erected in one of the garden divisions in 1924 and a cafeteria was opened adjacent to the sole surviving Tiltyard tower in 1932.

The parks, meanwhile, also became popular resorts for day-trippers and local inhabitants alike. Although Bushy Park had been open to the public from the early nineteenth century, Home Park only opened its gates in 1893. Both parks were well stocked with fallow deer, and from the late nineteenth century they began to harbour public recreation grounds and allotments. An eighteen-hole golf course was laid out in Home Park in 1895.

During the Second World War large parts of the parks were set aside for food production and a corner of Bushy Park was given over to the Allied Forces. Little irreversible damage took place during their occupation and disturbed land was reinstated by the early 1960s.

Gardens that 'Have not Broken with the Past'

In 1950, Mollie Sands commented in *The Gardens of Hampton Court* that though the gardens at the palace were thoroughly up to date and provided with everything necessary for the public that then enjoyed them, they had not 'broken with the past . . . as you walk through them you are reminded at every turn of their former owners'.[28]

Sands was of the opinion that when the palace ceased to be a royal residence, the direct connection with English history was severed. She did, however, propose that the story of the gardens 'would be worth telling from the point of view of English garden history alone'. In the event, an appreciation of garden history only began to influence the layout and interpretation of the estate from the late 1980s. Although one of the Tudor Pond Gardens was restored between 1949 and 1952, using archaeological evidence and early plant research, such attempts at informed restoration, as opposed to conjectural reconstruction, were not repeated until the advent of the restoration of the King's Privy Garden in the 1990s. Prior to this, the garden superintendents considered the grounds as independent of the palace and were inclined to indulge freely their personal whim in the layout and management of the estate.

The social character of the palace began to change in the 1950s with the decline in grace-and-favour occupancy, and in 1969 it was agreed by the Government that Hampton Court would henceforth be treated as an 'ancient monument' and not a living palace. Since then greater emphasis has been placed on the preservation of the palace fabric and its presentation to the public than on the courtly lodgings. The most significant impact of this shift in emphasis on the royal estate has been the loss of grace-and-favour gardens in and around the palace. Today there are only a handful of grace-and-favour residents at the palace, and only two – the occupants of Lady Mornington's apartments and Wilderness House – continue to have the use of private walled grace-and-favour gardens.

In March 1986 a serious fire swept through a range of apartments overlooking the Fountain Court. In its wake evolved a new era in restoration work at Hampton Court: the palace adopted a philosophy which proposed that historic investigation – both archival and archaeological – should precede repair and reconstruction, and that the results of this research should ultimately inform the restoration. These principles were also adopted in the future restoration of the Privy Garden and have been deployed in subsequent landscape improvements as well.

Hampton Court ceased to be managed by a government department in 1989, to be run instead by a government agency (Historic Royal Palaces Agency); and in 1998 the Agency gained independent charitable status to become Historic Royal Palaces (HRP). Since the early 1990s the fabric of the palace has been considerably improved through a series of major re-presentation projects, including the redevelopment of the Tudor Kitchens and the re-presentation of some of the state apartments. The re-creation of the King's Apartments to their appearance around 1700 is important in terms of the display and management of the royal gardens, since it presented the first opportunity to co-ordinate major building work and landscape improvements in a way which had not been seen at the palace since the time of William III; it also enabled the re-establishment of historic links between the King's 'Privy Lodgings', the Privy Garden and the River Thames.

18. The topiary giants
of the Great Fountain
Garden form a dramatic
setting for displays of
carpet bedding.

The garden today is a re-creation of the pleasance in *c*.1702 based on documentary and archaeological research.

The completion of the Privy Garden led directly to the development of a comprehensive strategy for the rest of the Hampton Court estate. The 'Hampton Court Gardens and Estate Conservation Management Plan' was published in outline in the *London Gardener* in 1997, and has informed the conservation and redevelopment of the estate since this time.[29] The document breaks down the royal estate into fourteen character areas and outlines distinctive conservation objectives and approaches for each; it also prescribes day-to-day and long-term management regimes, identifies opportunities for landscape restoration, repair and renewal, and sets standards for maintenance, conservation and presentation.

The Gardens and Estate Conservation Management Plan contains aims and objectives that reflect an awareness of the

gardens' and parks' ecological value. The public now often perceive Hampton Court and Bushy parks as 'wild' areas, or verdant oases amidst suburbia, which support a range of rare or dwindling ecologies. These distinctive ecologies, nonetheless, should be seen as the product of hundreds of years of human intervention and the imposition of successive waves of designed landscapes. Both parks are recognized as important sites both for the conservation of local biodiversity – due to their relative size and continuity – and for supporting habitats and species that are elsewhere restricted within the local area; they also possess extensive areas of open acid grassland – now rare within the metropolis – much of which has been continuously grazed by deer since the sixteenth century.

Hampton Court gardens and parks are maintained by a permanent in-house staff of thirty-nine – half the number employed on the estate in the early 1980s. This reduction in garden labour, and sweeping changes to the scope and scale of gardening

20. Gardener tending a bed by the Lion Gates.

activities at the palace, has transformed the estate management: since 1983 greater emphasis has been placed on staff development and training and the purchase of the best and most up-to-date garden equipment in order to make the team as effective and efficient as possible.

The Gardens and Estate Manager, Terry Gough, is directly responsible to the HRP Group Director for delivering the conservation, maintenance and business objectives identified in the palace's Annual Operating Plan. Terry and his operations and horticultural managers comprise the gardens management team, which runs day-to-day garden operations and superintends all events and work items relating to the estate. Six section supervisors oversee the operations and management of the estate's six management areas – the Great Fountain Garden, the South Gardens, The Tiltyard and Wilderness Gardens, the Twentieth-Century Garden, the Glasshouse Nursery and the Estate (which includes the park). In-house specialists are charged with machinery maintenance, wildlife management and tree work. External contractors carry out tree surgery and estate carpentry. Hampton Court is unique among the royal palaces in cultivating its own spring and summer bedding plants: over 100,000 plants are grown annually in the Glasshouse Nursery (near the Tudor Kitchens) to furnish the estate's array of lavish flower displays which have been continuously cultivated for over 160 years. The gardens and estate team also plants 70,000 spring flowering bulbs every autumn and manages a population of over 8,000 trees – the most ubiquitous of which are the European limes (*Tilia × europaea*) which are uniformly laid out in avenues criss-crossing the estate. Over the past decade the palace has also collected and over-wintered hundreds of exotic plants which are displayed every summer in the South Gardens.

The palace garden staff are given regular briefings on organizational matters and participate in specialist workshops aimed at developing and improving garden management and operations. Special emphasis is placed on historical technique and the application of traditional garden skills within the historic landscape. The gardens and estate team at Hampton Court also provides specialist advice and support to the gardens under the jurisdiction of HRP at Kensington Palace and the Tower of London.

Since the mid-1990s Hampton Court's Gardens and Estate Department has become a leader in the field of landscape restoration, conservation and management, and its policies, guidelines and practical experience have informed a range of historic landscape initiatives in Britain and abroad. The palace's garden managers have, for instance, forged close ties with a number of royal gardens which share similar interests and concerns, including Herrenhausen (Germany), Fredericksborg Castle (Denmark), Het Loo (Holland), Versailles (France) and Schlosshof (Austria); they have also played an active role in international garden symposia, such as the Baroque Garden Symposium, which for the past decade has met regularly across Europe to exchange management skills and to develop and review landscape conservation strategies. This new level of collaboration has inspired new professional partnerships and exchanges of landscape technology and management skill: members of Hampton Court's garden staff have, for instance, travelled to Het Loo and Fredericksborg to teach young gardeners traditional skills and to acquaint them with practical and theoretical approaches to historic garden management and conservation.

Recent efforts to conserve and restore the royal estate are a testimony to the enduring public fascination with Hampton Court: to many visitors the royal estate is a great emblem and monument of English history, combining picturesque and romantic elements of an ancient monarchy. As Ernest Law remarked in *The History of Hampton Court Palace* (1891), people everywhere have a special regard for Hampton Court as the palace and its parks and gardens are suffused and penetrated with the romance and poetry of the past. Indeed, as we have seen, for centuries visitors have observed that the royal gardens possess a captivating charm peculiar to themselves, retaining more of the form and spirit of former days than any others in England. These factors combine to form a picture of stately grandeur, enchanting beauty and repose which make Hampton Court one of the country's most popular tourist attractions, drawing over a million visitors every year.

The Privy Garden

To gaze over the Privy Garden from the lofty sash windows of the King's Apartments is to experience the most magnificent view of what was historically the palace's most intimate garden (fig. 21). This prospect – formerly the prerogative of reigning monarchs and their guests – is now available to all palace visitors. Few day-trippers who cast their eyes upon the vast geometrical garden which lies at their feet are, however, aware that the earth beneath the sprawling tapestry of flowers, gravel and verdure is inscribed with the scars of countless royal refurbishments. Were the Privy Garden a battlefield and its succession of plants and ornaments battalions of soldiers, its casualties would be incalculable. The benign appearance of this two-acre patch of green belies its tumultuous past: no division of the garden has been subject to more frequent, more idiosyncratic and more drastic re-orderings. No garden division has, however, enjoyed such a direct link to the monarch's privy lodgings. The Privy Garden has always been considered the heart of the royal garden estate as it was from the early sixteenth century to the early eighteenth century the exclusive resort of the reigning sovereign.

What we see today in the Privy Garden is a recent reconstruction of William III's garden as it is presumed to have looked at the turn of the eighteenth century: a great parterre gloriously embroidered with box and gravel arabesques, pierced by a round basin boasting a *jet d'eau*, dotted with shapely evergreen sentinels, urns and statuary, and framed by a pair of raised terrace walks – one bearing a green bower – and a bristling grey and gilt iron screen.

The Privy Garden is the largest but not the only component of a larger group of gardens, now sometimes referred to collectively as the South Gardens, that were laid out in the early sixteenth century. Although no longer the royal retreats that they once were, these pleasure grounds remain the most varied, horticulturally diverse and intensively gardened area of the sixty-acre palace gardens. In the late 1530s these gardens comprised three principal pleasances – the Privy Garden, the Mount Garden and the Pond Gardens.

It is generally assumed that these gardens, which lay adjacent to Henry VIII's newly erected privy lodgings, were the first to be formed on the south side of the palace. It is possible, however, that Cardinal Wolsey's earlier mansion had gardens here and that they,

too, were an integral part of his grand scheme for the redevelopment of the palace. The Cardinal had an extensive garden at York Place in Westminster, and his head gardener John Chapman worked at both of Wolsey's houses. Most contemporary ecclesiastical and courtier establishments on the Thames – such as Fulham and Lambeth palaces – faced the river and had extensive grounds running down to it. Given that Wolsey's palace at Hampton Court was built for the entertainment of royalty and foreign diplomats, and that his esteemed guests would ordinarily have arrived by barge, it is likely that ornamental planting was a conspicuous feature of the riverside approach to his palace.

The most compelling evidence we have to support this theory is the fact that the Cardinal built a long gallery on the site of the present Upper Orangery. Galleries were among the 'noblest roomes of Entertainement' of a mansion which gave elevated views over 'the flattest Embellishments of Gardens', such as 'Knotts', 'Fretts' and parterres:[1] Henry VII formed one atop a curtain wall at the Tower of London to overlook his newly refurbished privy garden there, and as early as 1523 Wolsey built a long gallery in order to survey his gardens at York Place. Sir Thomas More mentions the Cardinal's Hampton Court gallery in 1523. The feature was subsequently refurbished and extended by Henry VIII, suggesting that he may also have retained the earlier gardens.[2]

While further research into Wolsey's gardens might offer new insights into contemporary garden practices and design, it is unlikely to detract from the novelty of his successor's gardening achievements. Surviving accounts, topographical views and visitors' descriptions confirm that between *c.*1529 and 1536 Henry VIII considerably enhanced and improved what gardens he found at Hampton Court, making them the most extravagant and original in early sixteenth-century England. As Roy Strong remarks in *The Renaissance Garden in England*, the King's new gardens were the palace's 'most startling innovation. Nothing quite like them had ever been seen before and their design and layout are of major significance for the whole development of garden design in England down to the accession of James I.'[3] Palace gardens would henceforth be perceived as outward signs of regal magnificence.

21. Aerial view of the
Privy Garden taken
from the privy palace roof.

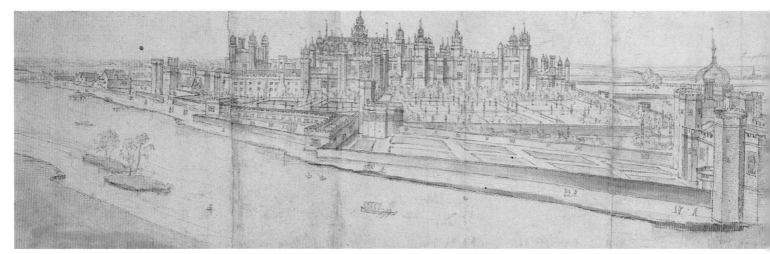

22. (left) Anthonis van den Wyngaerde's view of Hampton Court from the south, c.1555. The Privy Garden, the Mount Garden and the Orchard and Still House Gardens are depicted in the middle of the drawing.

23. (below) The Privy Garden today. The formal planting scheme was restored in the early 1990s to reflect the late seventeenth-century layout.

The Tudor Privy Garden

The Privy Garden – or the King's *private* garden – was the first of the south gardens that Henry VIII created. The immense pleasure ground was made for the monarch's private delectation and meditation, as well as for entertaining and impressing dignitaries; it was the site of extreme opulence and splendour and was full of extravagant features.

Contemporary accounts relate that it was laid out on a plot measuring about 300 × 200 feet – roughly half the size of the present-day Privy Garden – extending from the southern edge of the palace to the central fountain basin. The early garden was divided into square compartments by 180 carved and painted timber posts, 96 stanchions and 960 yards of rail painted in white and green chevrons. Thirty-eight of the posts were surmounted by the 'King's Beasts' in timber, which Henry VIII had commissioned in 1536 from one Harry Corant of Kingston. (They were complemented by an aerial menagerie composed of scores of beasts bearing the arms of Henry VIII and his wives Katharine of Aragon and Jane Seymour, which glowered from the palace roof tops. Twenty brass sundials, purchased in 1534 from the Westminster clockmaker Brise Angustyne, were also scattered throughout the gardens. The beds were planted with strawberries, roses, mint, sweet williams, carnations and primroses.

A bird's-eye view of Hampton Court and its surroundings in *c*.1555 by the Flemish draughtsman, etcher and painter Anthonis van den Wyngaerde portrays the new garden in considerable detail (fig. 22). His drawing is the earliest of a handful of surviving views of the royal demesne. The garden was encompassed by high brick walls against the sides of which were terrace walks, or raised earth banks. These terraces, edged with billowing foliage, wrapped around three sides of the garden, giving fine views over the gardens and outwards through shuttered windows to the park. Two banqueting houses were raised at the south-west and south-east corners of the garden.

Also discernible in the perspective view is 'Paradise', sometimes known as the King's Rich Chamber. This was a two-storey extension to the south-east corner of the palace, adjacent to the King's long gallery. The German traveller Paulus Hentzner remarked in *A Journey into England in the Year 1598* that in the 'certain cabinet called Paradise, where besides that everything

24. *Prospect of Hampton Court from the East Side*
(c.1665-70). Note the park-side pavilions of the
Privy Garden (left), and the long picket fence which
enclosed the Moat Ditch Garden.

glitters so with silver, gold and jewels, as to dazzle one's eyes, there is a musical instrument made all of glass, except the string'. The south-facing front of the small building had a loggia, surmounted by a balcony, which gave on to the adjacent gardens. These he described as 'most pleasant'. He admired, in particular, the 'rosemary so planted and nailed to the walls as to cover them entirely, which is a method exceedingly common in England'.[4]

While visiting England from his native Spain, Antonio Manrique de Lara, Duke of Najera, recorded in 1544 that the Privy Garden was 'extremely handsome, with high corridors and passages everywhere and in them there are various busts of men and women';[5] and in 1599 the Swiss topographer Thomas Platter, who was conducted around the Privy Garden by the gardener, observed:

> By the entrance I noticed numerous patches where square cavities had been scooped out, as for paving stones; some of these were filled with red brick dust, some with white sand, and some with green lawn, very much resembling a chess board.[6]

The 'patches' were presumably the knots created for Henry VIII that lay in the various garden compartments shown on Wyngaerde's view. Platter also describes the hedges and surrounds encompassing the garden, which appear to have been recast for Elizabeth I – they were, he remarked, 'very gay and attractive' and composed 'of hawthorn, bush firs, ivy, roses, juniper, holly, English or common elm, box and other shrubs'.[7] Sadly, we know little about the waterworks formed in the garden in 1591–2 to the designs of the tomb sculptor Garat Johnson the Elder, and another pair of fountains erected by the master mason Cornelius Cure in 1595–6 and 1598–9.[8]

The Mount Garden

Work began in the Mount Garden in 1532–3. This small triangular garden – which was raised in what is now the south-east quarter of the Privy Garden – lay between the Privy Garden and the edge of the Thames, and was circumscribed by high brick walls. One round and three quatrefoil-shaped two-storey towers were raised at the corners of the enclosure, giving it the appearance of a small, fortified garden.

The Mount itself was a prodigious earthwork, which erupted from the flat surroundings of the palace to give panoramic views over the gardens and the neighbouring countryside. Its summit – some forty feet above the garden – was crowned with a banqueting house known as the Great Round Arbour. Its hollow core was fitted with a subterraneous privy kitchen and cellars. Accounts show that 256,000 bricks were used in the construction of the garden. Sixteen posts bearing the King's ubiquitous beasts lined the rosemary-fringed paths that wound their way up to the summit of the giant swelling. The garden appears to have been planted by Edmund Gryffin, who replaced Wolsey's gardener Chapman as head gardener in 1533. Gryffin was assisted in his work by another gardener known only by his sobriquet, the 'French Priest'.

Wyngaerde's view of the gardens reveals the lower registers of the Mount and some of the planting to the west of it. However, much of the Mount and its ogive-domed banqueting house remain concealed by the imposing bulk of the Water Gallery. This brick building was raised in 1536 on the southern boundary wall of the Mount Garden and served as a boathouse, a jetty and as a riverside grandstand.

Elizabeth I employed the French gardener John Markye and his team of assistants between 1583 and 1586; they were paid a considerable sum for the purchase of timber poles to make arbours, box for hedging, several holly trees, a bay tree, an olearia tree, lavender plants, double primroses and daisies – presumably to decorate the various compartments of the Privy Garden. The Office of Works also provided new or replacement heraldic beasts for the Privy Garden and the Mount Garden.

According to a description by the English herbalist John Gerard in 1597, the Mount Garden was planted with yew, cypress and bay trees gathered from the gardens at Charterhouse and Richmond Palace. These evergreens were presumably the shrubs that were cut into the fanciful topiary referred to by Platter in 1599, who remarked:

> There were all manner of shapes, men and women, half men and half horse, sirens, serving-maids with baskets, French lilies and delicate crenellations all round made from the dry twigs bound together and the aforesaid evergreen quick-set shrubs, or entirely of rosemary, all true to the life, and so cleverly and amusingly interwoven, mingled and grown together, trimmed and arranged picture-wise that their equal would be difficult to find.[9]

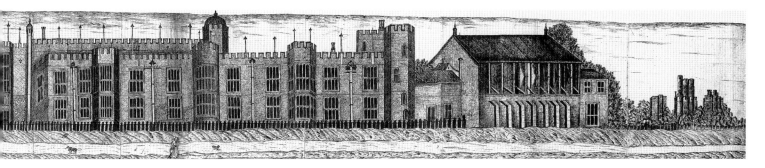

The Netherlandish painter, poet and draughtsman William Schellinks visited Hampton Court in 1662 and provides us with our most detailed account of the Mount Garden before it was demolished in 1690. He observed that, at the south end of the Privy Garden,

> One goes through a door up some steps to a very pleasant octagonal summer-house, which stands on a higher level; from which one has a view over the whole garden; in its middle stands a marble table on a pedestal, and its ceiling is painted with a heaven full of cupids. There is nothing but glass windows all round, and under them are nicely carved benches. Below this place is a deep vaulted wine cellar.[10]

The Orchard and the Still House Garden

These two gardens formed some time between 1538 and c.1558 lay between the Barge Walk and the former 'Great Wall' that defined the south side of the Mount Garden – more or less under what are now the southern quadrants of the Privy Garden. All traces of these productive grounds have vanished, having been demolished and excavated in 1690 to make way for the extension of the Privy Garden. Both grounds appear to have been originally laid out as orchards: the Orchard sat west of the Water Gallery and was cast into four rectangular panels divided into narrow beds, and the Still House Garden lay on the opposite side of the Gallery.

A small castellated tower raised upon the Great Wall at the north-west corner of the Orchard gave on to a covered bowling alley, or skittle ground. By the end of the sixteenth century this feature had become disused and turned into a store, and the quatrefoil-shaped tower at the south-east corner of the Great Wall had come to be known as the Still House. The *Parliamentary Survey* of 1653 informs us that William Hogan was granted the 'Office of Keeping the two little new gardens' adjoining the Thames, for the distilling of herbs for the Royal Household.

The Gardens after the Death of Elizabeth I

Surviving garden accounts suggest that the structure and much of the planting of the Tudor gardens were carefully maintained and embellished under James I.[11] Towards the end of his reign, the King commissioned George Hopton to reorder the beds in the Privy and Mount Gardens, adding five new knots to the Privy Garden and two in the Mount Garden. The most notable additions to the Privy Garden were two pairs of fountains that were erected between 1607 and 1616. The first pair was made of black and white marble with pyramids and the second possessed leopards' heads.

Charles I's improvements to the gardens were chiefly horological.[12] In 1625 Elias Allen – the famous instrument maker, and Master of the Company of Clockmakers of London – erected a horizontal sundial with fourteen brass gnomons on a great pillar of Portland stone. Where these were placed remains unknown. In 1631 the King commissioned nine large hemispherical dials and seven large plain dials from the mathematician John Marr; again, however, we do not know how they were disposed in the gardens.[13]

Oliver Cromwell's Garden

From 1653, Oliver Cromwell began to rescue the gardens from the years of neglect they had suffered during the Civil War. Once more, it was the south gardens – and the Privy Garden in particular – which became the focus of costly and fashionable improvements.

Somewhat surprisingly for a Puritan, Cromwell, like his colleagues John Milton and Bulstrode Whitelocke, greatly admired classical sculpture. No sooner had he begun to occupy Hampton Court than he instructed the removal of the finest classical statuary from the Privy Gardens at Somerset House and St James's Palace to the Privy Garden at Hampton Court.

The arrival of this statuary precipitated a simplification of the Privy Garden plan from its diffuse Tudor layout to a bold quadripartite plan with an imposing two-tiered fountain at its hub. The ground was cast into four large grass plots, each set with a classical statue at its centre – Adonis, Apollo, Venus and Cleopatra. The whole was circumscribed by broad gravel paths, and a 'Great Gate' was cut in the southern boundary wall to give direct access to the Mount Garden. The new layout appears to have been based on the 'great garden' at Whitehall which Cromwell had reconfigured between 1650 and 1651.[14]

The Arethusa Fountain, which arrived from Somerset House in 1656, was the most illustrious element of the new garden – a towering confection of black marble embellished with bronze sirens sitting astride dolphins, pairs of scallops supported by goats' hoofs, and four boys holding dolphins, atop which was 'a large

strong figure of a woman' known as Arethusa.[15] The fountain was subsequently remodelled in the late seventeenth century, when it became known as the Diana Fountain, and in 1714 it was recast and re-erected in Bushy Park, where it remains to this day. The original bronze and marble fountain, with its crowning bronze nymph, is attributed to Hubert Le Sueur and Inigo Jones, and is one of the greatest works of garden sculpture at Hampton Court.

The Restoration

John Evelyn visited Hampton Court in May 1662, a few days before Charles II and Catherine de Braganza and their entourage arrived for their royal honeymoon. Although his contemporary, Schellinks, remarked that the Privy Garden was 'very interesting and decorative', Evelyn conjectured that it 'might be exceedingly improved as being too narrow for such a palace'.[16]

Foreign visitors were generally impressed by what they saw. The French physician and diplomat Baron Balthasar de Monconys noted in 1666 that the parterre was 'quite handsomely done'; and in 1669 the Italian visitor Count Lorenzo Magalotti observed that the parterre was 'divided into very large, level and well-kept walks, which, separating the ground into different compartments, form artificial parterres of grass, being themselves formed by espalier trees, partly such as bear fruit, and partly ornamental ones, but all adding to the beauty of the appearance'.[17]

Magalotti also remarked that the beauty of the gardens was further augmented by fountains 'after the Italian style, whose *jets d'eau* throw up the water in various playful and fanciful ways'.[18] Only Evelyn observed that the Arethusa Fountain suffered from an insufficient water supply. He was, on the other hand, intrigued by the long verdant tunnel that surmounted the west terrace: this 'Cradle Walk', or what was subsequently known as Queen Mary's Bower, was in Evelyn's words a 'perplexed twining of trees' (fig. 25). Schellinks, too, noted in the same year that the bower was a 'very cool walk, so overgrown with greenery that no ray of light can penetrate through it', suggesting that the feature was already reasonably mature.[19] The terrace walk and its closely-set bower may, in fact, have Tudor origins. The bower which presently stands on the west terrace remains a pleasing and conspicuous element of the Privy Garden.

26. The Great Wall which separates the Privy Garden from the Pond Gardens, as seen from the west. Queen Mary's Bower is visible behind.

27. (overleaf) The west terrace, surmounted by Queen Mary's Bower. The present hornbeam bower was planted in 1995.

The east terrace of the Privy Garden was no less interesting than the west, possessing 'several little cabinets of diverse figures' which projected into the park from the brick cloister in the garden; the cabinets were 'round, square, cross shaped, which have as many little towers'.[20] Magalotti, too, noted the presence of 'some snug places of retirement in certain towers, formerly intended as places of accommodation for the King's mistresses.'[21] The Italian traveller's vision of a variety of towers and mistresses emphasizes the combination of splendour and seclusion that the gardens supplied.

Contemporary accounts report that many of the gardens' little towers were being refurbished: carpenters were making repairs to summer-houses in the Mount and Privy Gardens and masons were taking down a stone window in the King's Water Gallery in order to add a balcony next to the Thames. This balcony was subsequently gilded and appears to have given views over a small pleasance by the river's edge. When, subsequently, the Water Gallery was given over to Charles II's former mistress, Barbara Villiers, Countess of Castlemaine, the ground floor was converted into a dairy.

Lady Castlemaine appears to have ordered a series of garden improvements – most notably the planting of a vineyard east of the Water Gallery in the Still House Garden.[22] Although vine culture was common to most gardens of the period, the palace's new vineyard was the first English royal vineyard to have been formed since medieval times. The feature may have been planted by John Rose – one-time Royal Gardener and author of *The English Vineyard Vindicated* (1666). The present Great Vine – which is discussed in detail in the following chapter – is neither a descendant of the early vines nor planted in the same location.

The north-east corner of the Privy Garden was modified in the mid-1670s to receive the King's new building, known as 'Next Paradise'. The brick building was an extension of the royal lodgings; at first-floor level the new apartments opened into a broad wrought-iron balcony giving views over the Privy Garden to the south. A great black and white marble staircase led from the first storey to the garden level. South of Next Paradise was built the 'great neech' – a seating alcove – which gave views eastwards into the park.

William and Mary's Garden

The Privy Garden figured prominently in William and Mary's schemes to recast the south-east area of the palace. The sixteenth-century ranges containing the principal royal apartments were swept away and replaced with a new building to the designs of Nicholas Hawksmoor, then principal draughtsman to Sir Christopher Wren.[23] Wren's sketch designs of 1689 (drawn by Hawksmoor) show how the garden layout was carefully considered during the initial planning stages and how the central axis of the new quadrangle – the present Fountain Court – was to be aligned with the central axis of the old Privy Garden.

Although William and Mary were accomplished gardeners in their own right, they appointed a range of officials to oversee the garden refurbishment. From 1689 the Earl of Portland became Superintendent of the Royal Gardens; he in turn appointed the nurseryman George London as his deputy, as well as the architect William Talman as Comptroller. William and Mary's Dutch gardener, Hendrick Quellingburgh, was charged with the responsibility of maintaining the Privy Garden.[24]

Work on the new palace buildings began in May 1689 with the demolition of the Tudor south range. Progress was swift: by the end of the year the new south range was virtually complete. In the course of the building works, however, the Privy Garden was littered with temporary buildings and had become a store yard for building salvage and large consignments of new building materials; and thus it remained until the summer of 1690 when much of the material was removed and the royal labourers began to lay out the new garden.

While resident at Hampton Court, the Queen occupied the Water Gallery, which served as temporary lodgings as she supervised the building work in the gardens. During her tenure she built a grotto, a dairy and an aviary – for her collection of exotic birds – within the gallery, and commissioned the Huguenot blacksmith Jean Tijou to form a balcony to give views over the Thames.

Stephen Switzer wrote that William and Mary's Privy Garden was made 'with great dispatch'. This statement is not entirely true. Its redevelopment can be divided into two phases – the first from *c*.1689 to 1694, and the second from 1699 to 1702.

The building programme was presumably intended to progress steadily, but was interrupted by the death of the Queen in 1694.

Central to the first phase of the garden's redevelopment was the creation of a pair of terrace walks thrown up perpendicular to the palace, on the east and west sides of the garden (fig. 27). According to Switzer, raised terrace walks were 'necessary for the proper elevation of any Person that walks round his Garden, to view all that lyes round him'. They were also 'absolutely necessary, both as to Use and Beauty' as they were often built of 'Earth, Clay, Rubbish, &c. that necessarily comes out of the Cellars and Foundations'.[25] This was the case at Hampton Court, where spoil from a variety of demolitions was used to form garden terraces.

The western terrace walk in the Privy Garden was raised in 1689–90 after a towering red brick garden wall was completed (fig. 26). This wall – which still defines the eastern boundary to the Pond Gardens – was built on the western edge of the former bower and replaced an earlier timber fence. The new west terrace was first laid to grass but was soon crowned with a capacious 300-foot long green arbour framed with fir rails, oaken posts and circular ribs, and planted with wych elm. The new bower – known henceforth as Queen Mary's Bower – was doubtless contrived, like its predecessors, to screen the stoves in the Pond Gardens. The north end of the bower was dignified with a portico, emblazoned with a coat of arms. The hornbeam bower we see in the garden

30. A modern marble
copy of an original late
seventeenth-century
statue of Ceres.

today was planted in 1995 and is presumed to be the fourth incarnation of the original feature: the first was uprooted in the 1690s, the second suffered a similar fate in 1720 and the third fell victim to Dutch elm disease in the 1970s. The garden's east terrace – raised in 1691 – was, unlike its western counterpart, left unadorned, giving panoramic views to the gardens and the Home Park beyond.

Further progress was made once building work to the south range of the palace began to wind down. In June 1690 labourers began demolishing and levelling the Mount and dismantling the south and east garden walls and the Tudor garden towers. Towards the end of the year the Diana Fountain was dismantled, refurbished – its large brass shells recast by Josias Iback – and re-erected in the centre of the garden on the site of the former Great Gate at the south end of the garden. A pair of marble Great Vases made to the designs of the stonemasons Edward Pearce and Caius Gabriel Cibber were mounted on stone pedestals at the north end of the garden. Cibber's vase portrays *The Triumph of Bacchus* and Pearce's *Amphrite and the Nereids*; both may now be seen in the Great Fountain Garden.

The four rectangular panels of the parterre were also reformed and inscribed with arabesques of cut grass, or *gazon coupé*. Statuary does not appear to have been designed into the new garden. The southern garden boundary was altered and replaced with a trellis screen to conceal the scars of the recent demolitions. The northern end of the garden was terminated by the Upper Orangery – a glass-fronted arcade which formed the ground-floor level of the new south range of the palace. The orangery was linked to the King's bedroom and was built to receive citrus trees shipped from Holland. The various improvements to the gardens are captured in a plan made by Talman in 1699 and in a print by Sutton Nicholls of *c.*1695 (fig. 28).

Nicholls's view also shows four statues surveying the garden from the vertiginous vantage point of the central bay of the balustrade atop the south range of the palace. Wren conceived of the plan to erect figures in this location, which appear to have been raised in the early 1690s. Leonard Knyff's view of *c.*1702 portrays the stone-coloured lead statues of Fame, Mars, Victory and Hercules in greater detail (fig. 4).

William's Garden Improvements

Switzer remarked that upon Queen Mary's death in 1694 all the King's pleasures, including gardening, were 'under an Eclipse', and that his 'beloved *Hampton-Court* lay for some times unregarded'.[26] Only in late 1699 did William resume his work in the Privy Garden. William Talman and George London were retained to guide the King in his work, but to this team was added Henry Wise – London's partner in the Brompton Park nurseries.

Over the following two and a half years the Privy Garden was redeveloped in three distinct stages. The first stage appears to have been makeshift, and involved widening the central path, replanting the borders alongside it and building four flights of steps.

The second stage entailed extending the garden southwards as Wren had proposed in 1689, with a view to forming a great vista from the King's first floor apartments to the Thames. In July 1700, shortly after the Earl of Ranelagh had replaced Portland as Superintendent, the King ordered the demolition of the Water Gallery and other buildings that lay between the palace and the riverside and encumbered views to the south. Much of the building material was salvaged and the plants from the old Mount Garden were transplanted to the Lower Wilderness at the east end of the Long Water in the Home Park. Shortly thereafter an iron palisade was put up outside the Upper Orangery, a temporary fence was erected around the garden and the excavation of the soil from the southern end of the garden was begun. Adjustments were made to the terrace-walks and to the panels of *gazon coupé*, and pedestals were placed to receive the garden statuary. In early 1701 the fountain had been removed to the Fountain Court and Jean Tijou's wrought-iron screens – which had been removed from the Great Fountain Garden the year before – were set up temporarily to enclose the south end of the garden.

This second round of improvements failed to impress the King, who, on visiting the garden in mid-June 1701, found to his immense dismay that he was still denied a view of the river from his royal apartments. The level of the garden was too high. After three days of prevarication William resolved to embark on further improvements, ordering his gardeners to sink the ground yet again. In July, all the plants and lines of box were put into baskets and carried to the Lower Wilderness for safe-keeping, the ground was sunk and the rubbish carted away, the walks, verges, slopes and quarters were stripped and the materials stored for re-use. Roughly 40,000 cubic yards of soil and gravel were removed and the garden was lowered an average of three feet.

The sculptor John Nost was commissioned to design a new fountain for the King: his sketch model proposed to reorder the existing Arethusa Fountain and made provision for additional figures. The new fountain was completed by the end of the autumn, as were the steps and drains.

The garden was almost completely refurbished by the end of the year. The exercise caused innumerable problems but potentially awkward changes in levels were overcome through the introduction of parapets, steps and retaining walls. After the terraces were turfed, the paths laid out and gravelled and the great parterre was reformed, the plants were brought back and replanted in the Privy Garden: it took eight 'Luggage Boat Loads' and three 'Large Waggon Loads' to retrieve the round-headed and pyramid-shaped hollies, pyramid-shaped phillyreas and yews, clipped yews, round-headed buckthorn, lines of box and thousands of herbaceous plants from the temporary nursery in the park.[27]

As in previous phases of improvement, new sculptures were introduced on a lavish scale and others were swapped round. The Great Vases were removed to the Great Fountain Garden and two 'bronzed' statues took their place – one representing a 'blackamoor' supporting a sundial and the other an Indian slave in the same posture. Sixteen lead urns and four sundials were subsequently mounted upon marble pedestals on the steps leading from the Upper Orangery Terrace into the garden.

Five white marble classical deities were raised on pedestals in the centre of the grand design to bestow grace and majesty upon the whole. The King, who subscribed to the contemporary method of displaying durable memoirs of virtue, honour and valour, raised this clutch of figures – Bacchus, Ceres, Vulcan and a double figure of Apollo and Marsyas – in the four quarters of the parterre, and Apollo in the large, circular lawn at the south end of the garden. These noble decorations had been procured from Italy by the London merchants Robert Balle and Sir John Stanley. Carved Carrara marble facsimiles of the statues were placed in the garden between 1995 and 2000 (fig. 30); the weathered originals can be seen in the Upper Orangery.

The refurbished Privy Garden is depicted most reliably in Leonard Knyff's views of Hampton Court from the south and the east (figs 4, 5). The layout of the small residual triangular plot east of the new garden remained unresolved, and the Tijou screens, which Knyff shows as enclosing the south end of the garden, were not erected in the King's lifetime.

Few visitors today will appreciate that Jean Tijou's opulent screens, which are now such a conspicuous ornament of the Privy Garden, were not, in fact, designed for the position they presently occupy. Nor have they occupied their present position very long (figs 6, 32). The twelve ironwork panels, which were published in Tijou's *New Booke of Drawings* (1693), and produced in 1701–2 in his workshop on Hampton Court Green, were made for the 'circle of the Fountain Garden' on the East Front. In the event they were erected in the Great Fountain Garden for a short spell before they were despatched to their present location at the south end of the Privy Garden in 1702, where they remained until 1729, when they were re-erected on the park side of the Pavilion Terrace. By 1867 the screens were in a very poor state of repair and were again dismantled and removed, although this time to the Victoria & Albert Museum, where they were restored. Two panels were returned to the gardens in 1900, while the remainder, which formed part of the Museum's circulation collection, were loaned to galleries in Edinburgh, Wolverhampton, Sheffield, Nottingham and Dublin. The screens were finally reinstated in their present location by the mid-1930s.

The Eighteenth Century

The improvements to the Privy Garden were brought to an abrupt halt on the death of William III in February 1702. Although his successor, Anne, disapproved of the late King's extravagance, she resolved to complete the garden by erecting Tijou's iron screens at its southern end. William's temporary timber palisade was, therefore, dismantled and replaced with the iron screens that were painted and partially gilded.

The Queen professed to dislike Balle's five marble deities and refused to pay for them, declaring imperiously that 'he may have the statues again'. The marble figures, however, remained on their pedestals and the London merchant's claim was still undischarged in 1722.

The engraved view of Hampton Court by the French artist Jacques Rigaud published in 1736 shows the Privy Garden more or less as it must have looked when it was newly laid out in 1702 (fig. 31). There is, nonetheless, little evidence of Queen Caroline's alterations to the gardens of the early 1730s, when steps were removed from the centres of the terraces, the *gazon coupé* was grassed over and the beds (*plates bandes*) had been reconfigured.

How different is our next – and only reliable late eighteenth-century – view of the same garden by the topographer John Spyers (fig. 34). Spyers, a local nurseryman and surveyor who assisted the Royal Gardener 'Capability' Brown at Hampton Court from 1764 to 1783, shows the Privy Garden in his watercolour of *c.*1775–80 as trim but startlingly vertical in its development: four ranks of etiolated yew and holly sentinels surge skywards, their distended forms dwarfing the geometrical gardens at their feet. The shapes of these trees are clearly not the result of any mere lack of maintenance, but of some bold, purposeful, inventively whimsical planning on Brown's part. The whole looks like a vast ruined classical temple – the trees resembling relic specimens of antiquity; what were formerly lines of dwarf topiary have evolved into a living gallery of aged trees. The carved marble deities also conspire to complete the illusion of the ruined temple.

Spyers's distorted perspective, reducing the statues, and the 'blackamoor' and Indian slave sundials in particular, to the puniest of garden ornaments, emphasizes the impressive effect of topiary on such a gargantuan scale. His view suggests that Brown incorporated new ideas in the garden: a sense of the value of accumulated years of growth and vigour derived from a continuous tradition of cultivation. Whereas previous monarchs had repeatedly torn up the gardens of their precursors and redesigned them, George III allowed his Royal Gardener the scope to develop a slightly different approach: the earlier concern with splendour and pageantry was displaced by a respect for historical continuity. Such themes continue to play a central part in the perception of the gardens to this day.

Since earlier in the century, the Privy Garden had begun to be plundered for its ornaments, which were redistributed in other parts of the palace gardens and, indeed, further afield. The result of this process of removal was to accelerate the shift towards greater simplicity. By the late 1720s the Tijou screens had been

31. Jacques Rigaud's published view of the Privy Garden as seen from the Broad Walk in the Great Fountain Garden, 1736.

32. The Tijou screens, with a marble statue of Apollo in the foreground.

33. The entrance gate to the Privy Garden in the Broad Walk, c.1900.

34. John Spyers' watercolour view of the Privy Garden, c.1775–80.

re-erected on the Pavilion Terrace, and by 1816 the lead figures that crowned the parapet of the south range of the palace had been removed and relocated. Although the former were replaced by four smaller seventeenth-century marble statues by Pietro Francavilla, these too were removed in 1829 when George IV stripped the Privy Garden of its remaining ornaments to embellish the gardens at Windsor Castle. By 1832 only a single sundial remained – its pair having being removed in the same year to Kew.

The Nineteenth Century

The story of the south gardens from the late eighteenth century to the early twentieth century is one of piecemeal adjustments. The gardens were no longer subject to the improvements born of royal whim: the Royal Gardener and a clique of grace-and-favour busybodies and amateur gardeners ruled the garden. The new masters were considerably less ambitious and destructive than their royal precursors; under their gentle stewardship the gardens became a private sanctuary for passive pleasures and active recreation.

In 1849 the topographer John Fisher Murray remarked in his *Picturesque Tour of the River Thames* that 'a little beyond the southeastern angle of the garden front, a gate generally closed, but which will be speedily opened upon the summons of the bell, leads into the Private [Privy] Garden, without seeing which none can say that they have explored all the beauties of Hampton Court' (fig. 33). 'There are', he continued, 'some very fine holly trees in these gardens, with a number of pleasant walks, shelving banks of velvet turf, arbours, pleached alleys, one in particular distinguished as Queen Mary's Bower, and the like. If the weather be sultry, the orange trees will be ranged in order outside their winter-house.' Charles Knight – author of the *Cyclopædia of London* in 1851 – also extolled the gentle virtues of the Privy Garden: it was, he remarked, 'a very curious specimen of the old-fashioned, long-neglected, but now appreciated garden of a past age, with its raised terraces, and formal flower beds, and long arcades impervious to the noon-day heat'. Few commentators were as evocative as the Commissioner of Works, Sir Henry Cole, who had remarked in *Some Thoughts on Hampton Court Palace* (1843), 'the gardens'

35. Orange trees and
exotics set out on the
Orangery Terrace.

36. Pots of agaves and
palms arranged by the
Tijou screens.

37. Aerial view of
the exotics on the
Orangery Terrace.

terraces abound with picturesque spots, in which Watteau would
have rejoiced, as backgrounds for his satin and brocaded dames'.[28]

One would assume from reading these descriptions that the
garden had remained unchanged from the early eighteenth
century. But the pleasance bore no resemblance to gardens of a
'past age': its blowsy picturesqueness was entirely modern. The
entire perception of the garden had, however, changed – what was
formerly a great, flat parterre and subsequently a bizarre topiary
garden was now, according to the *Surrey Comet* (1882), perceived
as a 'sort of valley . . . planted, like the outer garden, with fine
variegated hollies and yews alternating, with flower borders,
fountains seen playing sweetly near the lower end'. Many
contemporary visitors agreed with the assessment of a contributor
to the *Cottage Gardener* (1887) that few 'garden scenes' were
invested with 'a richer, more varied, and more pleasing and restful
aspect' than the south gardens.[29]

In 1869 two marble statues by Robert Jackson, representing
'Spring' and 'Summer' – and also known as Flora and Adonis –
were mounted on the two northernmost plinths in the Privy
Garden. The allegorical figures later gave their names to the alleys
in the garden.

Within the empty triangular space east of the Privy Garden,
a lawn tennis court was built in *c*.1880 and kept up by subscriptions
from among the palace inhabitants. The court was surrounded by
an unclimbable fence that protected the residents from the prying
eyes of the public.

Gardens of 'an Irresistible Charm'

In 1893 the Privy Garden was handed over to the Office of Works
and opened to the public. The opening to the public of what had
previously been the resort of few precipitated a greater interest
in the layout and character of the garden.

Ernest Law, who had been brought up at Hampton Court
and who played an important role in the restoration of the palace's
fortunes from around 1900 through the publication of his three-
volume *History of Hampton Court Palace*, was a great advocate of
what he coined the 'old fashioned' character of the Privy Garden.
While London's royal gardens were generally laid out as artistic
landscapes enamelled with a profusion of brightly coloured
flowers planted in regular intervals in geometrical patterns, the

Privy Garden retained a sense of modest dignity. Ernest Law
remarked in 1891:

Visitors . . . to Hampton Court Gardens, whether amateurs of
antiquity, or intelligent working men, do not look for, nor wish,
nor care to find an imitation of the profusion of blossom and
gorgeousness of colour, that blaze in the flowerbeds of Hyde
Park. It is on this account, probably, that so many excursionists of
all classes always express their strong and decided preference for
the Private Gardens [the Privy and Pond Gardens] – as they are
called, though they are open to the public – which are much more
unaltered than the others, and in which very little bedding-out is
attempted: though a truly delightful effect is produced by the
number of old-fashioned English shrubs and plants, which are
arranged and disposed in the ancient style. These gardens retain,
indeed, more, perhaps, of the form and spirit of former days than
any others in England, the grounds being laid out in a way suited
to the variability of our climate: for winter, walled parterres and
sheltered alleys; for summer, grassy banks and plots, shady
bowers and nooks, refreshing fountains, and flowery arbours – all
of which give it an air of repose and seclusion, and an irresistible
charm, entirely unattainable by the most lavish expenditure and
display of modern horticultural art.[30]

The South Gardens may have appeared 'much more unaltered
than the others' on account of their architectural setting, but their
layout was nineteenth century. Nor were the old-fashioned plants
disposed in the 'ancient style'. Ernest Law replanted much of the
Privy Garden – keeping, however, the large, overgrown early
eighteenth-century yews and hollies – to create seasonal alleys
running parallel to the raised terrace walks. While some of the
planting played on the seasonal themes, much of it was, according
to the improver, 'grouped in well-favoured, conspicuous positions
in the warm and sheltered borders where many tender shrubs can
thrive'.[31] The great tubs of orange trees and exotics set out each
summer along the gravel walk immediately against the South
Front were the most faithful display of historic planting in the
gardens. This tradition was established in the early eighteenth
century and continues to this day (figs 35, 37).

Other adjustments were also made to the Privy Garden from
the end of the nineteenth century: in 1895 the lead statues of
Hercules and Mars which had once graced the parapet of the south

range were returned, although not restored to their former positions and in 1933 the bronze Venus de Medici and Cleopatra were also restored to empty pedestals in the 'Autumn' and 'Winter' alleys of the Privy Garden. In 1919, after the neglect suffered during the Great War, the vegetation of the garden was thinned, some of the 'missing yews' were replaced and the shaggy topiary was once again clipped. In 1946 the figure of 'Abundance' by Derwent Wood – now in the Rose Garden – was placed to the west of the central fountain. The most significant improvement was, however, the restoration of Tijou's wrought-iron screens.

The King's New Privy Garden

The decision to reconstruct the garden of William and Mary was taken roughly five years after a fire swept through the seventeenth-century King's Apartments on the south side of the palace on 31 March 1986. This disaster served to galvanize a radical reassessment of the presentation of the palace and its gardens, and ultimately resulted in what was then the most ambitious garden reconstruction undertaken in England.[32] As Simon Thurley remarks in *Hampton Court: A Social and Architectural History*, 'never before had a garden for which such superb documentary, archaeological and horticultural evidence survived been restored . . . [and] never before had such a methodical and scientific approach been taken to garden restoration.'[33]

Hampton Court was, at the time of the fire, in need of a thorough reappraisal: what had once been one of the country's most celebrated monuments was perceived to be less a former royal palace than a public picture gallery set in an expansive municipal pleasure ground. The aim of the proposed reconstruction was to revivify the fabric of the palace and the gardens and to re-establish the historic link and harmony between the King's 'Privy Lodgings' and the Privy Garden. This entailed the removal of the last remaining privately tended patches of the grace-and-favour occupants, their sheds, fences, pavements and ornaments, and the re-establishment of a new coherent landscape, with a clear identity, free of the accumulated clutter of centuries of uncontrolled use. No less important was the aim to re-establish the visual link between the palace, the gardens and the River Thames. The aim was shared by the 'Thames Landscape Strategy', which sought to restore the network of neglected historic vistas, avenues and

landscapes along and across the river from Hampton to Kew.

The garden rebuilding was a costly and lengthy enterprise. Work began in early summer of 1991 and was completed in July 1995 (fig. 40).[34] The full story of the restoration is related elsewhere;[35] a quick overview will, however, convey the scale and complexity of the initiative. After detailed historical research and trial archaeology was completed, and a strategy agreed by spring 1993, the Victorian shrubbery was clear felled. Archaeologists then proceeded to strip the whole ground to reveal the garden layout of 1702: tree pits, paths, flowerbeds, drains and brick foundations for walls, plinths and steps were found intact. Meanwhile special plants – including bulbs, perennials and evergreens – were being grown on in nurseries in Britain and the Netherlands to transplant into the new garden: thirty-three thousand box plants were struck to form the ten thousand feet of edging for the beds (*plates bandes*), and two acres of turf – comprising five varieties of grass characteristic of unimproved meadows – were grown on for the cut grass (*gazon coupé*). The Tijou screens were partially restored and gilded, the bower reconstructed and sixteen lead urns were copied from an original eighteenth-century prototype.

The most difficult and speculative aspect of the garden reconstruction was the production of the planting plan. Whereas we know what plants were grown in the gardens, we do not know precisely how they were laid out. The resultant scheme was, therefore, informed by contemporary documentary evidence from a variety of sources. Planting schemes were then tested in an experimental ground established in Home Park in spring 1992, and over the succeeding two years trials were carried out on the planting and maintenance of *gazon coupé, plates bandes*, paths and sand alleys. The final setting out of the Privy Garden began in March 1995 and was completed by late June, in time for its official opening by HRH The Prince of Wales in early July.

Over the past decade the richness of the garden has been enhanced by the display of exotic plants. Tubs and pots bearing over seventy varieties of hothouse plants are now lined out on the Orangery Terrace, along the paths and the base of the Tijou screens, and around the fountain basin and the statue of Apollo. Oranges in tubs embellish the corners of the *plates bandes*. There are also plans to enhance the floral interest of the garden beds by adopting a double rotation scheme.

39. (left) The Privy Garden in 1992, before its restoration.

40. (below) Setting out the Privy Garden in May 1995.

41. (overleaf) The restored Privy Garden looking east.

The Pond Gardens

The Pond Gardens are the most evocative and curious pleasure grounds at Hampton Court. Known originally as the Pond Yards on account of their fishponds – now sumptuous flower gardens – the diminutive, triangular slip of ground, tucked away behind the Privy Garden, and sandwiched between Base Court and the Barge Walk, contains some of the royal estate's most celebrated garden features.

The structure of the gardens has changed very little over the past five centuries: they retain the dwarf walls of Henry VIII's fishponds, their sturdy early sixteenth- and early eighteenth-century brick garden walls, the Banqueting House and the Lower Orangery. No less important are two of the garden's most distinguished horticultural wonders – the Great Vine and the Great Wisteria – both veterans of the eighteenth and early nineteenth centuries.

Henry VIII is presumed to have laid out the Pond Gardens. Early in 1536 three rectangular basins were excavated and their banks were planted with quicksets of woodbine, whitethorn and hazel. These hedges were replaced in 1537–8 by low brick walls interspersed with stone piers bristling with the King's ubiquitous heraldic beasts.[1] The Pond Gardens may, however, predate Henry VIII's improvements by almost two decades: surviving building accounts suggest that Cardinal Wolsey employed a workman named James Bettes to dig or repair fishponds at Hampton Court in 1518.[2]

The gardens' extravagantly ornamented ponds had a practical purpose: they supplied fish for the royal table. The largest basin was a *vivarium* or breeding pond, and the two smaller ones were *servatoria* or holding ponds. Fish that were selected for eating were transferred from the *vivarium* to the *servatoria*, where they were kept alive until required. The ponds appear initially to have been filled by bucket with water drawn from the Thames until a well was dug and a mechanical pump installed in the autumn of 1536. Henceforth they were fed by the overflow from the palace conduit, which directed water from the cisterns through the fountain in Fountain Court into the ponds and thence, by a series of sluices, into the Thames.

Queen Mary's Exotics

We know little about the Pond Gardens from the mid-sixteenth century to the late seventeenth century, when Queen Mary adapted them to indulge her interest in the cultivation of ornamental plants. The Queen was an enthusiastic gardener and was in fact the first sovereign to take an active interest in plant cultivation, as opposed to display.

It is a measure of the Queen's enthusiasm for her collection of plants and the great value and rarity of her vegetable charges that in 1691 she appointed Dr Leonard Plukenet as Queen's Botanist. The Queen's collection was almost certainly the finest in England: it contained unusual plants from Ceylon, the Cape of Good Hope, Virginia and Barbados, as well as the former collection of exotics accumulated by Gaspar Fagel, the one-time Grand Pensionary of the Netherlands. Much of this mercantile prince's impressive collection was painted by Stephanus Cousijns in a series of 133 plant portraits, collectively known as *Hortus Regius Honselaerdicensis* (1688). The specimens are portrayed in a range of lavish – if often grotesque – stone, earthenware and lead containers, which are presumed to have come to Hampton Court with the Pensionary's consignment of plants. The Queen's collection of East Indian plants was no less celebrated and was catalogued by Cornelius van Vliet in *Horti Regii Hamptoniensis* (1690).

Stephen Switzer wrote in 1715 that 'this active Princess lost no time, but was either Measuring, Directing, or Ordering her Buildings; but in Gard'ning, especially Exoticks, she was particularly skill'd'.[3] Almost immediately on her arrival at Hampton Court, the Queen raised three new glasshouses in the Pond Gardens to receive her collection of tender exotic plants and citrus trees that had been transported from her gardens at Honselaarsdijk and Het Loo in the Netherlands. The south-facing, stove-heated buildings were designed by the carpenter Hendrick Floris, and were praised in 1690 by the exotic plant collector Christopher Hatton as 'much better contrived and built than any other in England'.[4]

The character of the Pond Gardens was, in fact, dramatically transformed by the creation of a variety of new flower gardens: the ponds were drained and planted to form the Flower, Orange and Auricula Quarters; the broad rectangular plot which lay adjacent

41. The Pond Garden lies within the walls of a former fishpond. Henry VIII first established a garden here between 1537 and 1538.

42. Looking north-east
towards the palace
from the Pond Garden.

43. The early
eighteenth-century
Dolphin Fountain
in the Orangery
Garden. It may replace
an earlier fountain on
the same site.

to the Queen's new glasshouses became known as the Glass Case Garden; and new beds were laid out in the small triangular pieces at the south ends of the former ponds. The layout of these beds is clearly shown on Leonard Knyff's drawing of Hampton Court from the south and his view of Hampton Court from the west, of *c.*1702 (fig. 4).

The Orangery Garden

A few years after Queen Mary's death in 1694, her glasshouses fell into disrepair; they were demolished in 1701 and replaced with a single, more substantial brick building with capacious south-facing sash windows. The Lower Orangery, as it became known, is thought to have been designed by William Talman and was completed some time before 1702, when it is illustrated in Knyff's sketch of Hampton Court from the south. The new plant house superseded the Upper Orangery in the Privy Garden, which was given over to royal accommodation.

The garden which lay in front of the new orangery was also recast in 1701 and took the name of the Greenhouse Quarter or the Orangery Garden. A large rectangular apron was set out within low garden walls, a 'parade' was formed beside the building for plant display and several walks and pieces of gravel were laid down framing a pair of rectangular beds, or pieces for flowers, dotted with yew, juniper, striped box and evergreens.[5] Displays of bulbs were planted in the box-edged beds and borders in the early spring; these were, in turn, succeeded by ranks of exotic plants set in wooden tubs, simple glazed terracotta pots, or painted and gilded decorative vessels. The wall-mounted Dolphin Fountain and a large lead cistern are among the few early eighteenth-century features to survive in the gardens today (fig. 43). The topographer Thomas Cox noted in *Magna Britannia* in 1724:

> The Green-houses ... have Stoves under them, so artificially contrived, that all foreign Plants are there preserved in gradual Heats, suitable for the Climes of their respective Countries, where they naturally grow, and from whence they are brought.[6]

The Banqueting House and Aviary Garden

In 1700 William III gave orders for the construction of the Banqueting House and the King's Aviary beyond the Great Wall at the south end of the Pond Gardens. The ensemble was intended to form an elegant trianon, or rural retreat, and was modelled upon Louis le Vau's Menagerie at Versailles.[7] The handsome brick building designed by Talman, which still presides over the Pond Gardens, was raised on the Thames foreshore upon the foundations of a former mill house. New gardens were also laid out to the east and west of the building. The King's Aviary, also referred to as the Pheasantry, the Menagerie or the Vollery, lay to the east of the Banqueting House, on the site of the former covered bowling alley, and was a rectangular enclosure with an apsidal end. Here domestic and exotic fowl were kept in a double range of oak-framed hen houses and Pheasant Rooms. The houses had eighteen nest boxes and twelve oval drinking basins, and the surrounding garden – laid out in borders, grass plots and gravel paths by Henry Wise – possessed a fountain made of Dutch clinkers and tiles and pavements of Swedish stone. The garden to the west of the Banqueting House was laid out as an orchard. The whole ensemble is portrayed with great accuracy on Knyff's view of *c.*1702, and on an estate map of around 1714.

The aim of the Banqueting House and its gardens was to open views from the Pond Gardens to embrace the Thames. The two-storey Banqueting House was, therefore, projected boldly beyond the Great Wall, and thirteen large windows were punched at regular intervals through the wall to provide vistas over the Thames and the new riverside gardens from the Glass Case Terrace in the Pond Gardens.[8] A bronze bust of Flora was set above the building's north-facing stone doorcase, to survey the Pond Gardens. From the sumptuous interiors, graced with murals by Antonio Verrio, one still gains views up and down the Thames and over the adjacent gardens and riverside. The gravel walk atop the Glass Case Terrace has recently been refurbished, and the gate at its east end leading to the Privy Garden has been reopened. The terrace will soon be embellished with yew pyramids as it was depicted in Knyff's view. The steps and Purbeck stone apron on the north side of the building are original.

In 1746 the Aviary was dismantled and the windows in the Great Wall were bricked up before 1760. Henceforth the Pond Gardens would put their back to the river. The Banqueting House for many years remained unused and uncared for until the 1830s when it was refurbished and converted into a private residence. The building and its cycle of decorative wall paintings – which had been concealed behind wallpaper in the 1860s by a grace-and-favour occupant – were restored in the early 1980s. The Banqueting House opened its doors to the public from 1983. The Aviary Garden and the orchard today lie fallow with a sprinkling of trees, and are closed to the public.

The Great Vine

Since the late eighteenth century, there has been a great interest in the age, girth, extent and vigour of two of the Pond Gardens' horticultural elements, one a vast fruiting vine (fig. 45) and the other a giant flowering tree. Both of these leviathans live within a few yards of one another in the south-west corner of the Pond Gardens – one in a purpose-built glasshouse and the other in an open bed.

As already noted, a vineyard had formed part of the royal gardens in the seventeenth century. There is, however, no record of the further vine culture at the palace until 1768, when 'Capability' Brown planted a vine of the 'Black Hamburgh' variety in a disused glasshouse in the Pond Gardens from a slip off a vine at Valentines, an estate near Wanstead in Essex. In setting up this new attraction, Brown – possibly renaming the 'Grape Vine' as the 'Great Vine', even at this early stage, since he regularly incorporated such pieces of wordplay in his work – implicitly invoked the history of cultivation of vines at Hampton Court and so defined the gardens as the site of longstanding and continuous fruitfulness and abundance – a place readily associated with the Bacchic delights of classical mythology.

The celebrated vine was already a curiosity in 1798, when the *Gentleman's Magazine* published a note on the thirty-year-old tree, reporting that it entirely filled 'a grapery 24 yards long, and 6 yards wide . . . and has now upon it 1800 bunches of grapes, supposed to weigh one pound each upon an average, and to be worth altogether at least £400'.[9]

In 1825 Thomas Hardwick, Clerk of the Works at the palace, reported:

> The rain for these two winters past and particularly the last has penetrated through almost every part of the Lights [of the glasshouse], to the injury of this famous Vine; and the Master Gardener, Mr Pedley assures me that owing to the state of the Building there has been a deficiency in the quantity of Grapes

> this Season and that they will not last so long as usual for the supply of His Majesty's Table.

Hardwick put forward a plan to erect a temporary stage for the vine, to remove all the rafters, lights and sashes and to rebuild the house. The exercise cost £476 8s. 7d., and was completed by the end of March 1826.[10] The present vine house – the fourth on the site, the first being raised in 1698 for overwintering Queen Mary's exotics – was built in 1964 over the framework of the previous house erected between 1904 and 1906. Since 1904 the vine has been kept in 'solitary confinement' behind a glass screen to prevent the transmission of potential pests and diseases from neighbouring plants, and to protect the vine's fruit from the dust created by its many admirers.

Since the early nineteenth century, commentators have repeatedly affirmed the size and fecundity of the vine, often through detailed numerical calculations. The King of Saxony and his personal physician Dr Carus noted in 1844 that the 'immense vine' was an object of 'great curiosity' and that 'it occupies a house built for itself, has already reached an extraordinary age of seventy-six years, is 110 feet long, and often bears from 1200 to 1400 bunches of grapes'. The vine was shown on application to a gardener (fig. 47).[11] In Victorian times the Queen's Gardener used to charge 1d. for each visitor to the house. This perquisite was, however, abolished and the Vine House was opened for free. In 1920 the charge was reimposed and the ample proceeds were paid into the Exchequer.

The vine was so popular that in 1925 the visitors numbered 280,000, yielding about £1,170, which made it among the most popular and profitable elements of the royal estate. Indeed, the visitor numbers were so high that Lionel Earle, the First Secretary of the Office of Works, lamenting the public's lack of interest in the palace's canvasses by the Italian Renaissance artist Andrea Mantegna, noted in 1930 that 'such is the mentality of the ordinary British public . . . [that] the joy riders at Hampton Court will always be more attracted by the vine than by any Mantegna pictures'.[12]

The vine's grapes were formerly reserved for the sovereign's table at Windsor, though Ernest Law informs us that 'His Majesty always sent most of them to the hospitals.' From the early twentieth century the grapes have been sold to the public.

44. Aerial view showing
the Pond Garden with
its oval basin, and the
Banqueting House
beyond. The Aviary
Garden and the former
Orchard lie behind
the Great Wall which
projects on either
 side of the Banqueting
House.

45. The Great Vine –
possibly the oldest
living vine in the world –
has for almost two
centuries been one of
the most famous and
popular attractions at
the palace.

46. (below) The piece of ground beside the Vine House has traditionally been left uncultivated as the roots of the Great Vine lie beneath it. The Great Wisteria can be seen on the gable end wall to the right of the Vine House.

47. (right) S. Turrell Junior. was keeper of the Great Vine and his 'very good portrait' of his charge was described in 1841 as 'well worthy of a horticulturist's purchase'.

The vine crop is now restricted, through assiduous pruning, to roughly one thousand bunches, which yield about 500–600 pounds of grapes. These are harvested daily between the end of August and early September and sold in the palace shops on the same day they are picked. The vine is tended by the resident Vine Keeper, and has been for over 150 years when the post was created during the reign of Queen Victoria.

Since the late 1990s cuttings of the vine have been grown for sale and for presentation to visiting dignitaries. Shoots have, however, been planted since at least 1778 when a consignment was sent to Cumberland Lodge in Windsor Great Park. The closest living relation to the Great Vine may be the vine at Wrotham Park, Hertfordshire which was planted about 1785 – possibly on the recommendation of 'Capability' Brown.

The Great Wisteria

While the Great Vine is famous, and is to this day assiduously nursed by a resident keeper, its neighbour the Great Wisteria, which appears to have been planted a few decades after the vine, thrives on neglect and is now virtually unknown (figs 48–50).

Year in, year out, the Great Wisteria has but a fortnight to outshine its vegetable rival and become temporarily the most fragrant inhabitant of the Pond Gardens. Only during the winter months can one discern the writhing mass of this immense tree, which for almost two centuries has quietly embraced the east-facing Tudor brick walls of the Vine Keeper's house (fig. 46). For much of the year the sinewy framework of the colossus is concealed beneath tussocks of foliage, except for two weeks each May, when it erupts into flower and is, according to the *Gardeners' Chronicle* (1899), 'smothered with pendant racemes of sweetly-scented, peculiarly-tinted blooms' (fig. 50). The correspondent went on to

48. (below) The writhing trunk of the Great Wisteria.

49. (bottom) Late nineteenth-century photograph of the Great Wisteria.

50. The Great Wisteria in blossom.

observe that 'some of the plants are such veterans that in size and age they are little less remarkable than the famous vine, but of which a great deal more is heard'.[13] Ernest Law, writing in 1926, corroborated this claim: 'its age is probably not much less than eighty years; so it is interesting, like the Great Vine, in antiquity as well as size'.[14] Indeed, the Great Wisteria is every bit as impressive as the 'glory of Kew' – the Medusa-like giant which is purported to have been planted in 1820, and is the oldest surviving descendant of the first consignment of Chinese wisterias to arrive in England from Mr Consequa's garden in Canton.

The main stem of the wisteria was recorded in the 1920s as being some six or seven feet in girth. It is now considerably larger and so contorted that it is difficult to ascertain whether it is, in fact, one or several plants. It was also thus in the nineteenth century, when a French visitor marvelled at the 'enormous wisterias [which] spread gnarled branches over the gables'. Nor was the giant specimen in the Pond Gardens the only noteworthy wisteria at the palace; 'they appear to have been planted in almost every convenient situation', and were said to 'overflow even into the village'.[15]

The palace recently began a programme of striking cuttings of the Great Wisteria. Scions of the tree should, therefore, soon be available for sale to the public.

The Reform of Henry VIII's Pond Gardens

During the nineteenth century the Pond Gardens, like the Privy Garden, were the private resort of the palace's grace-and-favour inhabitants; as such they were subject to the personal whims and idiosyncrasies of the many people who staked their claim to parts of the grounds.[16] Although the Office of Works and the Royal Gardener retained overall control of the gardens, their efforts were largely restricted to keeping the Great Vine and one or two of the gardens in the former Tudor ponds.

Most of the late-Victorian improvements to the Pond Gardens by the Office of Works were of a whimsical, cheerfully trivializing kind, aimed at prompting a vague sense of English history. Pageantry and royal magnificence were set aside to make way for a more generalized evocation of English vernacular gardening: putti replaced deities, crazy-paving replaced gravel, and ornamental trees, rare shrubs and perennials replaced clipped

evergreens. As Ernest Law commented in 1900, the gardens at Hampton Court owed their prettiness to a range of 'accessories until recently too often despised' – embellishments

> outside the range of horticulture pure and simple – as dwarf terraces, enclosing walls, recesses, and niches of old red brickwork; balustrades, pedestals, steps, urns, vases, sundials, copings and carvings of stonework; ornamental gates, screens, railings, and wickets of wrought iron, and leadwork in moulded forms, such as pinnacles, vases, statues, cisterns and the like.[17]

The presence of these ornaments in the palace gardens did more to reinforce the impulse to create *petit bourgeois* prettiness than dignify what remained of the gardens' royal magnificence.

By the late 1910s Ernest Law, who had established himself as the champion of a version of the vernacular in horticulture and a creator of a generalized vision of English garden history, set about to enhance the illusion of the palace's historic gardens.

His improvements were doubtless galvanized by reports in the press suggesting that areas of the Pond Gardens were becoming rather shabby. The *Gardeners' Chronicle* reported in March 1919:

> The Dutch Garden [formerly the Orange Quarter, or middle Tudor fishpond] certainly does require attention. It has ceased to be 'Dutch' owing to the ragged and generally worthless character of the mixture of shrubs and small trees which occupy the beds. In our opinion this garden should be restored to what it was intended to be.[18]

The Office of Works proposed an elaborate scheme to revive what was known as the 'Dutch' or the 'Tudor Garden' – now often referred to, rather confusingly, as the Pond Garden. Although the design of about 1920 appears to have been based on careful observation of the remaining features of the Tudor pond garden and early building accounts, it is not an archaeological restoration but a fanciful reconstruction.

In 1926 the garden was replanted and its structure gently
modified – although not in the Tudor taste (fig. 52). The results were
much admired. The 1932 palace guidebook reports that 'the round
fountain in the middle is modern, and the leaden statue of Venus in
the yew harbour [*sic*] at the farthest end of the garden was sent from
Windsor and placed in its present position about thirty years ago.
The leaden figures of children representing the Seasons near the
gate are also modern additions.' The Venus had been extracted by
Ernest Law from 'Mrs Grundy's Gallery' – a famous repository in
which were stored statuary and pictures that the Housekeeper at
Hampton Court considered unfit for public exhibition.

The new garden layout comprised forty plant beds – each
containing no fewer than three varieties of flowers. The spring
and summer planting reflected Ernest Law's enthusiasm for 'old
fashioned' English plants, and created a varied and delicately
harmonious colour scheme.

The plants that are now used within the Pond Garden
displays are primarily cultivars of modern bedding plants. The
displays are changed twice a year, with a summer display of over
7,700 colourful plants such as heliotropes, geraniums, petunias,
marigolds and verbena. In the autumn the double display of almost
13,000 plants and 10,000 bulbs is planted with *Bellis*, *Erysimum*
mixed with *Viola*, hyacinths and tulips, giving a two-tiered display
in the spring.

Among the most remarkable attributes of the present-day
Pond Garden are the large wisterias which clothe its low walls, and
the ring of pleached limes that encompass it. These trees were
planted about 1704 as a windbreak, and have been pruned to their
present height for roughly three centuries.

The Elizabethan Knot Garden

The Pond Garden did not achieve the celebrity of Ernest Law's
Elizabethan Knot Garden. Laid out in the spring of 1924 and
modelled on the knot garden at Shakespeare's Garden at
Stratford-upon-Avon – itself a reconstruction by Law – this little
pleasance was promoted as the first knot garden made in England
since the time of the early Stuarts. The space was thought to
have originally been the location of Wolsey's former knot garden.
The beds of this garden – laid out by the 'wizard' Mr W.J. Marlow,
Superintendent of the Gardens, by direction of the Office of

54. The typical spring
bedding scheme in the
Pond Garden includes
10,700 wallflowers,
10,000 tulips and
2,450 pansies.

55. The Elizabethan
Knot Garden today.

56. (below) Postcard
showing the Elizabethan
Knot Garden shortly
after it was planted
in 1924.

57. (bottom)
Summer bedding
in the Pond Garden.

Works – were planted with what Ernest Law described as 'favourite flowers of the Elizabethans, such as white lily, lavender and rosemary'.[19] The patterns of the interlacing bands or ribbons were formed with herbs such as thrift, lavender-cotton, thyme, dwarf lavender and box, and the spaces between them were filled with masses of tulips, pink, blue and white hyacinths and daffodils.

Law reported in 1926 that the design of the knot garden was 'taken directly from those designed and published by the old masters on gardening of the time of Elizabeth and James I'. The piece of ground he converted was, he continued, 'formerly an ugly, shapeless plot, partly gravelled and partly planted with evergreens, lilacs, etc. In a straggling bed close up against and obscuring the beautiful oriel window and the fine old Tudor brick-work'.[20] According to *The Field* (1927), the new garden was 'looked upon more as a curiosity than anything else', although it was 'one of the best known' at the palace.[21]

Although the layout of the Knot Garden has not changed since it was laid out in the 1920s, the less robust hedging material such as the lavender and the lavender-cotton has been replaced with box (fig. 55). Double rotation planting is still practised in the beds, but the 5,000 bulbs and plants used in the displays vary from year to year and do not reflect Law's original Elizabethan palette.

The Greenhouse Quarter or Orangery Garden

Although the Pond Gardens were given over to grace-and-favour use from 1838, much of the collection of exotic plants remained intact at least until 1853, when it was described by Charles McIntosh in *The Book of the Garden* as having the largest collection of orange trees in England. The collection was subsequently much depleted but limped on until 1902 when the Lower Orangery was converted into grace-and-favour accommodation.

The introduction in the 1890s of beds for standard roses, gladiolas, anemones and phlox in the sunk garden adjacent to the Lower Orangery suggests that fewer exotics were set outdoors during the summer than had previously been the case; and we know from photographs that by 1900 the former display area was given over to lawn, although a few plants were placed on the Privy Garden terrace. Where the bulk of the exotics went after they were evicted from the royal gardens remains a mystery. We know, however, that two of the Queen's Judas trees were removed

58. The Lower Orangery was raised between 1701 and 1702, and replaced three earlier glass cases erected for Queen Mary. The area in front of it was formerly embellished with seasonal displays from the Queen's 'foreign plant collection'.

and planted in the Privy Garden. By 1919 the Lower Orangery had been converted into a picture gallery for the display of Mantegna's *Triumphs of Caesar* and it was opened to the public two years later (fig. 58).

The Flower Quarter

The Flower Quarter, which lies immediately adjacent to the base of the towering brick wall which supports the Queen's Bower in the Privy Garden, is the largest of the three walled gardens in the Pond Gardens (figs 59, 60). The garden – also known as the Long Quarter on account of its size – was created in this former fishpond in the late seventeenth century, and is shown on William Talman's map of *c.*1696 as possessing a pair of circular ponds. Knyff's view of *c.*1702 depicts what appear to be large flower-pots filled with

plants, suggesting that it may have contained a collection of shrubs, herbaceous plants and some succulents – some of which might have been overwintered indoors. By the 1730s the garden was divided into a series of rectangular beds, and by 1841 the area had been planted with fruit trees, as it has been ever since, and was, until the early 1990s, still partly given over to grace-and-favour gardeners. The garden within the walls presently lies fallow, although the long perimeter bed which runs along the garden's west wall has recently been planted with a herbaceous display.

61. Proposal for the
redesign of the Auricula
Quarter, 1903.

62. (right) The Auricula
Quarter today.

63. (overleaf) Spring
planting in the Pond
Garden.

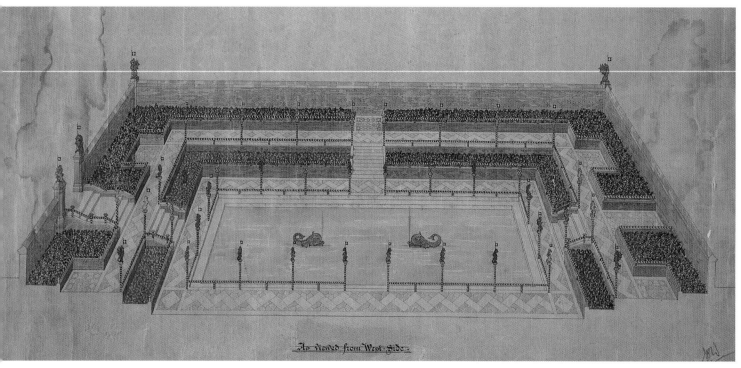

As viewed from West Side

The Restoration of the Auricula Quarter and the Orangery Garden

In 1903 the Office of Works put forward a fanciful scheme to refurbish the Auricula Quarter in the Tudor taste (fig. 61). The plan proposed the excavation of a large rectangular basin in the lower level of the two tiers of the garden and the deployment of a battalion of King's beasts to encompass the pond and the surrounding terraces. The scheme was shelved in 1909 as it was considered too costly. The proposal was, however, revived and recast after the Second World War: the new scheme was based on archaeological evidence and early plant research, and the layout was a re-creation of the garden as it was depicted by Knyff in c.1702 (fig. 4). The refurbishment went ahead, and *The Times* reported in November 1951 that the newly-restored sunken pleasance was formed of 'low box hedges cut in fancy shapes and a wide, red brick-dust surround'. A shingle and shell path lead to a central fountain.[22]

The garden today remains much as it was planted in the 1950s (fig. 62). However, the hedges now loom above the dwarf walls, making the central area more secluded than it was intended to be; they also obstruct views from the Orangery Garden to the Great Wall and the Banqueting House.

There are currently plans afoot to restore the Orangery Garden for the display of the palace's ever-increasing collection of exotics. The palace has undertaken extensive archaeological investigations and historical research to inform the proposed reconstruction. The Gardens and Estate Department began reassembling Queen Mary's collection of exotics in the early 1990s with a view to extending the present display in the Privy Garden, the Lower Orangery Garden and the palace interiors. Within the next few years hundreds of exotics which were known to have been cultivated in the late seventeenth century will be presented in facsimiles of their early containers in their original settings to evoke Queen Mary's garden at its prime.

The palace is presently preparing an overall strategy for the long-term refurbishment and maintenance of the Pond Gardens, with a view to restoring historic views and refurbishing neglected parts of the fabric, such as the Flower Quarter.

The Great Fountain Garden

To appreciate fully the Great Fountain Garden we must progress through the airy cloisters of the Fountain Court, eastwards to the Garden Vestibule. Here we gain a prospect of the theatrical spectacle of the landscape beyond.

Much of what we see today – the diagonal walks, the Broad Walk, the leviathan yews and the oval basin and fountain – are the relics of the early eighteenth-century Great Fountain Garden, a huge semi-circular garden laid out in the grand manner on a level plain between the palace and the park, stretching from the road to Kingston in the north to the Thames in the south. The Great Fountain Garden remains the most regal garden at Hampton Court, and its formal layout can be traced back to the reign of William and Mary, when John Evelyn recorded that 'spacious Gardens with fountains, was beginning in the Park, at the head of the canal'.[1]

The Moat Ditch Garden

What Evelyn doesn't tell us is that the origins of the Great Fountain Garden lie in a modest fourteenth-century ditch, which spanned the entire length of the palace's East Front. The Moat Ditch Garden was a long narrow pleasure ground cultivated in the rich silty deposits of the disused defensive moat. Prior to its creation, the open parkland of the Course and the Home Park swept up to the foot of the palace.

Historians have shown little interest in this unusual sunken garden – possibly on account of its piecemeal development, or its idiosyncratic nature. It was also known as the Balcony Garden because of its proximity to the large iron balcony that was projected off the east face of the Queen's bedchamber in about 1636. Although the first-floor balcony was doubtless contrived to give views over the park, its presence may have prompted the building of a garden in the ditch below.

It remains unclear whether the garden was the same Moat Garden described in an *Inventory of Oliver Cromwell's Goods* (1659),[2] or whether it took shape after 1662, when some of the bars, pillars, balls and rails of the balcony were painted and gilded in anticipation of the arrival of Charles II and Catherine de Braganza on their honeymoon. The refurbishment of the balcony certainly corresponded with the digging of the Long Water and the planting of the avenues in the Home Park – imposing landscape elements that will be dealt with in a subsequent chapter.

A contemporary view (1662) by William Schellinks and an anonymous *Prospect of Hampton Court from the East Side* (c.1665–70) depict the East Front of the palace as a parade of prickly Tudor and Stuart buildings huddled on a bleak grazing yard (figs 24, 66). The Moat Ditch Garden is barely visible, although heaps of disturbed soil, long runs of timber fencing and eruptions of billowing foliage betray its presence. Alas, there are no records to suggest what the garden actually looked like. However, given the irregular profile of the moat, we may surmise that the layout was reasonably informal.

The garden was enclosed on the park side by a fine spear-headed palisade which ran the length of the East Front, breaking only at the 'Course Gate' – now the Garden Vestibule; this was presumably put up to protect the garden from the deer and cattle that inhabited the park. The palisade was painted stone colour and white to match the East Front windows and the balcony doors, rails and balusters. The presence of the painted palisade and a makeshift garden may appear to modern eyes to compromise the dignity and magnificence of the place, but to contemporaries these features gave the east side of the palace an air of hospitable domesticity.

Other garden elements portrayed in contemporary views include panels of scrolled decorative plasterwork on the lower register of the palace walls and the silhouettes of cypress trees.

Parisian Echoes

The Great Fountain Garden succeeded the Moat Ditch Garden, and was contrived as part of a grandiose scheme to recast the Tudor palace and its setting. It was formed between 1689 and 1691 by diverting the Longford River and infilling the westernmost three hundred feet of the Long Water which projected into the great semi-circular apron east of the palace. The development of the new gardens was slow, and was to a large extent contingent on the progress of the building works of the palace. By the end of 1689 preparations were underway for the demolition of the whole of the eastern range, which overlooked the future Great Fountain Garden and the park. This work caused considerable disruption to the neighbouring area, as the Tudor buildings were cleared away, salvage and rubbish were removed section by section and new foundations were dug.[3]

64. View to the East
Front of the palace from
the Diagonal Walk.

65. Large tubs of agapanthus are placed around the perimeter of the oval basin of the Great Fountain Garden every summer.

66. William Schellink's view of the East Front of Hampton Court as seen from the Home Park. His sketch was made on 23 April 1662 – after the Long Water had been dug, but just before its flanking double avenues were planted.

The design of the capacious new parterre is generally attributed to Daniel Marot, a Huguenot who emigrated from France to The Hague in 1685–6 and who styled himself from 1689 as 'Architecte de Guillaume III, Roi de Grande Bretagne'. Nicholas Hawksmoor, working in Sir Christopher Wren's office, might also have played an important role in the garden layout: two designs prepared by him in the summer of 1689 show the Great Fountain Garden complete with its paths, beds, fountains, Broad Walk and the diagonal avenue.

The King and his circle of courtiers – most notably his Superintendent of the Royal Gardens, Hans Willem Bentinck – cultivated a lively interest in French engravings of garden architecture and ornament, collecting works by Charles le Brun, Antoine le Pautre, Jean Marot, Israel Sylvestre and Charles Perrault. These prints publicized the great flowering of garden art at the court of Louis XIV and served to encourage many to adopt the layout, decoration and iconography of French gardens. It is not, therefore, surprising to find that Hawksmoor's bold and curious remodelling of the east side of Hampton Court Palace owes a clear debt to Perrault's designs for the east front of the Palais du Louvre (1668), and Marot's gardens to André Le Nôtre's 'Grand Parterre' at the Tuileries.

Marot's bird's-eye sketch of 1689, his later, engraved plate entitled *Parterre d'Ampton Court* (1712), and Sutton Nicholls's published view of *c*.1695 suggest that William and Mary spared no expense to adorn their new garden (fig. 69). It was laid out in the form of a giant semi-circle, predetermined by existing rows of lime trees planted by Charles II in the 1660s. The area within its midst was laid out as a great parterre – possibly the largest ever created in England – inscribed with a central and radial gravel paths, *ronds-points*, basins and panels embellished with scrolls of fastidious broderie and *gazon coupé*. The grand design, enriched with pyramids of yew, globes of bay and holly, coloured gravel and grass, was relieved by a large oval basin and its Great Fountain at the midpoint of the broad central path aligned on the Long Water in the park. Marot's drawing depicts a long decorative iron screen separating the garden from the palace, its alignment following the eastern edge of the present Broad Walk, as well as two screens, or *claire-voyées*, marking the entrances to the Ditton and Kingston Avenues. This metalwork was executed by Jean Tijou (fig. 67).

Two concentric rings of fountain basins in the forms of circles, quatrefoils and octagons were among the garden's most novel and striking elements. Leonard Knyff's painted view of Hampton Court from the east of *c*.1705 shows glistening jets squirting playfully in the centre of each of the garden's thirteen pools – the simple columns of water complement the thrusting verticality of the yew sentinels and contrast sharply with the low relief of the parterre (fig. 5).

Statuary was raised in the midst of the gardens to evoke the memorable actions of great personages of Antiquity. A pair of marble Great Vases carved with bas-reliefs representing *The Triumphs of Bacchus* and *Amphrite and the Nereids* were removed from the Privy Garden and placed opposite the Garden Vestibule in the Broad Walk. Another pair with bas-reliefs depicting *The Judgement of Paris* and *Meleager Hunting the Wild Boar* stood at the bottom of the central walk.

Bronze statues of Antinuous, the Borghese Gladiator, Diana and the Farnese Hercules were also set on pedestals in the great parterre. The most celebrated of the group was the Gladiator, who formerly stood at the east end of the canal in St James's Park. Accounts of the time report that the figure caster Richard Osgood repaired the statuary – most of which had been 'melted and broke by the fire at Whitehall' in 1698. Hercules was given new feet and copper legs and hands; and Antinuous regained his legs and 'several other parts'. A few of the figures were cleaned with aqua fortis to make them 'look bright all alike'.[4]

High above the garden, in the pediment of the palace, was placed Caius Gabriel Cibber's carved bas-relief depicting 'Hercules triumphing over Envy' – a durable memoir of the virtue, honour and valour of William III.

Neglect and Improvements

Building work in the Great Fountain Garden came to an abrupt halt with the death of Queen Mary in 1694 and was only resumed in 1700. The aim of the next major programme of garden improvements was to expand the semi-circular garden to the north and south to include two oblong pieces of the park in order to establish a 'great walk' – now known as the Broad Walk – along the East Front.

The half-mile-long Broad Walk had been proposed by Wren's office as early as 1689 and was both a handsome and a

67. A late seventeenth-
century *claire-voyée*, or
screen, giving on to
Home Park from the
Great Fountain Garden.

68. John King's engraved
view of c.1700, showing
the Great Parterre –
now known as the
Great Fountain Garden.
The central oval basin
is the only water feature
to survive to this day.

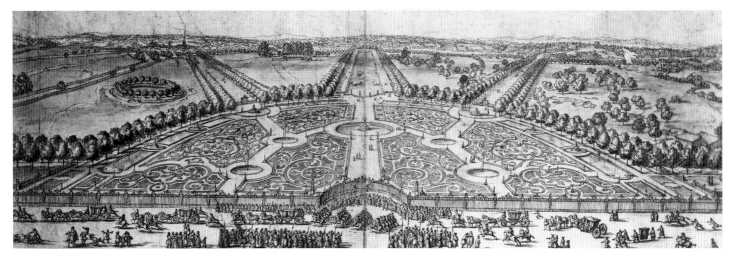

functional feature. The gravel walk, which runs parallel to the eastern leg of the ancient moat, was built to give access to the palace from the Kingston Road. Henry Wise superintended the building work, which entailed repositioning a 400-foot stretch of the Longford River north-west of the palace, digging a corresponding canal to the south-east of the Great Fountain Garden and the two semi-circular canals which still encompass the garden. Wise also dismantled and re-erected sections of the garden's original perimeter railings to form two return walls to enclose the two new oblong pieces. A gate – later known as the Flower Pot Gateon account of its eponymous ornaments sculpted by John van Nost – was inserted in the park wall where it joined the north end of the Broad Walk. The gate's piers still bear their original carved Portland stone panels and are surmounted with two groups of little boys cast in hard metal, supporting flower baskets (fig. 70).

Once this building work was completed, the divisions were levelled, turfed and bisected by the 40-foot-wide walk, which to this day extends from the Flower Pot Gate to the semi-circular terrace overlooking the Thames. The walk was flanked by long, narrow borders planted with large fine shaped yews, hollies, junipers and laurels interspersed with round-headed Cedars of Lycia and a range of flowers including tulips, crocus, snowdrops, white and yellow narcissus, Persian iris and polyanthus.

Some of the original features of the Great Fountain Garden were also improved during the building of the Broad Walk: a Derbyshire marble coping was set around the Great Fountain and a Ketton stone pavement was laid along the length of the East Front. Encouraged by the success of the elaborate waterworks at his palace of Het Loo, the King and Willem Bentinck – and possibly the new Superintendent of Buildings, Richard Jones, Earl of Ranelagh – also resolved to boost the water pressure of the fountains. Daniel Defoe informs us, that

> while the Gardens were thus [being] laid out, the King also directed the laying the Pipes for the [Great] Fountain and *Jette d'Eau's*; and particularly the Dimensions of them, and what Quantity of Water they should cast up, and encreas'd the Number of them after the first Design.[5]

The plumber Matthew Roberts was commissioned to lay new lead pipes and brass cocks for the fountains and to pave all the fountain basins with brick, and Stephen South was enlisted to repair the fountains. Despite these costly improvements, the fountains failed to play effectively. In desperation, the Office of Works consulted the hydraulic engineer Robert Alderney, who was asked to improve the ornamental fountains by lining the Great Fountain basin with clay. This, too, did little to enhance the vigour of the waterworks.[6]

As the East Front gardens began to take shape, the ground-floor apartments of the eastern range became the most desirable lodgings in the palace. From this time the most powerful courtiers at the palace – the Master of the Robes, the Lord Chamberlain and the Keeper of the Privy Seal – were assigned rooms overlooking the Great Fountain Garden and with easy access to the state rooms on the first floor. The apartments granted by the King to his 'favourites' – and the Earl of Albemarle, in particular – benefited from being both open to Fountain Court on the west and to the gardens and the garden gate on the east.

Fussiness, Costliness and Foreignness

The Great Fountain Garden became the subject of a lively aesthetic debate that revolved around the struggle for a national style of gardening. The controversy began in the very early eighteenth century, in the wake of the sweeping improvements to the pleasure ground made by Queen Anne.

In 1703 the Great Fountain Garden was remodelled, on the Queen's instructions, to reflect Nicholas Hawksmoor's second proposal of 1689 (fig. 73). The Royal Gardener, Henry Wise, supervised the 'sinking, new making and altering' of the gardens and it is presumed that the parterre de broderie, the *gazon coupé* and the fountains were removed by the end of the following year. An apron of Swedish limestone was also laid along the East Front for the display of tubs of orange trees during the summer. The gardens were again refurbished for the Queen in 1707 when Wise was paid for new turfing and gravelling the Great Fountain Garden. The lead pipes and brass cocks of the former fountains were also lifted. The only fountain to survive the refurbishment was the Great Fountain in the central walk, which remains to this day. The garden's statues were retained, although the Gladiator and his counterpart were repositioned, and a great many of the grand parterre's clipped evergreens were placed in rectangular beds edged with box.

69. Daniel Marot's
design for the Great
Fountain Garden, 1689.

70. (right) The Flower
Pot Gate forms the
northern terminus of
the Broad Walk.

71. (below) The Broad
Walk, looking south.

72. Anthony Highmore's view toward the palace, looking down the Diagonal Walk, c.1744. The conical-shaped yews shown on this print continue to thrive to this day.

73. (right) Plan showing proposed alterations to the Great Fountain Garden, 1703.

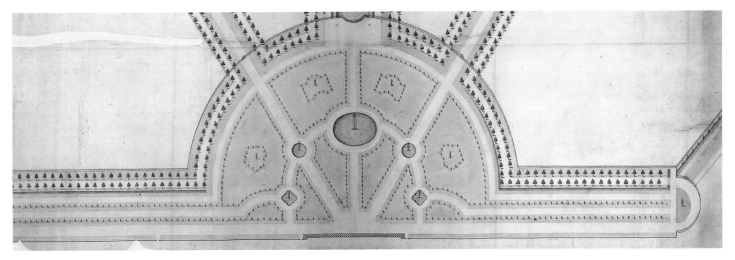

The transformation of the garden from a fussy and expensive layout to a simpler expression of grass and gravel appealed to the Queen's English taste. Proponents of this English taste, such as Stephen Switzer and Batty Langley, rejected the artful manipulation of natural materials into topiary, and the intricacy, extravagance and elaboration that English viewers registered in Dutch garden layouts.

Stephen Switzer, writing in 1715, expressed great pleasure that the fanciful box-work in the Great Fountain Garden had been pulled up and that the gardens were laid into a 'plain but noble manner'. A 'Regular Parterre, or Lawn, stript of all those Decorations, of tonsur'd Plants with which the Gardeners have heretofore loaded them, when smooth and even, and of a proper Proportion, strikes the Eye with a certain Reverence and Grandeur scarcely expressible'. The garden writer railed against the little niceties, the variety and the artificial rudeness of the Dutch taste, which came in with the Revolutio, and which were almost universally followed, remarking that though the gardens of Hampton Court were noble, they were nonetheless open to criticism: the pleasure gardens were stuffed too thick with box – a fashion brought from Holland by Dutch gardeners, who used it to a fault, especially in England, where good grass and gravel abounded. There was, he believed, nothing now so much wanting to complete the grandeur of the British nation as noble and magnificent gardens, statues and waterworks.[7]

The garden writer Batty Langley shared Switzer's distaste for 'that abominable Mathematical Regularity and Stiffness' in gardens. His patriotism led him to champion British gardening over all its rival traditions, remarking in *New Principles of Gardening* (1728) that the garden would have a very grand aspect were those trifling plants of yew and holly and their borders taken away, and replaced with plain grass. He also hoped that the plants which had been injured by intensive clipping might assume their 'proper and natural Shapes as soon as time can operate the same'.[8]

Daniel Defoe's earlier account of the Fountain Garden in his popular travel book *A Tour Thro' the Whole Island of Great Britain* (1724) was more conciliatory than Langley's. He admired the gardens and approved of the restitution of some of the old planting, observing that as the Queen disliked the smell of the box hedging, she had it pulled up and had the garden replanted.[9] Anne did not, however, have all the evergreen trees removed, which prompted the novelist Samuel Richardson's rebuke in 1742 that had the yews and hollies been 'thrown out and a finer Disposition made of the ground' it would have improved the view from the Queen's apartments.[10]

Suspicion of Formal Gardens

Few changes took place in the Great Fountain Garden after the late 1730s. Most of what we know about it during this period is based on topographical views: Bernard Lens portrayed the garden in 1733, Jacques Rigaud published an engraved view in 1736 and Anthony Highmore's detailed views were engraved by Tinney in *c*.1744 (figs 72, 74). The topographers portray the garden as a vast, flat, crisp and manicured expanse, dotted with clusters of diminutive figures in court dress – women kitted out in *robes à la française*, or in immense, cumbersome hoops, and men in tight-fitting frocks and tricorns – their sartorial absurdities reminiscent of the topiary which surrounds them.

From the second half of the eighteenth century, visitors registered intense unease with the quaint old-world arrangement, antique formality and mathematical character of the garden, which they perceived as grotesque, uninviting and distressingly neglected. The anonymous poem 'The Rise and Progress of the Present Taste in Planting, Parks, Pleasure Grounds, Gardens, &c.' (1768) summed up this sentiment:

> Here great Nassau the Belgian gardens spread,
> Yet Hampton-Court th' improving age misled;
> Long gravel walks with puerile knots of flowers,
> Of taste and grandeur still destroy the powers;
> With intersected plats of useless grass,
> Which seem to interrupt us as we pass;
> Garnish'd like Christmas brawn, with box or pews,
> With chearful hollies, and with gloomy yews:
> What tho' meandering Thames flows gliding by,
> Yet one dead level still offends the eye!
> We here fatigu'd the lengthening walk survey,
> That tonsured brushes, and parterres display:
> And pyramids in yew, that doleful stand,
> Like mutes and mourners in a fun'ral Band;
> When after dragging our tir'd legs a mile,

74. *An Oblique View of the East Front of Hampton Court with Part of the Garden,* after Highmore, c.1744.

75. (right) Thomas Rowlandson's *View in the Gardens in Hampton Court Palace,* c.1798.

76. (far right) View from the rooftop of the palace down the Kingston and Long Water Avenues.

Lo! Two pavilions in a wretched stile,
Thro' which we soon to rural meads retreat,
And what these gardens want, in them we meet.
Visitors to the palace were, nonetheless, bemused by its curious surroundings, and contemporary views – such as John Spyers's various watercolours (c.1775–80) and Thomas Rowlandson's engraved *View in the Gardens in Hampton Court Palace* (c.1798) – portray the gardens, not as quaint and mathematical, but *en déshabille*, like the groups of people who wander through them (fig. 75).

Spyers's watercolour of the middle of the Great Fountain Garden depicts the large oval basin and its fountain as a forlorn puddle pierced by a puny squirt; the pool is no longer encompassed by an ordered company of shapely yew sentinels, but by an undisciplined mob of monstrous shapes – sugar cones, pyramidal hats and gargantuan mushrooms – which sprout like rank weeds from the relict flowerbeds of the early formal garden.

A number of visitors to the palace were bemused by the garden. Thomas Jefferson – the future third President of the United States – who visited Hampton Court briefly in 1786, dismissed the Fountain Garden and the Privy Garden as 'old fashioned – clipt yews grown wild'; and the French traveller Louis Simond observed in 1811 that the garden was planted in the 'old fashion of strait walks', and the neglected topiary conjured an image of 'unlicked cubs, with their long hair sticking out on all sides'.[11] The London topographer David Hughson, on the other hand, provided a more useful advice for would-be copyists of the royal style of gardening: he opined in 1817 that the regularity and grandeur of the old-fashioned garden was 'more suitable to the magnificence of a royal palace, than the natural beauties of a private villa'.[12]

The Public Gardens

From 1832 the Great Fountain Garden was opened to the public, and became known officially as the Public Gardens. Its management was vested in the Office of Woods and Forests, who in turn appointed the surveyor and amateur naturalist Edward Jesse to the post of Surveyor of the Royal Parks and Gardens. Jesse immediately embarked upon the improvement of the gardens and appointed a Mr Johnson as head gardener.

A contributor to the *Gardener's Magazine* reported in 1833 that the gardens were 'excellent of their kind', but that it was to be regretted that 'they are not kept up, either with sufficient care in point of order and neatness, or due attention to their original form … the flowers and shrubs are straggling and tawdry, neglected or badly pruned, and either overgrown or deformed'.[13] This neglect had been arrested by 1837, when the same magazine reported that under the improving hand and the judicious management of the head gardener the gardens were being renovated and were 'beginning to assume a more pleasing character than they did a few years ago'.[14]

Johnson did not alter significantly the layout of the Great Fountain Garden, although he stripped the remaining old planting from the early eighteenth-century *plates bandes* and replaced it with showy bedding.[15] His floral schemes satisfied traditionalists and modern garden lovers alike as the 'bedding system' – the practice of planting tender plants outdoors during suitable seasons – made it possible to superimpose luxuriant displays within the existing eighteenth-century framework of the garden. Another contributor to the *Gardeners' Chronicle* remarked in 1841 that 'notwithstanding the gardens are laid out in a regular manner, the flowers and plants are in many instances so arranged that the formality is hardly perceptible, and the brilliant masses of colour distributed round the lawn offer a striking contrast to the dark green of the trees in the Home Park.'[16]

The oval pool at the centre of the garden was one of the palace's most publicized attractions. While the Great Fountain was little more than a pathetic squirt, its basin – referred to by the French botanist and water-lily specialist Joseph Latour-Marliac as 'Diogenes' tub' – was, from the 1840s, well stocked with remarkably fine goldfish and a number of choice and very beautiful water lilies. Life was not always rosy for the denizens of the pool: when they were not the prey of herons, they were victims of bureaucratic parsimony. In May 1847 the *Illustrated London News* reported that the 'spirit of Economy' had stopped an allowance formerly made for feeding the goldfish in the central basin: 'the famine is in their waters, and the finny people are represented as distressingly importunate, in their own way, to visitors'. It quoted from *The Times*:

We are credibly informed that half a hundredweight of gold and silver fish in the central pond of the gardens have for some time

been reduced to the alms of the faithful for their daily subsistence. The 'Board' acknowledges their need, but has resolutely declined to supply crumbs. The instinct of the tribe has been quickened into intelligence by such cutting severity, and any visitor may now see the party-coloured mendicants crowding up to the side of the pool in mute appeal from the tyranny of the Woods and Forests, and asking from private contributors the allowance they deserve from the Crown. There never was such retrenchment since Frederick the Great cut Voltaire's sugar.[17]

Sculpture and Fountains

Over the years the public cultivated an intense and lively interest in the character and layout of the garden – and nowhere was the fury of the debate more acute than in the role and display of sculpture and decorative ornament. The controversy was sparked by the conspicuous absence of garden statuary. In 1829 the statues in the garden had been expelled from their pedestals and were sent to Windsor Castle on the orders of George IV. Some of the plinths were adorned with feeble terracotta vases, while others remained for many years vacant. Commenting on the removal of the statuary, William Edward Trotter remarked in 1839 that the unoccupied pedestals gave to the grounds the appearance of a cemetery.[18]

The champion of the proposed restitution of statuary to the gardens was Charles Knight – a man of formidable literary energy, who poured his talents into producing popular educational books for the Victorian middle classes. Knight remarked in 1847 that the empty pedestals 'ought again to bear some classic burden'. Garden statuary could, he believed, serve an educational role and reinforce a sense of national identity:

We do not desire to see a chronic expense here incurred, like the cost of making the great fountains of Versailles play on fete days. We ask, only, that what has become a Palace for the people should not appear wanting in those decent ornaments which assuredly would not have been taken away had it remained a palace for the Sovereign. Restore the old statues, or give us something even more instructive in their place. Fill these gardens with such choice sculptures – we care not whether they are copies or originals – as may harmonize with the character of

the buildings. Do not fear that the people will mutilate or injure the very choicest works of Art.[19]

Finally, in 1864, replacement statues were raised upon the empty pedestals. The new works came from Austin, Seeley & Co., and bore no resemblance to the earlier copies of the originals: a playful group of cherubic boys occupied the pedestal which had once supported the brawny Borghese Gladiator, and the Farnese Hercules was replaced by Samson and the Lion (fig. 77). Two vases with goats' heads and handles, and two vases with handles and wreaths were placed in the garden, as well as a statue of the Three Graces at the head of the Long Water (figs 79, 78).

Knight also registered disappointment with the garden's principal ornament: whereas earlier visitors had remarked that the Great Fountain was in bad order, Knight condemned them as 'simply ridiculous'. The fountain was the garden's greatest deformity: this 'miscalled fountain' toiled away only to throw 'a few sputtering drops into the sunlight. . . . If the supply of water is limited – if hydraulic science cannot overcome the difficulties of producing lofty jets in a wide plain – let the fountains be obliterated, and the basins no longer deformed with these miserable pretences'.[20]

Ugly Old Trees

While some critics wrestled with issues of moral improvement, others took the flower gardens to task. Advocates of what was referred to as 'improved flower gardening' were of the opinion that the garden's enduringly formal layout, and its relict yews and hollies in particular, precluded the full potential of the gardener's art. Although the giant conifers were regarded as being in character with the place, they were 'highly detrimental' to the flowers and the displays: 'little or no effect can be produced with any amount of flowers in such a place as Hampton Court, where the flower-beds and borders are . . . smothered with useless, and very ugly old trees'.[21]

No one was as outspoken on the subject as Donald Beaton, whose name was regularly invoked as a standard for excellence in garden decoration.[22] He railed in the *Cottage Gardener* in 1856 that the effect of the garden was spoiled by the yews – 'every one of them being in the centre of a flower-bed, or in the mixed borders, where they carry the day, and with their gloom and shade hide and

76. The fountain
in the Great Fountain
Garden, c.1929.

destroy all ideas of effect from flower-planting'. The style of the garden was 'neither one thing or the other, but a bastard of bad taste and flat Dutch'. He helpfully recommended:

> A company of Sappers and Miners should be sent to there… to grub up every one of those Yews, root and branch; then the two flats on either side of the centre diverging walk from the palace entrance should be laid out in the true Dutch style of lace parterre, if it was thought worthwhile to retain that style. The Yews could be planted in other parts of the garden in the Dutch double-row style; they might even be reduced, by cut and clip, to fantastic shapes, the canal to be alive with sirens and water-kelpies; then with grottoes and a profusion of statuary, you need not go out of Middlesex to see a good example of the old Dutch style of landscape-gardening.[23]

A greater number of garden writers expressed their support for the mute regiment of ancient trees and desired to see them 'restored to perfect health, and free growth'. The enthusiasm for the preservation of the yews and hollies was fuelled by the topiary revival that swept across the country in the 1850s. Topiarian enthusiasm, in fact, still prevails at Hampton Court and has ensured that the giant yews and hollies have been spared a premature bundling to the woodyard. The trees are assiduously maintained today and are among the most curious and memorable attributes of the palace gardens (figs 78–80).

While there was disagreement in the mid-nineteenth century on the layout and composition of the garden's beds, there was a broad consensus that the 'gardening part of the business there is much better done than in any of our public gardens, not excepting the Crystal Palace'. The Crystal Palace was, for many, the apogee of flower gardening; setting Hampton Court in contrast to its unrestrained lavishness, commentators emphasized the taste and restraint of the palace's head gardener and his team of twenty gardeners. A contributor to the *Cottage Gardener* remarked that there were 'few enough [gardeners], goodness knows, for such a vast surface of flowers, grass and gravel'. There was also abundant praise for the head gardener's 'excellent plan . . . of naming every kind of plant which is bedded, by which all who can read may learn the names'.

Carpet Bedding

When, in the early 1870s, carpet bedding – a form of subtropical bedding in which dwarf plants and ground covers were shorn to create displays as uniform and even as carpets – was adopted at the palace it received lavish praise in the local press. The *Surrey Comet* reported in 1873 that the popularity of the novelty 'caused surprise' and that 'such crowds gathered round the beds that the turf was trodden almost out of existence, leading to the laying out of planks to protect the grass and enclosure of the beds with ropes'.[24]

The head gardener's innovation and floristic skills were, however, generally much admired. Nathan Cole – the champion of London's Metropolitan Parks and author of *The Royal Parks and Gardens of London* (1876), remarked that 'there are many points of attraction in this garden, but one of its principal features is the carpet and tapestry beds'. The new bedding displays were more than mere 'systems of decoration' – they had a moral purpose. Such efforts could not 'fail in exerting a beneficial influence in promoting improved habits, awakening new thoughts, and suggesting fresh subjects for the mental exercise of the million, who might otherwise be employed in the study of less desirable objects than those which nature provides and art cultivates'.[25]

The taste for exuberant bedding began to wither in the 1880s, to make way for a new, more cautious approach to gardening. Ernest Law remarked in 1891 that the 'original formal trimness' and the 'old fashioned air' of the Great Fountain Garden had suffered by 'attempts to follow the fluctuating follies of successive fashions in gardening, so that their archaic aspect has been unduly encroached upon, by efforts to vie with the costly pretentiousness of the modern style'. The rich masses of flowers in the beds did not entirely disappear, but their impact was dissipated by a re-appreciation of the other, more established elements of the garden which were thought to intensify the beauty of the whole – namely groves of lime trees, shelving banks of grass, winding streams, level lawns and walls covered with creepers and vines.[26]

'The Prevention of Vandalistic Alterations'

During the First World War, the celebrated flowerbeds at Hampton Court were turfed over and the houses and frames in which the summer bedding plants were nursed were devoted to tomatoes, potatoes and beetroot.[27] However, when the war was

over and there was no longer any need for economies of this kind, there was considerable public agitation for the restoration of the famous bedding.

His Majesty's Office of Works announced early in 1919 that the war-time modifications introduced to the gardens of Hampton Court might become permanent: that twenty-five of the thirty-seven flowerbeds along the East Front that had been turfed over were to remain thus, and that the rest might also be given a similar treatment. This plan, which they mistakenly imagined was a round of uncontroversial improvements, in fact struck at the very heart of the war-weary public – leaders in the press at once condemned the mean-spiritedness of the palace. The *Surrey Comet* launched the first salvo, publishing an editorial entreating the public to deliver the 'famous gardens at Hampton Court from the hands of the vandals'.[28] Its explosive rhetoric instantly begot a much-publicized debate on the benefits of public gardening. The *Gardeners' Chronicle* reported in spring 1919 that the 'furore' raised by these proposals revealed

> how strong is the affection among the people for that popular place of public resort. . . . Whether it is good taste or the reverse to have rich displays of flowers in beds more or less formal depends on what the canons of good taste are. In music, painting and architecture, we please ourselves, or ought to, but when the public are concerned we must please them, or they have a right to complain. We might with as much reason change the tune of the National Anthem to one of real Wagnerian strain, as change the flower gardening at Hampton Court.[29]

The publicity had the desired effect: in May 1919 the Office of Works published their revised proposal for a much reduced scheme in *The Times*, and in June an expert committee was assembled to consider the way forward. A white paper was subsequently produced, in which all the recommendations were approved and implemented – many of them still guide the garden displays to this day. There is not room here to enumerate the many recommendations. The aim was simple: as the garden designer H. Avray Tipping remarked in *Country Life* in June of the same year, the committee sought to re-establish a

> pre-eminence of fine form and simple dignity for the central section, contrasting with as much varied floral interest and rich colour in the side sections as is compatible with the spirit of

formalism which must be the dominant but not despotic note. An enhanced general effect with a curtailed list might thus be attained.[30]

By July many of the flowerbeds in the gardens began to take on the appearance of something approaching their former condition. Meanwhile, improvements continued apace throughout the gardens: the beds in the circumference of the semi-circle were reinstated and almost entirely devoted to spring and summer bedding, the plantations beyond the canal were preserved, the shrubs on the far side of the canal were thinned and all common plants were removed and replaced with choice suitable shrubs and bold-habited plants. In order to meet the strong public desire for flowers, all but four of the beds parallel to the Broad Walk were restored and new yews were planted to replace missing or decayed trees.

According to *Country Life*, the most dramatic step in the refurbishment came not, however, from the premeditated actions of experts, but through the 'fortuitous exigencies of war time': the turfing over of the flowerbeds beneath the now clipped but 'brooding yews' produced an effect 'a little sombre, perhaps, but full of restful dignity, of spacious presence in accord with the character of Wren's building and the gardening spirit of the time'. In order to relieve the cheerless appearance of the middle of the great semi-circle, tubs with flowering plants were placed round the oval basin.[31] This tradition continues to this day: tubs of agapanthus and lantana are ranged around the basin during summer months; the water lilies were, however, banished some years ago.

After the improvements had been made to the beds in the Great Parterre, the Office of Works turned its hand to the much-neglected Long Border. A contributor to the *Observer* remarked:

> The forlorn long borders that run North and South, parallel to the wet ditch, are excellently placed, and ought to be quite charming: frankly, they are deplorable. Rose bushes are dotted about in a spotty way, with herbaceous or bulbous plants among them and no hint that anybody dreamt of designing in line or colour. The so-called 'herbaceous border', eight feet deep, gives further opportunities which are missed. True, it is what is called 'a blaze of colour', but the effect is monotonous and meaningless, too often reminding one of a trial seed farm.

78. (far left) This group of cherubic boys is one of the statues introduced into the Great Fountain Garden in the nineteenth century.

79. (left) The Three Graces statue was placed at the head of the Long Water in the 1850s.

80. (below) Sir Henry Cole, writing as Felix Summerly, described the yews in the Great Fountain Garden in 1841 as 'peculiar, solemn, and mystic shapes'.

81. The Long Border after its restoration in 2002. The border lies on top of the Moat Ditch Garden which was destroyed in the late seventeenth century to make way for the new eastern range of the palace and the Great Fountain Garden.

82. (left) Watercolour view of the East Front by Ernest Arthur Rowe, c.1910.

83. (below) The fifty-two island beds in the Great Fountain Garden are double bedded. This view shows the summer bedding display and includes chlorophytum, pelargonium, canna lilies and abutilon.

There are very few perennials except phloxes in this bed, nearly all the plants being annuals or biennials… But the combinations are not beautiful, and plants of one season require a heavy expenditure, especially in labour.[32]

The Long Border which runs the length of the half-mile-long Broad Walk was recast in 1923–4 by Ernest Law: a new scheme of bedding-out was adopted and *The Flower-Lover's Guide to the Gardens of Hampton Court Palace* was published giving a full account of the bedding and a list of the flowers and shrubs. Law remarked that there were no gardens in England where the modern developments in bedding out and the planting of herbaceous and mixed borders had been carried out to so high a pitch as at Hampton Court. Indeed, he proposed that, 'to a great extent, the fashion was started here'.[33]

The border continues to dazzle garden visitors to this day (fig. 81). Between 1997 and 2002, fifty-two panels of the south herbaceous border were replanted to Ernest Law's designs of 1923. Wherever possible, original cultivars have been planted to replicate the effect of the early planting scheme and annuals and perennials have been intermixed to create bedding typical of the period. The north borders will also be refurbished in a similar manner.

'A National Monument to our Native Love of Gardens'

By the mid-1920s the grand aspect looking eastwards from the Queen's Apartments had been virtually restored. A London Underground poster of the period portrays the revitalized charms of the Great Fountain Garden: throngs of languid day-trippers mingle freely in the dappled light of the royal landscape (fig. 85). The image reinforces the invitation emblazoned on the poster – 'Hampton Court for cooling fountains, Sun and chequered shade, Walk in the alleys England's Kings have made'.

The Great Fountain Garden, more than any other part of the estate, was now also promoted as encapsulating the best of the democratic tradition of British gardening: to London's teeming millions they were, according to a contributor to *The Field* (1926), 'a perpetual joy' and a 'national monument to our native love of gardens', and to others – including American visitors and 'those from sun-scorched lands' – the gardens were a revelation of floral Paradise, and an evocation of 'Merrie England'.[34] The 'economical and showy' display of bulbs, annuals, biennials and perennials was

puffed in the popular press as inspirational for 'progressive suburban and country amateurs'.

The post-war refurbishment and its attendant publicity, not surprisingly, led to an increase in garden tourism; and with it came the wear and tear associated with intensive use. *The Sunday Times* announced in July 1920 that 'since the war . . . a return to something like the early Victorian disorderliness' was indulged by some visitors, who 'strew paper, orange peels and match-boxes in the gardens, and tread on the grass borders'. The Office of Works, therefore, re-erected the notice boards 'which for fifty years after the free opening of the Palace . . . stood in the gardens, appealing to visitors, in these terms: – "It is expected that the public will protect what is intended for public enjoyment". These notices were removed some twenty-five years ago, having, it was supposed, permanently effected their object.'

The *Daily Chronicle* reported in 1926 that the royal gardens attracted 'some 50,000 cockneys and north countrymen' every summer weekend – most of whom visited the Great Fountain Garden, and came to be educated in 'a more liberal habit of beds and borders', and who wished to see at first hand 'what can be done with these cheapest and easiest grown of annuals and others besides'.[35] While fewer of today's visitors may visit the Great Fountain Garden with a view to educating themselves in flower

HAMPTON COURT

For cooling fountains
Sun and "chequered shade"
Walk in the alleys
England's Kings have made.

**BY TRAM FROM HAMMERSMITH
WIMBLEDON OR SHEPHERDS BUSH**

UNDERGROUND

gardening, they nonetheless admire the ever-changing double
rotation displays which have become associated with the high
horticultural standards maintained by the palace gardeners.
Every year 31,500 summer bedding plants are set out in the Great
Fountain Garden's fifty-two beds; these are replaced in the autumn
with over 22,500 plants and 28,500 bulbs for the autumn and
spring displays.

Although the Great Fountain Garden suffered innumerable
privations during the Second World War, the fabric was restored,
much as it had been in the early 1920s, to reflect the guidelines
in the white paper of 1919. Not until 1987 was the garden subject
to another round of extensive improvements, when the Lime
Walks – which trace the outline of the little semi-circular canals
north and south of the Great Parterre – were felled and replanted
(figs 84, 86).

While the Lime Walks are now beginning to assume a degree
of maturity, it will be some years before they achieve the
picturesque character that made them so popular with the public.
Ernest Law remarked in the 1890s that 'no part of the Gardens of
Hampton Court have appealed more to the romantically inclined
than these delightful leafy groves. For more than two centuries
they have been the favourite haunt of love-making pairs, and
beneath their secluded shades protestations and vows of plighted
troth have been exchanged'. They provided, moreover, one of the
most popular vantage points of the palace. Many topographers
from the early eighteenth century onwards portrayed the palace
from the groves and noted the charms of the elevated Lime Walks
which bordered the little canal: Spyers's late-eighteenth century
view of the Lime Walk and subsequent sketches convey the bucolic
atmosphere of the terrace walk, where according to Charles
Knight, 'we may lounge away a summer afternoon upon welcome
seats under "boughs" which are not "melancholy"'.[36]

In recent years, two initiatives – one ephemeral and the other
permanent – were launched to mark the Golden Jubilee of the
accession of Elizabeth II. A pair of stately floral crowns was raised
in May 2002 at the origin of the *patte d'oie* – or goose foot of
radiating avenues – where it intersects the Broad Walk, framing
the view down the Long Water (fig. 88). The fifteen-foot-high
virtuoso displays of sculptural bedding, raised on carpet-bedded
pillows strewn with swags and crosses and bearing the mottos 'God

86. The southern leg of
the transverse canal.
The Lime Walks (left)
were replanted in 1987.

88. (below) The Jubilee Crowns by the East Front of the palace in 2002.

89. (overleaf) Spring planting in the Great Fountain Garden. Among the plants included in this display are hyacinths, wallflowers and bellis.

Save the Queen' and 'Long Live the Queen', were 'jewel bedded' with thousands of living dwarf bedding plants – sedums, sempervivum, aeoniums, alternanthera, helichrysum, echeverias and saginas – to evoke the brilliance and allure of the St Edward's Crown. Each crown was set with 15,000 plants, possessed drip and misting irrigation systems and weighed over five tons each when wet. A pair of similar vegetable sculptures were also erected at Waddesdon Manor in Buckinghamshire – in collaboration with Hampton Court – to mark the Jubilee and to celebrate the royal palace's and the Rothschild family's longstanding interest in the tradition of carpet bedding.

A more permanent note was struck in June 2002 with the refurbishment of the central fountain and its Victorian waterworks. The original display has, moreover, been enhanced with the addition of a central jet, which is intended to evoke the character of the early eighteenth-century display. The water now erupts more plentifully than it has for the past three centuries: the supply is mechanically pumped to the fountain, ensuring that the display will no longer suffer the rebukes of frustrated visitors.

The West Front

Throngs of visitors – whether foreign ambassadors and their retinues of attendants, or Cockney holiday-makers – have for almost five centuries approached Hampton Court from the west. Their first full view of the palace is the noble West Front and its forecourt setting (fig. 90). This view has changed considerably over the years as trees, shrubberies, buildings, railings and footpaths have come and gone, and generations of improvers have sought to confer ever greater degrees of dignity on the principal ceremonial approach to the palace.

In the early 1520s, Cardinal Wolsey's Great Gatehouse soared above a motley encampment of tradesmen's workshops and storehouses. By contrast, today we gaze, our view unencumbered, from Trophy Gate down the Causeway – or broad carriage drive – which leads to the bridge before the Great Gatehouse. As we process down the drive, our view to the right over the Thames and its opposite bank is partially obscured by a row of Norway maples – latter day replacements for a line of stately elms. On our left we see the long line of low brick barracks, now containing the palace Ticket Office and Shop, which reminds us that the West Front forecourt was once filled with troops protecting the Sovereign.

Although no longer known or perceived as a court, the West Front still serves as the palace's forecourt. The area, which has been known variously as the Long Courtyard, the Outer Green Court, Outer Court, Palace Yard and the Barrack Yard, remains the largest, greenest and most public of the palace's courts. This large trapezoidal area began to take shape in the mid-1530s when Henry VIII tidied up and formalized what had previously been a building site. A gate – known as the Outer Gate – was erected where Trophy Gate stands today, and a wall was built along what is now the north side of the Barrack Block, to the palace, to enclose the new forecourt. A new range – the Great House of Easement (a latrine block) – was also added to the western elevation of the palace front in order to restore the symmetry of the then lop-sided composition.

The court's principal ornament was, and remains today, the Great Gatehouse. This broad and imposing tower with four octagonal turrets and clusters of carved red-brick chimney-shafts was built by Wolsey in the early 1520s to mark the entrance to Base Court (figs 91–3). This building, being the front of the mansion house, was rendered even more impressive by the presence of the moat, which formed a deep and wide ditch between the first great

gate and Outer Court. The ditch was presumably crossed by a timber bridge; this, however, was replaced in 1536 by a stone bridge garrisoned by an impressive display of fierce heraldic beasts in carved freestone, including a bull, a greyhound, a dragon, a unicorn, a lion and a panther – all bearing shields blazoned with the King's and Queen's arms. Wyngaerde's view of the palace from the north (c.1555) shows the gatehouse, the bridge, the outbuildings and the court in considerable detail (fig. 93). A later view of 1669, taken across the Tiltyard looking south-east to the palace, also conveys the lofty grandeur of Wolsey's gatehouse.

The first surviving plans of the court date from 1689; they show the outline of the area, and the guard houses, which were first erected in 1661–2, and rebuilt in 1689 – the range of buildings replacing the Tudor north wall of the court. Curiously, the plans do not depict The Toye – the famous sixteenth-century tavern, or victualling house – which sat close to the Hampton Court Ferry, adjoining the south-west corner of Outer Green Court.

A survey drawing of about 1714 shows the court inscribed with three radial spokes projecting from a large *rond-point*. This formal landscape gesture – which appears strangely truncated and awkward within the confines of the narrow, irregular space – was contrived in imitation of the *patte d'oie* of the Great Fountain Garden. This scheme was laid out between 1699 and 1700 after the Tudor moat was filled in, and new ragstone paving was laid to form the Causeway between the outer gate and the semi-circular carriage sweep immediately in front of the palace. The Causeway, its radial arms and the *rond-point* were flanked with Portland stone bollards, which remain in place today.

Henry VIII's Outer Gate was also at the same time rebuilt in a more substantial manner. Four large brick piers were raised – the two inward ones framed the gateway and were adorned with the royal supporters – the lion and the unicorn – each holding a shield bearing the arms of Great Britain. The two outward piers were crowned with trophies of war – hence it was named Trophy Gate. The imperial supporters and the trophies were cast in 'hard metal' or lead by John Oliver, Master Mason, to the designs of the sculptor Grinling Gibbons.

From the late 1730s the buildings in the court were given over to grace-and-favour accommodation and became known as the

90. The Causeway
and the West Front of
the palace framed by
Trophy Gate.

91. The West Front;
 the large building at
the left is Henry VIII's
Great Hall.

92. (right) A mid-
eighteenth-century
view of the West
Front showing the
encroachment of
trees and shrubs
in the formerly barren
courtyard.

93. (below right) Detail
from Anthonis van
den Wyngaerde's view
of c.1555 showing the
Great Gatehouse and
Outer Green Court
(now known as the
West Front).

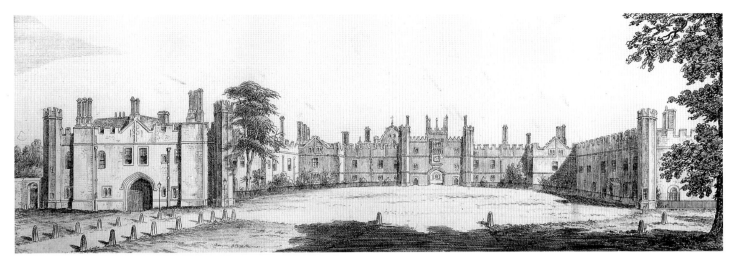

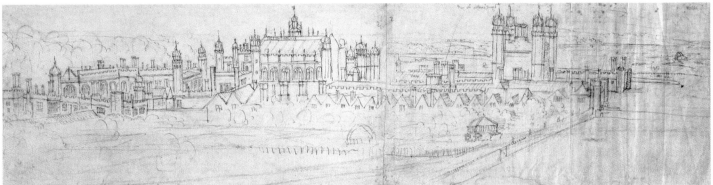

Trophy Gate Buildings. Watercolour sketches by John Spyers executed between 1775 and 1780 portray the court after it had been domesticated by the stately pensioners: iron and timber palisades had been erected and small gardens laid out by the guard houses and along the line of the former moat ditch, giving the court the appearance of a village green. The space exudes an air of gracious informality – the geometrical outline of the *patte d'oie* was lost as two of the diagonal spokes were grassed over and new paths were cast across the court. Spyers also depicts the refurbished Great Gatehouse. The building, having fallen into decay, was partly taken down between 1771 and 1773 and rebuilt. Sadly, it was not restored to its original form: its height was truncated by the removal of its two upper storeys.

The character of the court changed yet again when, in 1794, George III authorized the garrisoning of a troop of cavalry at the palace. The grace-and-favour residents in the horse guard stables (beside the guard houses) reluctantly surrendered their tenancies and their little gardens to the cavalry. *A Plan of the Trophy Gate Buildings* (1823, with later annotations) and Sayers's plan (1841) illustrate the jumble of yards, stables, small gardens and offices which encumbered the Outer Green Court; they also document some of the changes that took place from the late eighteenth century, including the giving over of much of the lawn to gravel to form a parade ground, and the setting out of railings on the south side of the court (fig. 193). The area south of the Causeway is shown as crossed by a diagonal path leading to the Barge Walk, and the old elms which line the tow-path are marked. The Toye is also gone, having been demolished in 1840.

There were several intermittent bursts of remedial works to the court after the palace opened to the public in 1838 – most of which were initiated to enhance the setting for tourists. For instance, by 1850 cast-iron lamps were installed to illuminate the Causeway, in 1877 a new iron railing was erected along the south side of the court, and in 1878 the Trophy Gate Buildings were demolished, a brick wall was thrown up between Trophy Gate and the Barge Walk, and the site of the Toye was enclosed, laid to turf and re-christened Toy Green in honour of the defunct hostelry.

In January 1881 the eastern end of the barracks, near the palace, was then converted into a canteen for the troops and subsequently provided refreshments for visitors. The canteen was closed down by the end of the year because of complaints about the behaviour of both the military and the day-trippers. It was reopened a few months later as a coffee and reading room for soldiers.

The cavalry and the tourists may have enlivened the forecourt, but their presence threatened the decorum of the palace. Two matters troubled the palace inhabitants: one Mrs Joyner had set up a fruit stall by Trophy Gate and 'loose women', too, had begun to congregate at the main approach and got into the habit of walking about the parade ground.[1]

The expulsion of the prostitutes appears to have been a protracted business. The problem lay in the fact that two government departments administered the court: the War Office was charged with looking after the barracks, while the Office of Works had jurisdiction over the rest of the fabric. The War Office, therefore, complained to the Office of Works in 1890 that the 'gathering of loose women about the Trophy Gate besides being

criticism, the residents evidently thinking that some vandalistic work was in progress.[3]

At this time, the gravel *rond-point* formed by William III extended right up to the walls of the palace, and the Great Gatehouse. Excavations carried out in 1872 and again in 1909, however, revealed that the course of the moat, its walls and the east end of the sixteenth-century bridge were still plainly traceable. The moat and bridge were, therefore, excavated. Sufficient remains were found to reconstruct the former bridge, although none of the original beasts that had embellished it was found. Replacements were designed by the heraldic artist and archaeologist, the Rev. J. Dorling, and carved by the ecclesiastical and heraldic carvers Farmer and Brindley. Further archaeological research was carried out on the bridge in the late 1990s, which resulted in the renewal of its walking surface.

After the First World War the Cavalry Barracks were used first as a storehouse, then as the record office of the Royal Tank Corps. Proposals by the War Office in the 1930s to convert the buildings into a Signal Experimental Establishment – entailing the erection of 100 radio towers – were quashed and the buildings were handed over to the Board of Works.

Over the past fifty years a variety of piecemeal improvements have been made to the West Front: trees have been planted adjacent to the south and west boundaries and shrubs have been trained up the south-facing walls of the Barrack Block. It is the long-term objective of the palace to resurface the Causeway with ragstone sets and to replace the line of Norway maples with limes.

an evil to the barracks has been of much annoyance to the residents of the Palace', and that they were considering 'the necessity of putting up gates at this entrance'. Gates were, in fact, put up in 1892 and a sentry posted at the gateway, but in the event these precautions were unnecessary as the women appear to have moved on.[2]

In October 1893 a proposal was put forward to abolish the fruit shop at Trophy Gate, to convert the drill ground into a grass plot and to provide a cavalry barrack yard at the rear – on the site of the present car park. These landscape improvements were completed by 1900. A correspondent to the *Journal of Horticulture* was also pleased to report in 1906:

> The main entrance has been altered with the most beneficial
> results. On the left we find the barrack building; on the right
> a strip of grass next the Thames. . . . the main roadway is now
> flanked on either side with placid, level stretches of green grass,
> in perfect harmony with the stately dignity of the ancient Court.
> The back entrances to the barracks were built up, and the level
> wall covered with Ivy and Ampelopsis. A line of standard
> umbrella-headed Acacias was also planted on this side; and
> this completed the alterations. The final result most admirably
> illustrates the wise judgment and taste of the instigators. The
> work, too, was carried through in the face of much local

95. This photograph of
1928 shows cars parked
in Outer Green Court
prior to the building of
the car park behind the
Barrack Block.

The Courts

The internal courtyards are the most underappreciated and misunderstood attributes of Hampton Court. We know surprisingly little about these spaces which have played an important role in the day-to-day life of the palace. What were once among the liveliest concourses of the palace precincts, filled with smells, din and litter, are now quiet and uninhabited yards; few possess features that evoke the richness of their former uses. For hundreds of years the palace's principal quadrangles – Base, Clock, Fountain and Chapel Courts – figured regularly in visitor accounts and were praised for their magnificence, grandeur and convenience. Only in the late nineteenth century, however, did visitors begin to register that the informal decoration of the courts – and the 'inferior courts' in particular – created a desirable air of comfort, homeliness and stately seclusion.

The courts were, in fact, for much of the palace's history, among the few outdoor areas within the royal estate where the resident population could indulge in small-scale private gardening. The gardens that were created in these spaces were necessarily ephemeral and *ad hoc* as they were often unofficial encroachments in paved enclosures which were – with few exceptions – little more than spacious light-wells to the palace's domestic offices, back-stairs, corridors and living apartments. Many of the residents, however, did what they could to improve the character of these bleak yards – planting flowers, shrubs, hedges and trees in pots and in the ground, and erecting rockworks, birdbaths and jardinières – as their decoration contributed to the comfort and convenience of the courts and to the character of the palace in general.

During the sixteenth and seventeenth centuries the principal courts were embellished with lavish fountains, statuary and occasional planting. The aim of these improvements was to confer dignity and magnificence on the monarch and his court. Roger North remarked in his survey of buildings from Henry VIII to Charles II (1698), that at Hampton Court 'we shall perceive more of the august than in any time before or since'; when 'the ancients, I mean our elder country men' built such 'lofty & noble' buildings, they laid them out 'so as to accommodate all orders of persons and occasions'. Hampton Court possessed what North referred to as 'a pompous walk', or an enfilade of spacious, formally laid out ceremonial courts which became increasingly grand as one

progressed from the West Front through Base and Clock Courts to Fountain Court.[1]

From 1737 the palace declined in royal favour, precipitating the colonization of the principal and inferior courts – and, indeed, much of the pleasure grounds – by the resident grace-and-favour population. This marked the beginning of the heyday of the palace's courtyard culture. Hampton Court possessed nineteen internal courts – some of which were so small and undistinguished as to remain nameless. These workaday spaces were henceforth cultivated with considerable vigour, regardless of their size or aspect. One need only examine John Spyers's watercolour views of the palace's courts of the late 1770s to see that curious, modest gardens abounded in every quarter. The impact of these gardens on the character of the palace and the built fabric itself was remarkable and, in official circles, occasionally worrying: it was observed in 1816 that 'in many parts of the Palace particularly the Courts, there are small Gardens with Trees, shrubs, Vines and Creepers trained against the walls, to the evident detriment of the Building'.[2]

After the palace opened its doors to the public in 1838 the grace-and-favour occupants, who had come to enjoy unfettered access to much of the parks and pleasure grounds, were forced to retreat from the 'public gardens'; and by 1897 their private outdoor refuges were reduced to a small slice of the Privy and Pond Gardens and most of the internal courts. These so-called 'crowded-up old bits of garden',[3] nevertheless, continued to flourish and remained lively resorts of their *de facto* guardians until the late twentieth century, when the grace-and-favour population began to dwindle. There are now few reminders of their long and fruitful occupation.

Unravelling the histories of the palace's internal courtyards is not easy, as there are few records of their numerous informal garden layouts. Moreover, the names, functions and positions of these spaces have changed several times over the centuries. These reflect the changing functions and appearances of the courtyards and are a tribute to the versatility of these open spaces and to their importance in the palace layout and its rigorous social order.

97. Cadell and Davies's
published view of 1800,
looking west from
Clock Court through
Base Court to Outer
Green Court.

Base Court

Base Court – whose name derives from the French *basse*, or lower court – was laid out by Cardinal Wolsey in *c*.1514 in imitation of the great outer courts created by Archbishop Morton of Canterbury and his successors at their palaces at Lambeth, Croydon and Otford. The large new quadrangle covered what had previously been the western leg of Lord Daubeney's late fifteenth-century moat, which the Cardinal had filled in the same year. The court's enclosing buildings were laid out to accommodate the Cardinal's guests and the court was paved with cobbles. Although described in a maintenance agreement in 1702 as a 'garden area', there is no evidence to suggest that the court ever had a garden. The central pavement did, however, in the mid-eighteenth century acquire a green patina of moss and grass – probably through neglect – which led to it being referred to as Outer Green Court.[4]

Throughout the eighteenth and nineteenth centuries the court was compared to the finest collegiate quadrangles of Cambridge and Oxford, and was praised for its spaciousness and uniformity.[5] Two features of its architectural setting were particularly admired: Anne Boleyn's Gatehouse and the glazed terracotta roundels of the Roman emperors, commissioned by Wolsey in 1521 from the Italian sculptor Giovanni da Maiano.

For centuries a lively debate ensued on the nature of the original surface material of the court. It was commonly – although mistakenly – held from the eighteenth century that in the sixteenth century the court was turfed. The 'white cobbled court', however, remained paved until 1891, when it was replaced – on the advice of several archaeological societies – with a pair of large grass panels. This improvement was reported in the *Gardeners' Magazine* (1892) as a slight but important change.[6]

The grass plots remain to this day (fig. 99). The Hampton Court Music Festival has been held annually each June in Base Court since 1993; the court is transformed into an outdoor auditorium with the erection of grandstands and a stage.

Clock Court

Clock Court – known variously as Second Court, Fountain Court, Conduit Court or Middle Quadrangle – is so called after its sixteenth-century astronomical clock. The present court was laid out by Henry VIII in the 1530s, and was formed by uniting Wolsey's Inner and Little Courts.

The court's clock was made for Henry VIII in 1540 by Nicholas Oursian, and probably designed by Nicholas Kratzer. The giant timepiece still presides over the stony court and is set above the gateway on the west side of the Inner Gate – framed by flanking turrets. It shares this wall with a pair of early sixteenth-century terracotta roundels of emperors Vitellius and Augustus – related to those in Base Court – which frame a red terracotta display of Wolsey's arms affixed to an archiepiscopal cross, supported by two cherubim and surmounted by a cardinal's hat.

Although the clock is now the principal ornament of the court, it was not always so. During the sixteenth century the court had two fountains – the first built in *c*.1536 for Henry VIII and the second in 1584 for Elizabeth I.

The first fountain was raised shortly after the court was paved with 'hard stone of Kent' and is clearly shown in a drawing by Anthonis van den Wyngaerde (fig. 98). The fountain rises boldly from a stepped hexagonal plinth, surmounted by a large lantern-like superstructure crowned with an ogee dome embellished with figures and finials. The whole resembles a great, fanciful table fountain.

We know considerably more about its successor. This New Great Fountain was completed in 1584 and was also presumably raised on the site of Wolsey's gallery. The ingenious waterwork was supplied with water by the Kingston Hill to Hampton Court conduit, and the design of the feature itself was probably the work of the Master Mason Cornelius Cure. Cure was described in 1596 by Lord Burghley as 'honest, erect and full of invention' and as having 'seen much work in foreign places'.[7] According to the Netherlandish visitor Lodewijck Hugen, Cure's *gioco d'acqua* – or water trick – was put into action by 'turning something' in a closet overlooking the court. Jacob Rathgeb – secretary to the Duke of Württemburg – writing in 1592, was also amused by the waterwork, which he reports was contrived to 'make the water to play upon the ladies and others who are standing by and give them a thorough wetting'. He described the fountain as 'splendid high and massy', and surmounted by a figure of justice.[8] The Brandenburg lawyer Paulus Hentzner – the travelling companion of 'a young Silesian Nobleman' – was no less impressed, remarking in his *Journey into England in the Year 1598* that most of the area is 'paved with square

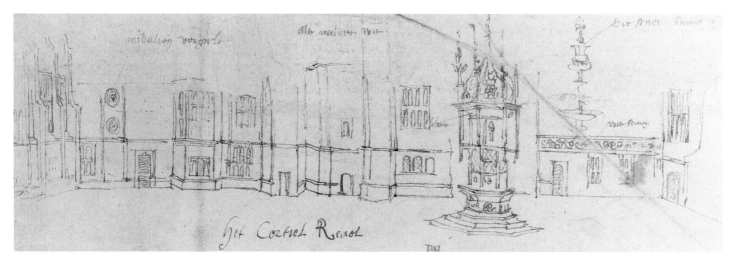

stone; in its centre a fountain that throws up water, covered with a gilt crown, on the top of which is the statue of Justice, supported by columns of white and black marble'.[9]

We know little about the fountain after 1653, when the court is described as 'paved with stone (with a fountain standing in midst thereof)'. There are, however, references to a 'maze' in the court. These presumably refer to the New Great Fountain, which may have been recast.

There are fewer references to the treatment of the remainder of the court. We know, however, that in 1662 masons were relaying the pavement which led from the 'Court into the Parke'. This reference serves to remind us that before the palace was extensively rebuilt in the 1690s, this court was an external court – like the Privy Garden – and lay adjacent to Home Park.

The giant Portland stone colonnade that straddles the south side of the court to form an approach to the King's Staircase remains the most imposing element of the court. This screen, which was raised to mask the irregular though picturesque range of buildings behind, is surmounted by vases, various masks and trophies of war and was designed by Hawksmoor.

John Spyers's view of the court shows the presence of *ad hoc* planting (fig. 100). A few wall plants are shown growing at the foot of the western range and at the base of the Great Hall. The planting is less intentional than serendipitous. The walls of the court were clad with Boston ivy until the early twentieth century (fig. 101). The court is now entirely paved in stone and no longer boasts vegetation or fountains.

Fountain Court

The present Fountain Court – the second courtyard on this site – has been known variously as Inner, Cloister, Cloister Green, Great or Quadrangle Courts. It was formed in the late seventeenth century on the site of an early sixteenth-century courtyard, which had itself supplanted Henry VIII's knot garden.

We know little about the early knot garden, which may, in fact, have been created by Cardinal Wolsey as early as 1515; it is first described in an account of *c*.1532 as lying between the Chapel and the Long Gallery. The garden and its surroundings were, in any event, reconfigured in January 1533 to make way for a completely new courtyard to house a new suite of lodgings for Anne Boleyn.

The construction of this court was the first initiative in Henry VIII's rebuilding of the palace. The new building layout also set an important precedent in royal domestic planning: henceforth the private lodgings of the king and queen would be arranged on a single level facing each other across a garden courtyard.

The new buildings that encompassed the court on its east and west flanks were raised on arches, which gave rise to the name of Cloister Green Court in the seventeenth century. A *Parliamentary Survey* (1653) describes this easternmost quadrangle of the Tudor palace as the 'first court within the said house' and as being 'one other green court', suggesting that it possessed sufficient verdure at the time to merit such a name.

When, in 1689, the early sixteenth-century ranges along the north, east and south sides were demolished and the court rebuilt, a colonnaded cloister was also added to the Tudor block between the present Clock and Fountain Courts. King William conceived of the new garden quadrangle as the centre of his new court, where he could surround himself with friends and retinues of confidants, resplendent with noble titles and working or semi-honorific offices.

Hawksmoor's original plans for the replacement courtyard were, in fact, much more ambitious than those which were realized. As with Henry VIII's earlier building campaigns, the transformation of the palace was contingent on the creation of new internal courtyards. The architect's quadrangle was to be one of three new courts, the largest and grandest of which was to be a new north-facing forecourt. The scheme entailed the destruction of the whole extent of the old palace, except the Tudor hall, which was to become the focus for a new northern approach. A quadrangle to the south-east of the new north-facing forecourt – which later was, in fact built, and became the Fountain Court – was to provide accommodation for the royal family and principal courtiers; further accommodation was to be placed in an open courtyard to the south-west. Instead, much of the Tudor fabric west of the new court was retained and Hawksmoor was instructed to proceed with the plan for a new quadrangle, incorporating the existing western range of court within the scheme. The great benefit of the new scheme was that it formed a stately and axial link between Outer, Base and Clock Courts and the Long Water in Home Park.

98. (left) Anthonis van den
Wyngaerde's view of Clock
Court from the west, c.1555.

99. Base Court
looking east.

100. John Spyers's
watercolour view of
c.1775–80 shows the
presence of informal
planting in Clock Court.

101. George II's
Gatehouse in Clock
Court, c.1900. The walls
of this court and others
were smothered
with vines and creepers
in the late nineteenth
century.

Work on the new court began in spring 1689, when the King ordered that the court be excavated and sunk a foot deeper. At first the Fountain Court was little more than a builder's yard. As the south, east and north ranges of the Tudor palace were demolished to make way for the new quadrangle, the central court was used primarily to stockpile materials. Only in early 1700 did the court take on the appearance of a royal palace and residence, in time to receive the King and court in April of the same year.

From December 1701 labourers were employed in digging the fountain in the quadrangle, and the basin with a marble coping was formed to receive it. In the same year a golden figure was placed in the court. Accounts for making and planting the garden record that a large square of grass was laid out round the fountain, surrounded by borders planted with box edging, in which were eight laurels, eight yews, eight phillyreas, four striped hollies, and four Swedish junipers.[10] A 'hedge' made of poles and wires was erected around the central area to protect it from dogs (replaced with an iron railing in 1796), and the cloisters were paved with Swedish limestone flags – which remain to this day.

Although the quadrangle was generally well-inhabited, some sections of its perimeter accommodation were not so grand. The status of the apartments was partly determined – as with all the palace courts – by the views they provided, and there was a distinct preference for outward facing rooms in the south and east ranges which overlooked the gardens. All the first rank courtiers obtained suites that included rooms with garden views.

Visitors appear, however, to have been preoccupied primarily with the architecture of the quadrangle. For instance, in 1732 the travel writer John Macky compared Fountain Court to a '*Piazza*; tho' by the Lowness of the Pillars, it looks more like a Cloister than a Royal Palace'. And Bickham states that at the centre of the court is a 'round Bason, and four large Lamps on Pedestals of Iron-Work; and on the right Hand, over the Windows, are the twelve Labours of *Hercules* done in *Fresco*'.[11] The panels were painted by the French artist Louis Laguerre between 1691 and 1694. They remain *in situ*, although they are much faded.

The only view we have of the court of this period dates from c.1730–40, which portrays the central area as chaste, if arid, with a simple circular basin and fountain; the evergreens which had been planted in the court in the early eighteenth century appear to have

vanished. Spyers, too, presents the central area in the late 1770s in the same manner; he, however, shows that the four 'pedestals' had been removed. The large quadrangle, in fact, could hardly have changed much by 1801 when it was described – as Base Court had been almost a century earlier – as 'remarkable for nothing extraordinary but its spaciousness and uniformity'.

By the 1840s the court had a sombre and melancholy air: the central area was laid to grass and gravel and an iron railing confined people to the perimeter colonnade. Although some visitors, like Sir Henry Cole, reported that the so-called cloisters afforded a 'welcome retreat, cool and refreshing, when the sun shines hot and scorching', more were inclined to ridicule the

102. A postcard showing Fountain Court in the late nineteenth century. W.H. Hutton remarked in 1897 that in the palace courts the artist found a subject 'at every turn', and that each court had its own charm.

court's central basin, which was described as a 'watery prison' for its captive carp and goldfish, and its fountain as a dribbling squirt unworthy of such lofty surroundings.[12]

The most striking and universally admired attribute of the court was the display of potted plants formed in the early 1850s and arranged in a double row around the central basin. Donald Beaton reported that the large pots filled with geraniums and 'pillar Fuchsias' were just like 'exhibition plants, they were so perfectly trained'.[13] Ernest Law, who refurbished the garden in the late nineteenth century, also noted the important role of plants in enlivening the court. He declared in 1888 that the area's 'bright flower-beds and grass-plat, and its broad gravel-walk next to the building, presents a fresh and pleasing appearance'.[14] A near contemporary view of the court shows how Ernest Law encompassed the central basin with a ring of alternating rectangular beds of flowers and round studs with statuesque yuccas (fig. 102).

Eleanor Vere Boyle, who knew the palace gardens intimately through the recollections of her grandmother who was a grace-and-favour inhabitant, remarked in her book *Seven Gardens and a Palace* (1900):

> The pillared Garden Cloister of Hampton Court was no doubt designed as a fitting entrance or exit for the Court to pass through, to and from the gardens. And thus, unaltered, it remained up to the late 'sixties', or possibly later. Then, when the palace grew to be more and more 'A People's Palace', this spacious, stately vestibule became a receptacle for the storing of garden chairs, piled up to the very ceiling. Shop counters were placed there, and photographs sold. And where once statues stood in the niches in the walls of the inner semi-circular alcove between the Fountain Court and the Clock Court, there sat a poor old woman who sold fruit.[15]

The court is now as polished as many an Oxbridge quadrangle (fig. 103): the central area is laid to closely mown turf, the fountain plays daily, and four stone pillars surmounted with giant lanterns rise pertly from the angles of the court. The dull lustre and the worn surface of the cloister's flagstone floor bears witness to the countless people who have filed through the stately quadrangle on their way to the Great Fountain Garden and park beyond.

Chapel Court

Chapel Court – which has also been known variously as Princess Court, Prince's Court or the Princes Garden – is among the palace's largest garden courtyards and has occasionally been the setting of minor displays of royal pageantry. The final element in Henry VIII's ambitious transformation of the palace, the court was enclosed in 1537 when the north range was raised on the site of a former garden wall which divided the Chapel's northern precincts from the Privy Orchard. The court was paved in 1603.

The court took its original name from Prince Edward's (later Edward VI) nursery – which enclosed and overlooked the central area. Like Base, Clock and the Fountain Courts, Chapel Court has a distinguished architectural setting, being enclosed on the north by the Prince's lodgings, on the east by the west wall of Henry VIII's tennis court, on the west by the Great Council Chamber and on the south by the soaring buttressed north wall of the Chapel Royal. The central area was, however, for many years undistinguished, being described in 1653 as one of 'severall other buildings, with the severall yards or courts lying betweene and amongst the sayd buildings'.[16]

The court is presumably one of the two spaces singled out by Lorenzo Magalotti in 1669 as 'being much superior to the others in size, as well as beauty, contain the gardens, which are admirably laid out'. If so, this layout only lasted until the early eighteenth century, when it was replaced by a small orchard. The court is included in a list of the palace's garden areas in an agreement with Henry Wise, who in 1701–2 was paid for removing rubbish from the court, and bringing in '376 Solid yards' of 'good Earth for borders and Plantations', and planting twelve standard cherries, six peaches, sixteen plums, twelve pears, eleven apricots and eight dwarf cherries.[17]

Spyers portrays the central area in the late 1770s in a pair of handsome watercolours. The views looking to the south and the north of the court show that it was almost entirely laid to turf. Two stone footways bisect the central area – one links the north and south ranges and the other runs perpendicular to these buildings and is aligned on the entrance to the tennis court on the eastern range. Two trees are shown on either side of the east–west path. Spyers's record of the northern range is particularly important as it is the only view of the Prince's apartments before

105. (right) Chapel
Court from the
south-west.

106. (far right) Chapel
Court as seen from
Prince Edward's
Lodgings, c.1890. The
garden was then in
grace-and-favour
occupation.

they were substantially damaged by fire in 1886 (fig. 104). Sayers's *Plan of the Royal Park at Hampton Court* (1841) shows the courtyard garden more or less as it appeared in the 1770s (fig. 193).

Chapel Court was the only large quadrangle in the palace to have been wholly colonized by grace-and-favour inhabitants. When it was invaded remains a mystery, but Ernest Law published a view of the court 'as seen from Prince Edward's (Edward VI) Lodgings' in 1890, by which time the garden is unrecognisable from earlier descriptions (fig. 106). It is portrayed as possessing a sprinkling of curious island beds flanked by a ring of ponderous ivy arches; a small fountain basin is set with planting and sits atop the remains of a tree stump in the centre of the garden, and an ivy-encrusted, skeletal tree rises like a menacing colossus from the corner of the garden. This fanciful garden layout may have been influenced by Ernest Law and was presumably intended to complement the Tudor surroundings of the ancient courtyard.

A late nineteenth-century photograph shows half the central area laid to pavement and the other thrown into garden. The garden is divided into two symmetrical halves – only one side being visible – surrounded by billowing shrubberies and vine-covered walls and separated by a central path aligned with the portico set in the wall of the former closed tennis court. This chaste and quaint layout appears to have been short-lived, as by 1900 the topographical artist Herbert Railton portrayed the garden as an unruly tangle, complete with clothes drying on a line.

The court has seldom been the site of any great excitement. However, it became newsworthy in 1953 when it became infested – like the Chapel Royal – with swarms of pigeons. The Ministry of Agriculture proposed a range of unsuccessful measures but the problem was only solved in 1965 when exterminators were called in to trap the birds. It was generally agreed that the £140 spent on the extermination exercise was not good value as it only resulted in the removal of sixty-three birds and the palace received a lot of bad publicity.[18]

Until recently the court had a melancholy appearance. It was partitioned into two roughly equal areas divided by a timber palisade: the west side was laid to granite sets and the east side possessed a rectangular lawn encircled on all sides by shallow beds planted with an array of withered herbaceous perennials, shrubs and small trees (fig. 105). The area will be transformed into a handsome pleasance in the autumn of 2005 with the implementation of a new scheme contrived by Dutch garden designer Piet Oudolf in collaboration with the palace's Gardens and Estates team. The new layout draws upon known eighteenth- and nineteenth-century views of the court when it was in grace-and-favour occupation: low ivy arches will separate the broad cobbled pavement from the garden and perimeter beds will be filled with a range of unusual shade-tolerant herbaceous perennials and grasses which enclose a central lawn dotted with a pair of low yew cylinders.

The 'Inferior' Courts

A handful of records survive that throw light on the informal domestic-scale gardens created in some of the palace's 'inferior' courts. Lord Chamberlain's Court was the first in a sequence of inferior courts formed from 1529 by Henry VIII when he enlarged the existing kitchens. Access to the court was gained from the Seymour Gate which now opens on to the West Front, above which were situated the offices of the Green Cloth – the body responsible for the complex task of purveying food for the court. Other domestic offices associated with the kitchens were also situated in this court, including the jewel house, the spicery, the chandlery and the coal house. Spyers's views of the late 1770s show small patches of grass growing through the pavement and shrubs growing at the base of some of the enclosing walls. The court was paved with cobbles in the nineteenth century and has never again appeared as picturesque as it did in gentle decay in the late eighteenth century.

Master Carpenter's Court – or the Second Inferior Court – was enclosed by the pastry house, the confectionery, the boiling house and the back of the north range of Wolsey's Base Court. Late nineteenth-century views portray the court richly clothed in climbing plants and vines. By the 1920s, however, the court had been stripped of its luxuriant growth.

Fish Court, which adjoined Master Carpenter's Court, was a long narrow yard which gave on to the site of the palace's wet and dry larders. The court appears always to have been paved, although views from the late nineteenth century to the mid-twentieth century depict window boxes projecting from the first-floor windows and large, bold displays of potted plants. In 1912 London

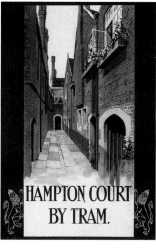

HAMPTON COURT
BY TRAM.

107. (far left) Master Carpenter's Court looking south-east

108. (left) London Underground poster advertising the domestic charms of Master Carpenter's Court, 1912.

109. (below) John Spysers's view of Master Carpenter's Court of *c.*1780 records the presence of small *ad hoc* gardens in what are now hard paved courts.

Transport used an image of this intimate domestic space and of Master Carpenter's Court – so evocative of Tudor street scenes – to promote tram travel to the palace.

Chocolate Court lies at the opposite end of the palace, near the south-east angle of the cloisters in the Fountain Court. It is so-called on account of its proximity to the former Chocolate Kitchen. It is first referred to in 1701 when £20 was spent cutting three new doorways out of the Earl of Albemarle's adjacent lodgings into the court. The new doors presumably led directly from the Earl's enormous suite of rooms to the cloisters and the garden gate that led to the Great Fountain Garden. This humble paved court – which was never previously open to the visiting public – has recently been taken into the palace's gardens exhibition space and has been embellished with a range of artefacts – including a short run of picket fencing, wirework seats, garden tools, potted plants and a Victorian plant-stand, which are intended to evoke the character of one of the palace's small courts at the turn of the twentieth century when they were colonized by grace-and-favour occupants.

Lady Mornington's Garden is unusual among the inferior courts as it is almost entirely given over to planting. This little walled garden at the north-east angle of the palace – encompassed

110. (right) Lady
Mornington's Garden
lies behind the high
brick walls which line
the west side of the
Broad Walk.

111. (below) Robert
McQuoid's watercolour
view of Lady
Mornington's Garden
from the Broad Walk
in the Great Fountain
Garden, c.1860.

by the Prince's Lodgings, the Tennis Court and the Broad Walk –
takes its name from its most famous inhabitant, the formidable
Countess of Mornington – mother of the Duke of Wellington –
who resided here between 1795 and 1831. An engraving of the East
Front of the palace, published in Lyson's *Middlesex Parishes* (1800)
shows dense foliage frothing above the courtyard's wall and is
portrayed in Sayers's plan (1841) as possessing a large oval pool
(fig. 193). The garden was best known in Victorian times for the
majestic catalpa which embowered it (fig. 111). The tree was
planted by Lady Mornington herself. This souvenir of her long
spell of grace-and-favour occupation was, however, 'reduced to
little more than a bare stump' by the 1920s.[19] The garden remains in
grace-and-favour occupation and its layout is one of the few to
retain a domestic character.

The Wilderness

The Wilderness is really a 'wilderness' in name only. Although the layout, character and function of this immense plantation have been transformed dramatically since the late seventeenth century – when it first became known as the Wilderness – the name has persisted and its connotations have evolved to accommodate the changing nature of the concept.

The Wilderness is the name given to the large skewed rectangular piece of ground north of the palace, sandwiched between the glasshouse nursery and Hampton Court Road. The garden, which now resembles a meadow, is criss-crossed with broad rectilinear paths and sprinkled with trees and shrubs. It is celebrated and popular for two reasons: it contains the world-famous Maze (fig. 112) and every spring the garden's large central lawn erupts with millions of brilliantly coloured bulbs. The garden is something of a curious hybrid as a result of organic change – its grassy expanses and open tree planting evoke the informality of the former Tudor orchard, its Maze and paths are relic features of its late seventeenth-century geometrical layout, and the garden's massed display of naturalized spring bulbs is a legacy of 'wild gardening' made popular in the 1870s. One of the most historic areas of the gardens, the Grove, is now, however, almost imperceptible: this geometric plantation was formed at the same time as the Wilderness, but it is now indistinguishable from its surroundings.

The Wilderness has been a plantation of one form or another for at least five hundred years. The earliest recorded plantation is the King's New Orchard – also known as the Great Orchard and later the Old Orchard – which was then encompassed by Home Park to the east, the Kingston road to the north, the Tiltyard to the west and the Tudor dry moat ditch to the south. The new orchard appears to have been an extension to the King's Privy Orchard (now the Glass House Nursery). In 1531 a team of gardeners set about planting 200 young oak and elm trees, 400 apple trees, 600 cherry trees, as well as six consignments of apples, pears, cherries, medlars and crab apples from Chertsey Abbey; a handful of service trees and hollies were also planted. The trees were set in open ground sown with grain. Part of the area was cultivated as a pleasure ground and possessed a pond, at least one arbour and a large circular banqueting house with its own kitchen, raised up on arches.[1] At about the same time a drawbridge was thrown over the dry moat, connecting the New Orchard to the King's Privy Orchard. The south-west corner of the New Orchard is depicted in Wyngaerde's view of Hampton Court from the north (fig. 126).

The New Orchard remained an orchard in name until the mid-1680s when it was recast by Charles II or his mistress Barbara Villiers, Countess of Castlemaine, to form a 'Wilderness', which was a large geometrical woodland garden contrived for the purpose of entertainment or contemplation. John Evelyn, who was on intimate terms with the King, and was well acquainted with the palace gardens, remarked in *Elysium Britannicum* (c.1658–1702) that a typical wilderness

> has a perfect resemblance of the Universe it selfe, of which contemplative men & such as best know how to enjoy the virtuous delights of Gardens are never sated, but find always something of new and extraordinary to entertaine their thoughts withall. And now, though of all formes of Gardens, we find the Square to be the most usuall; yet the oblong, & parallelogram, which is one of its species, is doubtlesse more convenient as to the circuit of the out Walles; because of protracting the Walkes, Allys, and prospects.[2]

He expressed his esteem for 'the naturall decorations of Groves, Labyrinths, thicketts . . . which after a wonderfull diversitie from the compt, polite and uniforme partes of the *Walkes* and *Parterrs*, is of all others the most noble, sollumne and divertissant of Garden ornaments', and recommended that these gardens should be laid out on the flanks of great parterres, opposite the gate to the mansion but at some distance from it.

The building of the Hampton Court Wilderness appears to have been completed by 1686, when an estimate for repairs to the royal parks records that a payment of £60 was made toward the fencing of the 'new Plantation in the Old Orchard'.[3] Site plans and surveys of the Tudor palace executed by Nicholas Hawksmoor corroborate that the imposing formal plantation was certainly in place by the early summer of 1689. The Wilderness Wall, which runs parallel to the Hampton Court Road, is, for instance, denoted on his surveys, as is the garden layout.

The presence of this new plantation appears to have been a crucial impediment to the realization of Hawksmoor's ambitious proposal of 1689 to create a new processional route to the north side of the palace. The mile-and-a-half approach was intended

to march southwards from Teddington Gate in Bushy Park, across Middle Park to the Kingston Road and thence through the Wilderness and the Melon Ground, to terminate in a capacious new *cour d'honneur* on the north side of Henry VIII's Great Hall. The Great Avenue scheme – now known as the Chestnut Avenue – was, however, only partially completed; no sooner had a handful of trees been planted than the King abandoned his plans. In the event, George London planted the quadruple lime and chestnut avenue between the Teddington and the Kingston Gates, but here it ended abruptly at the foot of the Wilderness Gate. Thus what might have been the most regal landscape gesture ever contemplated at Hampton Court was, and remains to this day, unresolved.

After the northern approach scheme was put to rest, the King embarked on a new round of improvements to the Wilderness: in 1701 an arbour was built on the north side of the plantation, a new walk was laid out and its borders were filled up with good earth to receive sixty-six striped hollies and forty bay trees which were planted against the walls. Turf was laid in the walks, gravel was laid in the circle at the centre and fine, screened gravel was used to dress the walks about the circle and other places. A large yew tree, nearly thirty feet high, was planted at the centre of the plantation. Two turf verges were also formed in the Wilderness. The Grove is only mentioned in building accounts of 1702, when it is referred to in a maintenance contract of the Queen's plantations.

Leonard Knyff's views of Hampton Court from the south and the east (figs 4, 5) show the Wilderness and the Grove in handsome bird's-eye perspectives in relation to the palace and the parks. The Wilderness is roughly centred on the Tudor Great Hall, its great bulk stretching the breadth of the palace and surging northwards to the edge of Bushy Park and its quadruple avenues. Two features of the Wilderness are clearly depicted: Wilderness House (fig. 115) and the precursors to the Lion Gates. Wilderness House sits in the north-west corner of the garden: the brick dwelling dates from the late seventeenth century and was the residence of the head gardener until the mid-nineteenth century when it was given over to grace-and-favour lodgings. 'Capability' Brown lived here from 1764 to his death in 1783. The house and its gardens remain in grace-and-favour occupation to this day. The modest gate – then known as Wilderness Gate – that Knyff depicts on the garden's

north boundary was formed in *c*.1701 by removing some very large plants to form an approach into the Wilderness; it later gave way to the resplendent Lion Gates which were erected by Queen Anne in the last year of her reign (fig. 114). The wrought-iron gates to this grand entrance were erected under George I and have historically been the source of much ridicule, as they do not correspond to the tall Portland stone pillars.[4]

A plan of *c*.1714 shows the Wilderness and the Grove in great detail and suggests that the two woodland gardens were originally distinct plantations (fig. 113). The Grove was dissected by twelve narrow walks, which divided the long rectangular plantation into thirty-six woodland compartments. The Wilderness, on the other hand, was apportioned into four large trapezoidal divisions by two broad diagonal walks, one of which was aligned on the Lion Gates. These divisions were, in turn, subdivided into smaller compartments encompassed by narrow, straight and meandering walks which opened into an array of open rooms or cabinets. Four of the compartments possessed mazes, only two of which were of any consequence – Troy Town (a horticultural contrivance laid out in concentric circles of espalier work) and the half-acre labyrinth that we now know as the Maze. The remaining woodland compartments were enclosed by pales and hedges, each with its own gate. Dozens of large clipped yews were dispersed throughout the cabinets and woodland. The plan shows very clearly that the broad diagonal alleys were laid to turf, while the smaller ancillary walks were laid to gravel.

Little is known about the specific character of the planting or the decoration of the gardens. The walks may have been lined with hedges of hornbeam and the compartments planted with an agreeable confusion of trees. Records suggest that lines of hornbeams were taken up from the Privy Garden and planted in the Wilderness in 1701; that box and other unspecified plants that grew in the Little Garden by the Water Gallery were also taken up and placed in the Wilderness; and as late as 1714 a hedge of 'very large evergreen plants' was formed on the north side of the Wilderness facing the Lion Gates – presumably to block views to the palace. Switzer proposed in *Ichnographia Rustica* in 1718 that yew, hollies and other evergreens could be introduced sparingly into wildernesses with great effect. This was, he assured his readers, 'entirely pretty and new in Gardening'. Such evergreens,

if 'planted large, viz. seven or eight Foot high, will soon form themselves, by little cutting, into Arches, Vaults, Groves, and all the other Beauties we borrow from Architecture'.

It would seem likely that the Wilderness and the Grove's little rooms, or cabinets of retirement, were furnished with statues, urns, vases, or little fountains, but again there are no records to prove this was the case. There are payments recorded to Thomas Highmore for painting tubs for the greens and painting 'twice over' the new arbour by the road to Kingston with an iron-coloured oil paint.

Daniel Defoe, who endorsed the late King William's desire to rebuild the north side of the palace, approved of the Wilderness, but suggested that the costly new enterprise was little more than a decorative screen. He remarked in *A Tour Thro' the Whole Island of Great Britain* (1724) that the espaliers in the Wilderness were so high that they screened 'all that Part of the Old Building, which would have been offensive to the Sight'. The garden was, however, 'not only well design'd, and completely finish'd, but is very well kept, and the Espaliers fill'd exactly, at the bottom to the very Ground, and are led up to proportion'd Heights on the Top; so that nothing of that kind can be more beautiful.' [5]

By the 1740s the taste for geometrical wilderness gardens had begun to wane and the trim plantations at Hampton Court gained some detractors. Samuel Richardson remarked in the revised edition of Defoe's *Tour* (1742) that when the Wilderness was planted it was

> thought one of the finest disposed Parts of the Garden. But as the whole Contrivance of the Plantations is in regular strait Walks, bounded on each Side by tall clipped Hedges, which divide the whole Ground into angular Quarters, to every Person of Taste it must be very far from affording any Pleasure, since nothing can be more disagreeable than to be immured between Hedges, so as to have the Eye confined to a strait Walk, and the Beauty of the Trees growing in the Quarters, intirely secluded from the eye. And at the same time as you are walking in this unmeaning Plantations, you are denied the benefit of Shade, being confined to these regular Walks, where it would be deemed an unpardonable Fault, to suffer the neighbouring Trees to diffuse their Branches over these shorn Hedges; so that, in the midst of a Wood, a Person may faint for Shade in a sultry Day, the Air being excluded from these Walks by the taller Trees

in the Quarters; and pent up Air is much more troublesome in hot Weather, than the Heat of the Sun in the most open exposed Plain. [6]

Succeeding garden improvers, and 'Capability' Brown in particular, addressed some of these criticisms. Spyers's views of the late 1770s show that although the Wilderness and the Grove retained something of their original formality, their planting was more unruly. The artist's view of the middle of the Wilderness portrays the giant yew – which was formerly clipped into tiers – grown out, and neatly clipped hedges suppressing a profusion of luxuriant foliage (fig. 117). In 1774 the architect Sir William Chambers observed that 'Master Brown has put padlocks on the wilderness at Hampton Court where he breeds turkeys'. [7] Spyers's other views of the Wilderness are equally revealing: one shows how the towering banks of foliage of the Wilderness and the Grove framed a magnificent *coup d'œil* of the palace and another depicts the western edge of the Wilderness, the Tiltyard tower and Brown's ballroom extension to Wilderness House.

By the early nineteenth century all consensus on the purpose or correct expression for the Wilderness had disappeared. William Trotter invoked Defoe, remarking in 1839 that it was 'planted by William the third to hide the incongruous character of the northern side of the palace'. Sir Henry Cole, however, writing in 1843, proposed a novel interpretation: the 'shade of the numerous groves of full grown trees' was a 'place for "whispering lovers" made'.

The anonymous author of *London and its Vicinity* (1851) was less susceptible to the languid charms of the Wilderness. It was, he remarked, 'only a subordinate and inferior part of the whole [palace gardens], and which might be removed without any loss, beyond the shadiness of the walks which it affords'. The garden was not, in fact, removed, but recast. From the late 1850s the Wilderness began to revert to 'Nature' under the stewardship of the Garden Superintendent James Donald. It became a completely different sort of wilderness – a 'wild garden', or a woodland garden embellished with naturalized exotics, sub-tropical planting and foliage plants. A correspondent of the *Gardeners' Chronicle* reported in September 1859 that 'evident improvements are in actual operation' in the Wilderness. 'Old walks which through time had become more like ditches than walks are being filled up with brick rubbish and surfaced with gravel, and the shrubs along

115. (far left)
Wilderness House was
formerly the residence
of the Head Gardener.

116. (left) J. Black's
'View at Hampton
Court' showing the Lion
Gates in the Kingston
Road, c.1779.

117. John Spyers's
*View of the Middle of
the Wilderness Garden
at Hampton Court,*
c.1775–80

their sides are being rearranged. Wild flowers might also be
introduced with advantage to this part of the garden.' In the event,
wild flowers were not introduced, but great drifts of daffodils
were planted from around 1900 to well into the mid-twentieth
century (fig. 119).

The Wilderness was again improved at the turn of the
twentieth century, this time by J.A. Gardiner, the then Garden
Superintendent. Mature trees were felled or pruned to increase
the light in the garden and new garden features were introduced.
In 1907 *The Garden* reported that 'not many years ago the quarter
called the Wilderness was a very uninteresting part of the garden,
with gravel walks winding among Laurels and other ordinary
shrubs. At the present time its features are really more in

conformity with wild nature than before, for it is planted with a
representative collection of flowering and foliage shrubs, and in its
centre, on the site of a former rubbish heap, has been constructed
a rootery [a folly made of tree stumps] and this is planted with
Ferns, Alpine, and trailing plants. Tall bamboos, pillars of
Wichuriana Roses, species of Rubus, Clematis, &c. are planted
thereabouts.' Not everyone was so favourably impressed by the
transformation of the formerly overgrown garden into an idealized
woodland. An enraged correspondent to the *Journal of Horticulture*
remarked in 1908: 'why should the arboreal grandeur of our fine
trees be so ruthlessly destroyed? The beheading that goes on is
wicked. Much has yet to be taught to the ordinary man in charge
of a park or garden in the art of arboriculture.'[8]

118. The Wilderness, c.1900. Compare with fig. 117 to see how the view had changed since c.1780.

Nevertheless, by the 1910s the Wilderness had become among the most popular areas of the garden. A correspondent to the *Morning Post* in 1913 exclaimed:

Visitors who enter by the Lion Gate cannot hurry through the Wilderness to see the achievements of Art when Nature seems to be beckoning them at every turn. The Wilderness is not all her work, but she has been allowed to have her way, even to indulging her preference for wild parsley and dandelions. They flourish in the uncut and luxuriant grass under the trees; and one has to admit that the light delicacy of the one as it is seen in the background and the golden masses of the other flashing in the sunflecks, while bluebells intensify the colour of the dappled shade, prove that decorative gardening is not the sole province of man. Of course, he has a large share in constituting the Wilderness, but he has kept his work in subjection. Mr Marlow, the superintendent of the Gardens, may seem to be an autocrat when it comes to selecting the colour-harmonies for the formal beds, but he recognizes that he has a chief, and the Wilderness is his tribute of loyalty. His only province here is to help, and whether he adds a sprinkle of white narcissus to nod above the high grass or provide further diversity in white and pink wild-hyacinths, graceful blooms, and flowering shrubs he does it all to accord with Nature's ways. As an example of the intelligent and sympathetic production of a natural effect the Wilderness is unsurpassed.[9]

The *Gardeners' Chronicle* reported in 1919 that the Wilderness – like most of the palace gardens after the First World War – was in need of considerable improvement: 'The noble Lion Gates are demeaned by a wretched tea garden just outside them, and immediately inside there are only rubbishy trees, unworthy of an ordinary spinney.'[10] Among the changes was the transformation of the rootery (formerly Troy Town) into a sunk rock-garden, known as the Glen. The topographer Edward Yates observed in 1935 that the rockery had a 'stream trickling through it – turned on by a tap. Narrow, flag-paved walks wind amongst the rocks, and here there and everywhere are ferns, grasses, and those brilliant, often very small flowers peeping out from or covering the grey masses amongst which such plants thrive'. The informality of the composition was, Yates explained, especially precious where most of the gardening at the palace was on a grand scale; even the stones

of the rockwork had an interest for many and were evidently part and parcel of the old Tudor palace.[11] During the late 1990s, the Glen was reduced in size and new plants and grass paths were introduced.

Yates also observed that the Wilderness then, like today, was a popular spring pilgrimage site: 'except the maze, [the garden] has nothing formal about it. It is a modern "wild garden" and in spring one of the most beautiful spots anywhere near London, the fine trees just bursting to leaf, flowering shrubs in perfection, and the wide spaces of grass carpeted with primroses, harebells, crocuses, narcissus and daffodils growing in wild profusion as nature intended.' About the same time as the publication of Yates's book, lilacs were planted in great profusion in the garden, and they, too, became a favourite with the public.

From the 1950s a number of facilities were built in the garden for the benefit of the visiting public. Ice cream kiosks were raised in Moat Lane and at the Lion Gates, and three blocks of lavatories were placed in disparate parts of the garden. New planting was also introduced: a laburnum tunnel (fig. 122) was made by the Lion Gates, new specimen trees and bulbs were planted in the central lawn and carpet bedding was introduced into the small beds beside the Lion Gates. In the 1970s a well was dug in the Grove, which now supplies the water for the irrigation of the entire royal gardens.

In the wake of the recent reconstruction of the Privy Garden, the palace has considered the feasibility of returning the Wilderness to its early eighteenth-century appearance. There are, however, no plans currently afoot to recast the garden. Notwithstanding, Historic Royal Palaces is committed to gaining a better understanding of the surviving garden fabric, and to this end proposes to commission archaeology to determine how much of the early infrastructure lies beneath the surface of the garden.

121. A postcard
showing visitors to
the Maze, c.1900.

The Maze, Hampton Court Palace.

The Maze

Hampton Court Maze is the oldest planted maze in Great Britain, and is the most popular attraction of the palace gardens. Hardly a visitor arrives at Hampton Court who has not heard of the celebrated labyrinth, or who does not long to thread his or her way through its half-mile of well-trodden paths. Unlike other areas of the royal estate, the Maze is not an object of pilgrimage because of its noble antiquity or its historical associations: it is famous because it is an object of curiosity to visitors of all ages and interests. Indeed, the Maze was conceived as a puzzle for entertainment in the Wilderness. For these reasons alone, the attraction has transcended taste and fashion and has been largely unaffected by the changes which have taken place in the rest of the Wilderness.

The Maze appears to have been an original attribute of the Wilderness, laid out by 1686 – possibly on the advice of John Evelyn. The labyrinth was well formed by 1710 when the German traveller Zacharias Conrad von Uffenbach remarked on its presence. There were, he observed, two mazes – 'one in the form of a circle and the other of a triangle.' The triangular maze was the 'largest and best'.[12] The circular maze he referred to was Troy Town and the other was presumably the trapezoidal-shaped labyrinth that has survived to this day.

In the absence of surviving documentation of the building of the Maze and the principles underlying its design, we must turn to

John Evelyn, who provides clear instructions in *Elysium Britannicum* for the creation of 'Labyrinths and *Dædales* which in English we mean by Mazes'. There were, he observed, two methods:

> They are made either by cutting them out of larger thicketts, or else are sowne & planted in formes and plotts contrived with the greatest intricacy, windings & meanders leading to a certaine Center in imitation of that famous Labyrinth of Creete so much celebrated by the Poets: one Aker of ground set out for this work is capable continuing a walke of a mile in circute provided the palisads or hedges be not over thick.[13]

Mazes experienced a revival in the wake of the new labyrinth at Hampton Court.[14] Even Stephen Switzer, who remarked in 1715 that mazes were 'calculated for an inferior class of people', was forced to revise his opinion, dedicating a chapter in *Ichnographia Rustica* (1718) to their design, nature and use. Mazes were associated with antiquity, historical continuity and social pedigree, and as such became objects of intense horticultural interest. It is a measure of the public's enduring fascination with Hampton Court Maze, and the pleasures of popular antiquarianism that in 1747 it became the subject of a verse which celebrated its metaphorical richness, and in 1785 the antiquary Daines Barrington speculated, mistakenly, in the learned journal *Archæologia* that the 'mighty labyrinth' was 'possibly as old as the time of Henry the Eighth'.[15]

While the Wilderness may have lost its way in the early nineteenth century, its ample labyrinth remained a curious and

entertaining anachronism and was, as it remains, chiefly valued as a source of amusement. As early as 1818 *Leigh's New Picture of London* provided a plan of the curious maze that afforded great amusement to its juvenile visitors. *The Mirror* subsequently published a plan in August 1825, remarking that it was an object of great attraction to visitors, who would be sadly bewildered were there not a guide at hand to direct their step.[16] Most commentators agreed with John Fisher Murray, who remarked in 1849 that it afforded much amusement to crowds of holiday folks, 'looking on while beaux and belles lose themselves and each other in its intricate doublings and circumvolutions'.[17] No Victorian guidebook to the gardens was complete without a description or a plan of this great and popular wonder.

Edward Jesse tells us in 1839 that the Maze was open at all times, except during divine service, and that a small fee was expected by the gardener. The keeper was appointed to take charge of the Maze. One Serjeant Dobson held the post from the 1850s: he was allowed a livery, but no emoluments beyond what he received – one penny per person. The pecuniary incentive appears to have been a terrible temptation for the Serjeant, who in July 1856 was reprimanded 'for allowing persons to enter the Maze after the prescribed hours'. From the 1880s the Maze admission charge was no longer payable to the gardener, but paid into the Exchequer. The proceeds have always been substantial, as over 150,000 people annually make their way through the Maze. The Maze and the Great Vine are, in fact, the only elements of the gardens that have over the past century regularly produced profits.

The Maze became truly famous in 1889 when it featured in Jerome K. Jerome's *Three Men in a Boat*. We are told of the difficulty of the accident-prone Harris in navigating the Maze, even with the assistance of a map: as he threads his way purposefully through the labyrinth a procession of lost souls fall in behind him. It soon, however, becomes apparent that Harris is no more able to find his way through the labyrinth than his new companions. The keeper eventually rescues the disillusioned crowd and their hapless guide.

The increased fame of the Maze ensured that it would remain unchanged while its surroundings were drastically refashioned. As William Holden Hutton remarked in *Hampton Court* (1897): 'among all changes [to the palace gardens] the Maze has survived'.

Although 'something of the formality of the "wilderness" still remains, it has not been unaffected by the influence of the "landscape gardeners", who came before long to destroy all the symmetry they could. But whatever audacity may have been done in the "Wilderness" by cutting down hedges and allowing trees to grow with comparative freedom, no one has been hardy enough to disturb the Maze.'[18]

Unfortunately the Maze soon became a victim of its own success: by 1895 Ernest Law estimated that some ten million people had wandered through it since it was first set out. Not surprisingly, Emily Constance Cook noted in her guidebook to the palace that the labyrinth was 'now rather dilapidated with much use'. By 1908 it was replanted – possibly for the first time since the early eighteenth century – as a correspondent to the *Journal of Horticulture* for the same year remarked that 'the maze still goes on', although it was 'rather a mistake that it should be renewed with all sorts of shrubs instead of one only'.[19]

In 1932 the hedges were again renewed, this time with a mixture of yew, holly, privet and hornbeam. The new clipped hedges were six feet high so that no one could look over them and two feet thick so that no one could look through them.

The Maze has been subject to various piecemeal improvements since the 1930s: the paths were Tarmacadamed in the 1950s and in 1963 the hedges were again grubbed up and replanted for the first time entirely with yew. The post of gardener-keeper was abolished in the mid-1980s and the raised platform from which he guided lost people was dismantled at the same time (the ticket office at the entrance to the Maze, however, remains). The pair of horse chestnut trees that formerly stood in the centre of the Maze came down in the mid-1990s and they have not been replaced.

Although the Maze is in reasonably good condition given its constant robust use, the palace has recently embarked on a range of improvements to enhance this popular attraction: the yew hedging is being reinvigorated and in some stretches replanted; the path surfaces are being renewed with bound gravel; the centre of the Maze is being refurbished, and new interpretive material is being made available on the history of the Maze and the surrounding Wilderness.

A harassed school teacher from Hayes
Took her children to Hampton Court Maze,
They got thoroughly lost
At a moderate cost
And then had a wonderful time admiring
the Great Vine and imagining Henry VIII
serving double faults on the Tennis Court.
It was easy to get there, too — Green Line
Coaches 716, 716A, 718 and 725 run to the gates.

123. Frederic Henri Kay Henrion's poster design for the Hampton Court Maze published by London Underground, 1956.

124. (overleaf) Spring flower display in the Wilderness.

The Tiltyard

In early summer 1537 the surveyors William Clement and Christopher Dickson set out an area measuring 450 feet by 1,000 feet to receive Henry VIII's Tiltyard. Tiltyards – enclosed areas for tournaments between two men on horseback armed with lances – were at the time a common feature at most of the greater houses around London, and the one at Hampton Court was the last one to be built by the King. The dimensions of the enclosure were determined by the tiltyard at the King's palace at Greenwich, although at Hampton Court the width may have been adjusted to incorporate two existing arbours in the neighbouring New Orchard for the purposes of converting them into viewing towers. By 1541 three additional towers had been erected – possibly for the contemplation of scenery and gardens as well as for the spectatorship of jousting. In the event, they were inhabited as court lodgings. The Tiltyard was first used in November 1569 for Elizabeth I's accession-day tournament.

Wyngaerde's view of *c.*1555 shows the Tiltyard a few decades after it was formed – a clutch of crenellated towers soar above the bleak expanse of the yard, dwarfing the encompassing walls and neighbouring trees and buildings (fig. 126). Beyond the eastern wall we can discern the frothy foliage of the Great and Privy Orchards.

The Tiltyard lost its function when the sport of jousting became obsolete in the late sixteenth century. In the Dutch traveller Abram Booth's drawing of Hampton Court from the north-east of *c.*1630–40 the Tiltyard towers are portrayed as thrusting pertly from the dense cover of the neighbouring orchards (fig. 127). His view was composed shortly before the Tiltyard was described in 1653 as a parcel of pasture ground enclosed within a good brick wall, containing five brick towers with lead roofs – two of which straddled the perimeter wall facing the Old Orchard. Inigo Jones refurbished the towers in 1628 to receive Charles I's retinue of physicians, apothecaries and laundresses. One of these towers has come down to us and now forms part of the Tiltyard tearoom.

The area appears to have been kept clear as a piece of waste ground, occasionally serving as a store yard for old stone, until it underwent some modest improvements in anticipation of the arrival of the court of Charles II. Early in 1662 a guardhouse, or Court of Guard, was erected at the south-west end of the area and soon thereafter a few enterprising people set up booths and victualling houses to serve the resident cavalry. A view of the north side of the palace taken in 1669 shows the newly erected buildings.

In the early 1690s the vacant ground was metamorphosed into a princely kitchen garden for William and Mary. Knyff's early eighteenth-century views show the eight-acre rectangular piece of ground cast into six equal parts separated by high brick walls. Each of these six so-called 'divisions' was laid out with broad perimeter walks lined on both sides with fruit trees – those in the narrow beds beside the walls being trained against them. It is tempting to compare the new garden to the Potager du Roi at Versailles, which was built for Louis XIV to the designs of Jean-Baptiste de la Quintinie between 1677 and 1683, especially given George London and Henry Wise's familiarity with de la Quintinie's treatises on the making, ordering and improving of fruit and kitchen gardens.

Surviving accounts do not relate what was planted until 1702, when Queen Anne had the ground dunged, dug and cropped with 'Severall varietys of Eatables, the most proper for her Majestys use', and planted with hundreds of fruit trees, including apples, peaches, plums, figs and quinces which were pruned and nailed to the garden walls.[1]

After the departure of the court from the palace in 1737, the Tiltyard once again lost its way. This eventually prompted the Office of Works to lease its kitchen gardens: from the 1760s the Tiltyard and the adjacent Melon Ground were united under a single mantle – sometimes called the Fruit and Kitchen Gardens – and were leased to local market gardeners. In time, this arrangement became the source of friction between the custodians of the royal estate and their tenants. Although the tenants were let the gardens on the condition that they would undertake to supply plants for the gardens and keep the gardens to an agreed standard, they were also free to pursue their own private business on the side. This inevitably led to a conflict of interest as the market gardeners took a greater interest in their private enterprise than they did in their obligations to the palace.

Although the kitchen gardens were let for much of the eighteenth and nineteenth centuries, the Office of Works took the opportunity when leases fell in to improve or renew the garden fabric. For instance, in the early 1840s the gardens, which were reported to have fallen into a poor state of cultivation, were

125. The ring of
magnolias in the
Tiltyard.

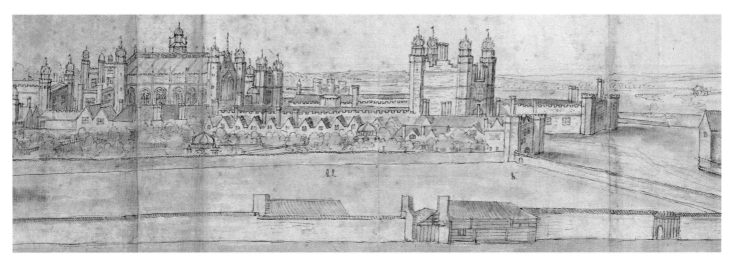

put back into complete working order, and in the late 1840s the forcing-houses and the Cherry House were repaired in the Melon Ground and new glasshouses were raised in the south-east division of the Tiltyard – now the Rose Garden.[2] Heating flues were also laid into the internal garden walls of the Tiltyard for the benefit of the wall-trained fruit some time in the mid-nineteenth century.

We know few details about the palace's leased kitchen gardens, and the Tiltyard in particular, as they were managed as private concerns behind high garden walls. One exception, however, is the garden run by Thomas Jackson, a nurseryman and seedsman from Kingston. Jackson leased the Tiltyard and Melon Ground in 1850 and his floristic skills and success with forced strawberries, cherries 'and other things in that line', earned him the praise of the discerning garden critic Mr Donald Beaton.[3] In 1881 Jackson's achievements in the Tiltyard were once again commended in the garden press. A correspondent of *The Cottage Gardener* observed:

> the garden is very extensive, and contains a good quantity of glass; in fact some twenty men are employed in these gardens. The ground was well cropped with the best of vegetables, and large squares were devoted to Seakale, Asparagus, and Strawberries . . . the walls are covered with old fruit trees, which

had formerly the spurs a great distance from the wall; they have not been well cut back, and good crops of fine fruit are produced close to the wall. The vineries are rather numerous, and some of the Vines are very old, but were carrying heavy crops of good average fruit. . . . Several houses are devoted to Peach and Nectarine trees.[4]

Shortly after this report was published, Jackson & Sons were forced to surrender their lease, and the land reverted to the Office of Works, which was eager to redevelop part of the twelve-acre gardens for the benefit of the visiting public. In the event, these plans came to nothing and the gardens were let in the mid-1890s to the nurseryman Mr James Naylor. Naylor was a cunning and industrious tenant, who obtained permission to convert the old Tiltyard Tower into a residence and to sell produce at Trophy Gate. In 1899 he was requested to surrender the two southernmost divisions of the Tiltyard to make way for the barracks parade ground, which had been ejected from neighbouring Outer Green Court. Naylor, whose 'Royal Nurseries' made a handsome profit, refused. His obstinacy held up the redevelopment of the Tiltyard for over two decades.

The first comprehensive redevelopment proposal for the Tiltyard was put forward in 1923 by F.E. Carter, Bailiff of the Parks, who proposed to create a recreation centre in its midst.

He recommended that three of the six compartments should be devoted, one to each, to hard tennis courts, putting greens and bowls – thus keeping all noise at a distance from the Gardens and the residents at 'A' [Wilderness House]… The sections on the east would be laid down to g[arden] shade trees and flowering shrubs being planted on it; gravel walks provided parallel to the walls, against which would be trained attractive climbers and shrubs. No bedding out is suggested… The house ('B') [the Tiltyard Tower] now occupied by Mr Naylor could be adapted to form a refreshment establishment with rooms for the staff, a large verandah, and free lavatory accommodation for both sexes.[5]

Two entrances to the Tiltyard were proposed – one from Hampton Court Green to the west and the other from the gardens to the east, at which turnstiles should be fixed. It was reported that 'taking into consideration the enormous crowds which visit Hampton Court in the summer and which now have to obtain refreshments in the somewhat squalid shops of the neighbourhood … a large rent would be obtained from a suitable establishment in pleasant surroundings.'[6] The plan was revised the following year, to make provision for car parking in the lower garden behind the Barrack Block. Cars had previously been parked in Tennis Court Lane and Outer Green Court.

Naylor was finally removed in early 1925, and the Office of Works immediately embarked upon the transformation of the nursery ground into the 'Tiltyard Gardens'. Later that year, the Tiltyard Tower was converted into a teahouse, with lawns, trees and flowerbeds in front. Tennis courts were formed in the north-west division and a putting green was laid out adjacent to the 'Teahouse Division' (formerly the site of the Tiltyard's towers). As E.M. Keate remarked in *Hampton Court Palace: A Short Popular Guide* (1932): 'thus in the great Tilt Yard of Henry VIII, built for the warlike sport of his day, made once more the scene of – more peaceful – sport, nearly four hundred years later.'

In 1926 the Office of Works decided to impose a fee of one penny per head for admission to what they called the 'transformed Tiltyard'. Although the *Surrey Comet* praised the 'pleasant refreshment rooms' that were formed in the Tiltyard Tower, it condemned the 'last word in Departmental niggardliness' which penalized visiting families.[7]

The two remaining divisions reverted to the Office of Works before 1934. One of them was laid out as a rose garden (figs 131–2). 'It was a happy inspiration', wrote Edward Yates in *Hampton Court* (1935), 'that came to a twentieth-century gardener to lay out a garden in which old roses were to provide the chief attraction'. The garden was laid out in a 'most attractive' manner, 'with no formality – there is enough of that in the various gardens already'. The shrubs were, therefore, 'tastefully set about the lawn' in clumps and their blooms were 'not the latest wonder of the rose shows but the old roses about which the memory clings, roses t hat call forth recollections not only of old-world gardens … but also of old and kind friends who delighted in telling of times more remote.'[8]

This informal layout was, however, abandoned in 1937 and the garden was reconfigured in a geometrical pattern. The new scheme gave over a greater area to grass, and provided axial vistas along the new grass walks. The borders were made on more generous proportions to accommodate larger specimen rose shrubs as well as small species and hybrids.[9]

Although many of the beds retained their displays of hybrid tea roses well into the late twentieth century, the easternmost bed had been planted with small flowering trees in the 1970s; these were felled in 1998 and the bed was replanted with old roses and English roses, and the beds were edged with box; the western end of the garden was replanted in a similar fashion three years later. The garden's southern boundary was replanted in 2002 to screen the car park: the existing box hedge was pulled up and replaced with a line of espaliered limes and underplanted with yew. The limes will be kept trimmed to the height of the existing garden walls, and the yew will be loosely cloud pruned. The stone statues of Flora, Adonis and Abundance were placed in the garden in the early 1990s when they were removed from the Privy Garden.

The only other statuary on display in the Tiltyard is the Portland stone sundial which sits – rather curiously – in the shade of a giant cedar of Lebanon, opposite the Tiltyard tearoom (fig. 130). This dial once belonged to the celebrated eighteenth-century actor/manager David Garrick, who had it erected in the pleasure grounds of his Thames-side villa in nearby Hampton. It was presented to the palace in 1929 and bears the inscription 'David and Eva Garrick, Hampton-on-Thames'.

131. (left) The south-east division of the Tiltyard before it was converted into the Rose Garden, 1934.

132. (below) The Rose Garden, looking south-east towards the Great Hall.

133. The Victorian
Water Tower in the
Glasshouse Nursery,
seen from the
Rose Garden.

134. (below) A spring
display of wallflowers
and tulips in the Tiltyard.

134. (below) A spring
display of wallflowers
and tulips in the Tiltyard.

135. (right) The
pavilion in the
Herbaceous Garden.
The crenellations of
the Tiltyard Tower can
be seen beyond.

The putting green was given over to herbaceous borders in 1950; its handsome pavilion built in the 1920s was, however, retained – as were its public lavatories. The tearoom was expanded and recast in 1964 by Trusthouse Forte and was again refurbished in 1995. In 1998 a pair of long, buttressed serpentine yew hedges were planted around the tearoom terrace, and espalier fruit trees were planted on the south-facing wall of this garden division. The perimeter beds are lavishly planted with subtropical bedding schemes in the summer.

The Herbaceous Garden has remained more or less unchanged since it was established in the late 1930s (fig. 137). The central area is laid to grass with large rectilinear perennial beds, and the western edge – adjacent to the lavatory block, which abuts the western boundary wall – is a dense shrubbery. At the south-west corner of the division is a gate which leads to the Vrow Walk (fig. 136).

The provision of car parking for visitors and improved circulation of traffic have always been difficult matters to resolve. Early on, vehicles were parked in Outer Green Court, and subsequently in Moat and Tennis Court Lanes. This *ad hoc* arrangement was formalized in the 1950s with the transformation of the south-west division of the Tiltyard and the neighbouring parade ground into a car park.

The palace presently has plans to improve the visitor facilities in the Tiltyard. Foremost is their wish to restore one of the divisions to a kitchen garden to evoke its former use. It is also hoped that car parking will one day be phased out from the area. In accordance with the objectives outlined in the 'Gardens, Estate and Landscape Conservation Management Plan', the tennis courts in the north-west division – which were never very popular – were removed in 2003. The area is now laid to turf.

136. (right) The gates in the Herbaceous Garden leading to Vrow Walk and Hampton Court Green.

137. (below) The one-acre Herbaceous Garden in the Tiltyard provides later summer interest in the palace gardens.

The Glasshouse Nursery

The Glasshouse Nursery is among the oldest continually cultivated and most private divisions of the palace gardens. Its historic importance has been determined by its proximity to the Tudor Kitchens: for centuries it supplied fruit and vegetables to the Royal Household. Formerly known as the Privy Orchard, the Kitchen Garden, the Melon Ground and the Forcing Ground, the area still supplies plants and flowers for the royal estate and is the heart of the garden establishment at Hampton Court (fig. 138).

The four-acre ground is enclosed by high brick walls and is not open to the public except by special appointment. It contains a great number of outbuildings dating from the nineteenth and twentieth centuries, which chart the horticultural and technological development of the estate. Most of these are occupied by offices or services which are critical to the day-to-day running of the gardens and the palace – including the Garden Manager's office, machine stores, workshops, potting sheds, the boiler house, old fruit stores, petrol and oil pumps and tanks, the palace's refuse tip and the gardeners' mess. The leaning brick and timber tower which sits north-west of the Works Yard, off Moat Lane, is the most conspicuous feature associated with this workaday quarter (fig. 133). Known as the Victorian Water Tower; the building's reclining posture can be explained by the fact that it was built atop the old moat ditch and is suffering from subsidence.

Immediately to the south of the Glasshouse Nursery is Tennis Court Lane. This slip of ground adjacent to the Tudor Kitchens was given its name in the nineteenth century on account of the succession of royal tennis courts raised in its precincts. The lane was formed in 1737 upon an encroachment in the Melon Ground. Known in the eighteenth century as North Inferior Court, the area came to resemble a village street with workshops and store yards and, from the 1840s, the palace school. Like many of the palace courtyards, the area once boasted a handful of informal grace-and-favour gardens. It is now largely given over to pavement. Beyond the Georgian House (originally the New Kitchen – now in part a Landmark Trust Property), and concealed behind brick walls, lie the tennis club garden, the pleasure ground of the Georgian House and the so-called staff garden. Although these gardens and, indeed, the whole of the Glasshouse Nursery are presently closed to the public, they warrant our attention as they have played a critical role in the development and maintenance of the royal estate.

Recent archaeology suggests that the origins of the Privy Orchard lie in the early to mid-fifteenth century: it occupied the northern half of a large moated platform. The southern half contained a dwelling-house with a chapel, garden and a pigeon house. By the late 1520s the Privy Orchard was enclosed with walls, and a gallery and an open tennis court were raised at its western end. The gallery gave views east over the neighbouring Course (now Home Park), and the Privy Orchard to the west. It is not clear when the first tennis court appeared at Hampton Court, although it is conceivable that Daubeney built one some time around 1500, or Wolsey after 1514. Between 1531 and 1533 Henry VIII – a keen tennis player – built a second, indoor court at right angles to the Chapel Royal, just south of the Privy Orchard. This space was given over to other uses in the 1620s, and the indoor court was moved to occupy the site of the earlier outdoor court. The present tennis court was built for Charles II in the early 1660s. It is the fourth to be built on the site and is associated with real (royal) tennis through the survival of the seventeenth-century court where the tennis club is based.

Accounts indicate that in 1531 seven King's beasts in timber were set up in the Privy Orchard. Wyngaerde shows the area in c.1555 as thickly planted with billowing trees, through which emerge the domed roofs of a pair of arbours. In 1537 a covered bowling alley was laid out across the ground for Henry VIII. The long, slender building was built perpendicular to the palace and stretched from the Prince's Lodgings to the orchard's north boundary wall, creating what was to become a permanent division in the Privy Orchard. By the mid-seventeenth century the area was described as a kitchen garden, and later surveys suggest that the bowling alley had been converted into forcing houses and the area to the east of it laid out as a garden. This pleasure ground became known as Tennis Court Garden and survives to this day, tucked away between the west wall of the Tennis Court and the brick Victorian garden walls at the west end of the Glasshouse Nursery.

By the third quarter of the seventeenth century the so-called Kitchen Garden had become know as the Melon Ground, reflecting the court's infatuation with that fruit. John Evelyn was among the first English garden writers to praise the virtues of this expensive and prestigious fruit in its many forms and to promote its cultivation in the royal kitchen gardens. In 1658 he published

138. Looking south
from the Nursery
to the palace.

139. The area now
occupied by the
Glasshouse Nursery has
been in continuous
cultivation for upwards
of eight hundred years.

140. (left) Looking west down Tennis Court Lane in 1928. The Glasshouse Nursery is situated on the right-hand side of the lane.

141. (below) Detail of one of the glasshouses given over to the cultivation of Queen Mary's exotics.

The French Gardiner, which included a treatise entitled 'Of Melons, Cucumbers, Gourdes, and their kindes', and he subsequently published an essay on some directions 'concerning the ordering of melons' in *The Compleat Gard'ner* (1693).

Leonard Knyff's perspective views of Hampton Court from the south and from the east (figs 4, 5) show the Melon Ground as being marshalled into three great divisions flanked by two narrower beds. These views depict the area after William III trebled the size of the palace's productive gardens by turning the eight-acre Tiltyard into a kitchen garden – a grand gesture which doubtless had repercussions on the layout and management of the Melon Ground. In Knyff's views the 'lights' of the brick melon pits are highlighted in bright white, as if reflecting the summer sunshine. The ground is laid out in the 'best Figure for a Fruit-Garden', being, as Stephen Switzer remarked in *Ichnographia Rustica* (1718) 'a Square about half as long again as Broad'.[1] It is, moreover, enclosed on the north and west sides by brick walls set with trees in borders, behind which are rows of espaliered trees – presumably to protect the garden from the wind. The garden's cherry and vine houses are depicted in the north-west corner – their location calculated to maximize the sun they got. The Tennis Court Garden is also delineated and appears to be divided into two large divisions – each possessing a quadrupartite plan.

John Rocque's *Plan of the Royal Park and Gardens of Hampton Court* of 1736 depicts the arrangement of beds and buildings in the Melon Ground and the open character of Tennis Court Lane. The survey also records the arrival of two new buildings: the New Kitchen – today known as the Georgian House – designed by Colen Campbell and built by the surveyor William Benson for George I in around 1716, and the communal lavatory, or 'necessary house for persons of fashion', completed two years later.

John Spyers's views of the late 1770s are the most revealing topographical records of the Glasshouse Nursery precincts. His view from the north-east portrays the palace and the New Kitchen looming above serried ranks of etiolated fruit trees; and his north-west view paints an even more melancholy picture of the royal Melon Ground – long rows of hotbeds emerge from rank grass, and a mutilated tree and a derelict cart underline the decrepitude of the garden, which from the 1760s was no longer in

control of the Master Gardener Mr Brown, but let by the Office of Works to local market gardeners.

The topographer's views from the east and the west of the North Inferior Court illustrate the future Tennis Court Lane in considerable detail: the court lodgings at the base of the Prince's Apartments are graced with small shrubberies contained by white-painted palisades; the New Kitchen is enveloped by neat grassy panels; and the communal lavatory is represented as something approaching a Romanesque mausoleum. Very interestingly, most of the ground surface of the court is shown as given over to grass interlaced with narrow, rutted gravel tracks. While the grass has doubtless colonized the court rather than being deliberately sown, its presence – and that of a quarry of discarded masonry at the foot of the Neo-Palladian villa-like kitchen – gives the court the air of a scene from Classical antiquity.

By the late eighteenth century the remains of the old moat that ran along the northern and eastern flanks of the ground were filled in, and its northern arm was planted with trees and shrubs to become Old Moat Wood. Henry Sayers's detailed plan of 1841 shows how the once open nursery ground was becoming increasingly covered with glasshouses for the cultivation of cherries and figs, pit houses for melons and pineapples, as well as stables, offices and buildings for fruit storage and plant propagation (fig. 193). A broad slice of the western end of the nursery was also given over to a new works yard. Old Moat Wood was threaded with serpentine paths, Moat Lane was formed on the north side of the works yard, and the Garden Manager's Office was raised in the north-east corner. The New Kitchen's garden is portrayed as a pleasure ground, and the Tennis Court Garden as an orchard.

From the middle of the nineteenth century the nursery was known as the Forcing Ground and was given over to the cultivation of vast quantities of bedding plants for the palace gardens. Potting sheds and offices were built along the northern wall and in time this area became the centre of horticultural operations at Hampton Court. Few gardens in England at the time produced so large and diverse a range of bedding plants as Hampton Court. The palace, in fact, still ranks among the country's leading in-house nurseries, growing over 140,000 spring and summer bedding plants under glass every year. Several houses are also given over to the propagation and over-wintering of Queen Mary's collection of exotic plants (figs 141, 143, 144).

Late nineteenth- and twentieth-century surveys of the area document the loss of open beds and the relentless march of glasshouses, stores and ancillary buildings across the site. Most of the early plant houses were renewed in the twentieth century and replaced with glass and aluminium structures – some of which are pioneering in their layout and construction. The character of Tennis Court Lane also changed significantly in the 1920s when it was first used for public car parking (fig. 140); this practice was discontinued in the 1970s. The lane is no longer open to the public.

Over the past fifty years, as garden operations have become more complex and mechanized, the need for greater space for the cultivation of plants and the storage of tools, machinery and vehicles has increased. Being surrounded by high walls, the area has had no scope for expansion, so from the mid-1940s onwards some functions have been transferred to Stud House Nursery in Home Park. At various times over the past decades proposals have been put forward to relocate the whole of the estate's garden operations to Stud House Nursery, to make way for the expansion of the tennis club. Fortunately, these have come to nothing.

The palace is currently exploring the possibility of opening a limited area of the Glasshouse Nursery to the visiting public, so that they might gain a 'behind-the-scenes' look at the horticultural hub of the estate. This initiative might encourage greater investment in the careful refurbishment of the area's most outstanding features, as well as safeguard the future of this historic area, which for almost eight centuries has enjoyed a close and fruitful relationship with the palace and its precursors.

142. (left) Moat Lane
was formed in the
eighteenth century
upon the former line
of the Tudor moat.

143. (below) Prickly
pears flourishing in
the Nursery.

144.(overleaf) Exotics
being grown on in the
Glasshouse Nursery.

Hampton Court Green and the Vrow Walk

Visitors to Hampton Court might be forgiven for thinking that the flat and featureless field that lies west of the Tudor walls of the Tiltyard and the leafy fringe of the Vrow Walk has little historical interest. This twenty-nine-acre green is, however, of greater importance than the visible fabric obviously suggests and has a long and distinguished association with the palace.

The bleak expansiveness of the centre of the green belies a rich legacy of temporary uses: for hundreds of years it has been a lively place and the site of work and play – a resort of tradesmen, troops, sportsmen, gamesters, costermongers and grazing animals – and has at one time or another been littered with the detritus of their occupation. The green, however, bears few scars from its intensive, varied and continuous use: fairgrounds, barracks, workshops, timber yards, gravel pits and car parks have come and gone and the green remains the open field it ever was. By contrast, the margins of Hampton Court Green are crowded with a range of more permanent structures dating from the sixteenth to the nineteenth centuries that chart its changing fortunes – inns, dwelling houses, stabling and workshops used or enjoyed by the sovereign and a handful of royal officials including the Master Carpenter, Mason and Locksmith, the Comptroller of Works, the Palace Clerk of the Works and the Surveyor of the King's Works.

Long before the Knights Hospitallers owned Hampton Court, the area now covered by the green had been part of a long arable field running parallel to the Thames extending from Hampton Court to Hampton Village. Some time before Henry VIII became Lord of the Manor, a track was formed along the south and east sides of the green – now the Hampton Court Road – and part of the field was enclosed as pasture land for the Hospitallers' sheep, or Wolsey's or Daubeney's animals – the horses, mules and other cattle necessary to a large household.

Hampton Gate at the west end of the green was erected before 1529 to stop grazing animals from wandering into Hampton Town. This gate – which was abandoned in 1810 and has long since vanished – admitted people to the green or Bushy Park and was operated by a gatekeeper who resided in a small timber shed beside it. There was also a conduit head by the gate, presumably to water travellers' horses. The green continued as pasture for about three hundred years, except in the 1650s during the Protectorate when the pasture was in abeyance. The green, like the neighbouring park, was also sometimes used for archery practice.

Accounts show that 'victualling houses' – inns or taverns which supplied the food and drink for the royal workforce – were set up in the middle and on the edges of the green in the early sixteenth century. These included Great and Privy Bakehouses, a Poultry Office (for the preparation of chickens), a Scalding Office (a boiling house), a Knife House and a woodyard that had formerly occupied a part of Outer Green Court – now the West Front of the palace. In 1536 they were relocated to the south-west corner of the Green.

The Royal Mews – which consists of two buildings – has always been the most distinguished ensemble on the green (fig. 146). The King's New Stable, which stands on the south side of the green, about two hundred yards west of Trophy Gate, was built in 1537 for Henry VIII to the designs of the Master Mason Christopher Dickinson. Dickinson was responsible for the design of some of the King's most important buildings between 1529 and 1530, and his square courtyard plan for the stable was at the time novel in England and appears to have been influenced by the royal stable erected at Fontainebleau for Francis I. On the abandonment of the palace as a royal residence in the late 1730s, the Keeper of the Royal Mews was permitted to convert the east side of the King's Stable into an inn, known as the Chequers. This was given up in the 1840s. The mews is now the headquarters of the Horse Rangers Trust.

The red-brick building adjoining the King's Stable is the Queen's Coach House, or Great Barn, built by Elizabeth I in 1570 (fig. 147). The erection of this building had a considerable impact on the future development of the green and the palace, as the Queen's preference for travelling overland instead of by barge led to a change in its approach roads and a decline in importance of the Water Gallery south of the palace. Hampton Court Road which divided the palace from the green – would henceforth become a busy thoroughfare.

From the early 1660s soil and gravel were frequently excavated from the green. Charles II, as Lord of the Manor, had the right to do this. He, and later William III and Queen Anne, did so with great liberality. Large pits were dug on the north-east side of the green and great quantities of gravel were extracted for walks in the gardens and for surfacing the roads. In 1707 the accounts report

145. *The First Grand
Match of Cricket
played by Members
of the Royal Amateur
Society on Hampton
Court Green*, 1836.

147. (left) The Queen's Coach House was built in 1570 for Elizabeth I. The building forms part of the Royal Mews and lies west of the palace in Hampton Court Green.

148. (below) Bernard Lens's *A South View of the Camp on Hampton Court Green*, 1731.

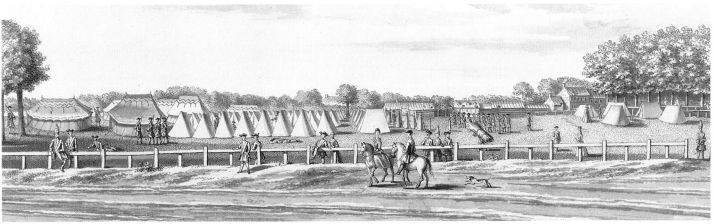

that the Old Gravel Pit was so depleted that gravel had to be imported from pits at a distance of two and a half miles from the palace.

Material was not only excavated from the green, but dumped on it as well. For instance, in 1700, '1,277 yards of rubbish' were removed from Outer Green Court; likewise, many loads of building spoil from the demolition of the Tudor state apartments were tipped on the green to fill the gaping gravel pits. One of these disused quarries can be clearly seen on Knyff's painted view of Hampton Court from the east (fig. 5); this large depression was later used to advantage by the architect Thomas Wright of Durham, who created a sunken garden and a small lake in its midst when he landscaped the grounds of Hampton Court House in the 1750s.

The green became a giant royal workshop during the rebuilding campaign of the palace that began in 1689. This work prompted a great influx of people associated with the building trade, many of whom set up temporary booths and sheds on the green to act as workshops or places of refreshment. They, in turn, are said to have attracted 'many vicious and idle people' to the neighbourhood who pilfered and stole some of the palace's building materials. A survey of the late seventeenth century indicates that there were over ten temporary buildings scattered on the margins of the green. Some of these premises can be seen on Knyff's bird's-eye view of Hampton Court. In the east view, the artist portrays the green as a noble paddock with a handful of trees scattered on its western and northern margins and a single round

plantation opposite the Royal Mews. The range of red-brick buildings depicted on the south side of the green includes the Royal Mews, Old Court House (Sir Christopher Wren's house) and Faraday House (so called after 1867) – their capacious gardens stretching southwards to the Thames. Later in the eighteenth century the Royal Gardener 'Capability' Brown set up his yard on the south side of the green, which became the base for his extensive landscape operations.

Hampton Court House remains to this day the largest premises to have been built on the green. The house was raised in the 1750s by George Montagu Dunk, second Earl of Halifax (then Ranger of Bushy Park) for his Irish mistress, on an encroachment on the green. The garden possesses a terrace walk, a pond and a grotto decorated with shells, spars and minerals. The grotto was refurbished in the 1980s and the house is now a preparatory school.

During the reigns of George I and George II the green was occasionally used as a camp for the military. The First Regiment of Guards was encamped there in 1716, and George II gave orders in 1728 for a battalion of guards to be encamped on the green and to provide the guard whenever he was in residence. An engraving by Bernard Lens from 1731 depicts a rather decorous encampment on the green radiating around a halberd and a cone-shaped tent emblazoned with a royal coat of arms (fig. 148).

From 1794 George III sanctioned the posting of a Troop of Cavalry to Hampton Court. The troop took over the King's Chaise Marine House (coach house), which stood on the green against Bushy Park wall, and converted it into barracks. The building

remained until 1811, when it was rebuilt. These barracks were demolished in 1932 and are now the site of the present car and coach park at the west end of the green.

The green, inevitably, played a role in a range of military events; it served not only as a parade ground, but also as a regimental recreation ground for football, cricket and other sports. During the Crimean War part of the green was given over to the army for training troop horses; in 1899 and 1901 villagers assembled in its midst to cheer soldiers departing and subsequently returning from the Boer War; and during the First World War both the Army and the Navy held recruiting meetings on the green.

From the mid-nineteenth century the green, like the palace grounds, became a popular resort for the urban working classes. Many clubs or societies in the metropolitan area had annual outings to Hampton Court, which included a visit to the palace or a game of cricket on the green, followed by dinner or supper in one of the local hostelries (fig. 145). In a letter to *The Times* (1873) headed 'Hampton Court Green' the correspondent refers to the 'tens of thousands of smoke-begrimed toilers of London… who indulge without let or hindrance in kiss-in-the-ring and the various other amusements which used to characterize the long-suppressed fairs of the metropolis'.

The crowds that assembled were not always orderly. Mr Herbert Cornewell – a grace-and-favour resident of the palace – wrote to Viscount Palmerston in 1854 complaining of the 'annoyance caused to himself and his family by the improper conduct of people who assemble for the purpose of recreation on Hampton Court Green during the summer months.' The most serious disturbance to take place was a riot which broke out in 1879, and which was only subdued when the constabulary and the 18th Hussars from the barracks on the green were summoned.

There were, of course, regular planned, popular events that caused minor local disturbance. Every Easter from the mid-nineteenth century onwards, Hampton Court Green was transformed into a fairground. Although a local byelaw prohibited gambling, betting, playing with cards or dice, begging or telling fortunes on the green, the Metropolitan Police found it difficult to apprehend people as the majority of the stallholders were 'travelling showmen who reside in caravans, having no permanent place of abode'. During the Easter bank holiday in 1930, charges

were nonetheless brought against twenty people apprehended for unlawful gaming. Police reports singled out 'Win-a-lot, Wheel-em-in, Electric Discs and Ringing Coins' as among the most vicious pursuits. The Office of Works appears to have been ignorant of or to have turned a blind eye to these innocent amusements, and was requested by the police 'to refrain from letting the ground to persons using it for games offering cash prizes'.

The green has undergone few dramatic changes since the 1930s. In the 1980s a car park was built at the west end of the green, and more recently horse chestnut trees were planted along the north and west boundaries. The green remains enclosed on the south and east sides by a low post and rail fence, and the central area is the site of summer funfairs and temporary overflow car parking.

The Vrow Walk

A letter published in *La Correspondence Secrete du Comte de Broglio* (1724) relates that 'His sacred majesty [George I] spent many hours of the day in the sweet companionship of his ugly fat mistresses.' Frau Schulenberg was, the Count remarked, 'of a yellow complexion, and so unusually tall and lank as to be popularly known as the "Maypole"'. The other companion who kept the King company in his retirement at the palace was Frau Kielmansegge, who was called 'Elephant and Castle' on account of her great corpulence. The tradition is that they used to promenade up and down beneath the broad spreading branches of the chestnut and elm trees there, waiting for the return of the King, when he had driven out; and that it was thus designated Frau or Frow walk, which was corrupted by the commoner people, by mistake or in derision, into the name 'Frog Walk'.

What is now known as the Vrow Walk has a double line of trees tracing the north and west perimeter walls of the Tiltyard. The horse chestnuts that presently line the walk were replanted in the 1970s.

The Parks

The Early Years

For hundreds of years the parks at Hampton Court were the retreat of English monarchs. The brick-walled enclosures were formed to protect and preserve 'venison and vert' – that is, red, fallow and roe deer, and the timber and undergrowth which fed them – for coursing, shooting and hunting.[1] These field sports were enjoyed by the sovereigns for recreation as well as for health.

The Manor of Hampton Court is now composed of two main divisions – Bushy Park and Home Park (formerly House Park), separated from each other by the Kingston Road, lying respectively to the north and south. Their present size and configuration were established by Cardinal Wolsey between c.1514 and 1529, when he enlarged his predecessor Lord Daubeney's 300-acre park to enclose an additional 1,700 acres with timber paling. He later subdivided them with brick walls into smaller enclosures. Bushy Park was partitioned into three parts of nearly equal size: Hare Warren to the east, Upper Park or Old Park to the west and Middle Park lying between the two others. Home Park was bisected into the Course next to the Kingston Road, and Home Park proper, bounded on the south by the River Thames. One of the dividing walls between the Course and Home Park can be seen on Wyngaerde's drawing of the north of the palace (fig. 126).[2]

In 1539 Henry VIII set about extending the boundaries of the parks to indulge his interest in stag hunting. An Act of Parliament was passed which made Hampton Court the centre of an honour, or a collection of royal property holdings. This princely manor, decent and convenient for a King, encompassed tens of thousand of acres and stretched all the way to Windsor; it also contained a ten-thousand-acre chase, or private forest, which was enclosed with a wooden pale. The King enjoyed the use of this giant forest until his death, upon which the pale was dismantled, the deer removed and the land 'dechased'.

The palace's parks had been predominantly in arable use before they were emparked and were part of a great open field system that covered much of lowland England. Of the two parks, Bushy retains the greater evidence of its early origins and is a remarkably large and well-preserved example of an everyday agricultural landscape of the medieval period. Traces of prominent banks known as field baulks abound; these defined individual field strips or, to use their technical name, furlongs. Less conspicuous

undulations associated with ridge and furrow cultivation can be readily detected beneath the closely cropped grass of the eighteenth-century Lime Avenue which stretches from White Lodge to the Royal Paddocks in the east. The boundaries and freeboard (the land outside the park fence) of the three original divisions of Bushy Park are also very much in evidence – that of Old Park being the most obvious, with its roughly circular shape still defined by the north-west section of the park wall. A row of hollow holm oaks and stubby English oaks set on the northern freeboard of the Old Park are among the most ancient and stately trees in the park.

Much of the history of the parks has been guided by the management and decorative display of water. The earliest water supply was possibly installed by Cardinal Wolsey, who drew water from the springs at Hampton and in Upper Park. The palace's supply was, however, much improved from about 1538 when Henry VIII began to extract water from the springs on the top of Kingston Hill, about three miles east of Hampton Court; here the water was collected in brick conduit heads, or small buildings which incorporated settling tanks to avoid sediment in the water, whence it was conveyed in lead pipes through Surbiton and Kingston to Home Park, and ultimately to the palace. The drop was 129 feet – sufficient to supply high-pressure water at second-floor level. This source supplied water for all the palace's decorative pools and fountains until 1639. The remains of three of Henry VIII's conduit heads survive: Ivy Conduit is privately owned and lies in the grounds of a school; Gallows Tamkin is situated within a golf course; and Coombe Conduit – which is the best preserved of all – is in the care of English Heritage (fig. 153).

Charles I and the Commonwealth

In 1638 Charles I directed a commission to consider how part of the waters of the River Colne in Middlesex might be taken over Hounslow Heath into the parks at Hampton Court to bring water to the ponds in the parks and the fountains in the gardens. The King and Queen, who were acquainted with some of the most celebrated contemporary waterworks in France, appear to have wanted to create water gardens along the same lines at Hampton Court. The works to the new river involved cutting a twelve-mile channel from Longford to the palace, a great part of the distance

152. The Longford River is managed by the Royal Parks Agency. Indeed, to this day three keepers are employed on a full-time basis to maintain the river, cleaning grates and sluices, cutting its grassy banks and weeding and de-silting the bed.

153. Coombe Conduit was built by Henry VIII to supply water to the palace. The conduit survives to this day.

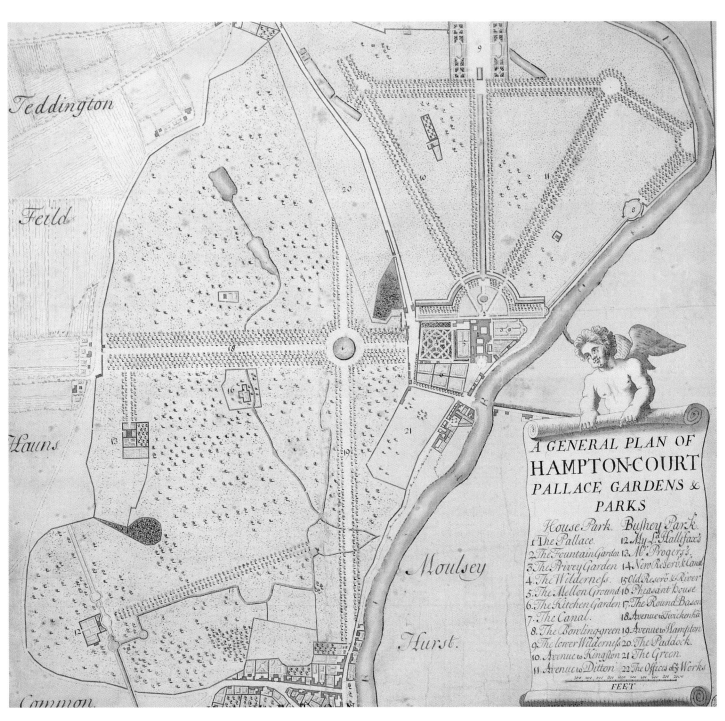

A GENERAL PLAN OF
HAMPTON-COURT
PALLACE GARDENS &
PARKS

House Park.   Bushey Park.
1. The Pallace.   12. My L? Hallifax's
2. The Fountain Garden   13. M? Proger's.
3. The Privey Garden   14. New Reserv? & Canal
4. The Wilderness.   15. Old Reserv? & River
5. The Mellon Ground   16. Pheasant house
6. The Kitchen Garden   17. The Round Bason
7. The Canal.   18. Avenue to Twickenha?
8. The Bowling-green   19. Avenue to Hampton
9. The lower Wilderness 20. The Paddock.
10. Avenue to Kingston   21. The Green.
11. Avenue to Ditton   22. The Offices of Works

FEET

being taken up by deepening, broadening and banking up of an existing branch of the Colne; extensive use was also made of the medieval field baulks in Bushy Park to form a natural course for the river. The artificially raised canal has a very gentle descent, dropping a mere thirteen feet from its source at Longford Point – near Heathrow Airport – to the Thames north of Hampton Wick. The entire length of the channel was originally, and remains to this day, insulated on both sides by a freeboard enclosed by quickset hedges, ditches and fences (fig. 152).

The course of the new river was laid out by Nicholas Lane, and cut under the supervision of the Commissioners of Sewers. Work began in October 1638 and finished in July of the following year. Since then the channel has been known as the King's River or Longford River and recently as 'the King's giant hose-pipe', and has supplied water to the ponds and ornamental waters at Hampton Court.

In 1652, Parliament resolved to sell Hampton Court and Bushy Parks and the following year the Surveyor-General for Land Sales, Sir William Webb, compiled a full and accurate land survey. The *Parliamentary Survey* of Hampton Court provides detailed descriptions of the parks and ascribed values to their 'Timber Trees and other Trees, Woods, underwoods, Bushes, Shrubbs, Wild Beastes, and all other commodities, and advantages, privileges, franchises, and Immunities'. By the close of 1653 Home Park had been reserved from the sale, but Bushy and the title of the manor and honour were sold; they were, however reacquired at great expense by the spring of the following year and vested in Oliver Cromwell and his successors. The estate was spared, but at a great cost: during the turmoil that ensued between Charles I's death in 1649 and Cromwell's installation at the palace in December 1654, a large proportion of the ancient oaks had been felled for timber, leaving extensive areas bleak and treeless.

During his tenure, Cromwell restored the flow of the Longford River, which had been interrupted by local inhabitants. He also diverted the river into Hare Warren and caused two ponds to be dug there, which were known as Hare Warren Ponds – subsequently corrupted to the Heron Ponds and now known as Heron and Leg of Mutton Ponds. Cromwell also barred the passage of an immemorial right of way across Bushy Park, which led to considerable public discontent.

Charles II

After the Restoration the story of the park is one of reconstruction, consolidation, reinvention and new building – and mostly on a princely scale. The improvements were begun by Charles II, who cast a long piece of water flanked by a great avenue across Home Park to establish a tenacious grip on the demesne. The upshot of this regal flourish was that Home Park became an extension of the pleasure ground, while Bushy retained much of its extensive landscape character.

The great tree-lined canal, or Long Water, which straddles Home Park was contrived by André Mollet in an attempt to reform the park after the neglect and depredations during the Commonwealth (fig. 155). Mollet's layout of a canal lined with double rows of lime was derived from an earlier design published in *Le Jardin de Plaisir* (1651), which, according to Evelyn, was applied with great success at St James's Park in 1660–1. The French gardener remarked in his treatise:

[A] royal house must be sited to best advantage, in order to ornament it with all things necessary to its embellishment: of which the first is to be able to plant a big avenue with a double or triple row of female elms, or lime trees (which are the two species of tree which we esteem most suited to this effect) which must be placed in line at right angles to the front of the chateau.[3]

Although Hampton Court had not originally been sited with a view to forming an imposing canal and attendant avenues, the open parkland which lay east of the palace provided an ideal setting for such a grand gesture. Mollet was presumably responsible for determining the alignment of the canal on the Queen's Rich Bedchamber and may have had a hand in the decision to erect, or possibly refurbish, a first-floor balcony overlooking the new design. Hendrick Danckerts's painted view of the East Front (*c.*1670) shows how, when the scheme was first implemented, the canal terminated rather abruptly, short of the long, straggling and asymmetrical palace front (fig. 155). When the east side of the palace was demolished and rebuilt to Hawksmoor's designs in the late seventeenth century, Mollet's grand gesture guided the planning of the new east-facing apartments and, indeed, the layouts of the Great Fountain Garden and the new Fountain Court.

The Long Water was dug under the direction of Adrian May – supervisor of the French gardeners at the palace and overseer

155. Hendrick
Danckerts's view of
the Long Water and
the Long Water
Avenue, c.1670.

156. Bushy House,
Bushy Park.

157. (right) Detail from
Daniel Marot's design
for the Great Fountain
Garden, showing Stud
House in 1689 (centre
middleground).

158. (far right) Leonard
Knyff's *Hampton Court
from the West*, 1707,
showing the radiating
avenues and the Pavilion
Terrace (right).

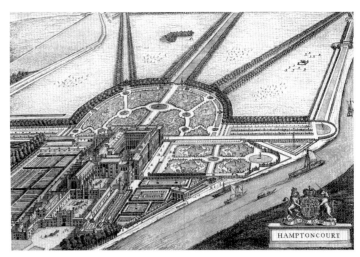

of the King's gardening improvements at St James's Park and Greenwich. Excavations began in the winter of 1661–2 and were completed some months later. A new transverse canal was created to divert the flow of the Longford into the new canal. Soon after the Long Water was completed the flanking avenues were set out and planted. This work, too, was supervised by May and his assistant Adrian Pratt. The lime trees for the avenues were procured in the Netherlands.

John Evelyn remarked in June 1662 that 'the Park formerly a flat, naked piece of Ground, [is] now planted with sweete rows of lime-trees, and a Canale for water [is] now neere perfected'.[4] He later noted in his transcript of *Elysium Britannicum* (*c*.1658–1702) that the canal at Hampton Court was the equal of the 'noble Piscina' in the Gardens of Fontainebleau; at 105 feet wide and 3,800 feet long, it was longer than its antecedents at the Chateaux of Fleury and Fontainebleau and in St James's Park. Such ornaments as the Long Water were seen by Evelyn as 'greately contributing to the perfection and accomplishments' of a garden. They served as noble embellishments to a royal garden, and were designed to be

> of such a capacity as may serve not onely to keepe a good quantity of Carps, Tench, Trowts, Pike or other fish, but for to saile and row about with a Pleasure Boate built of some antique shape, or Pinnace like, with a Cabine, gunns, sails, streamers, and other ornaments fit for the divertisements of Ladys, and entertainements upon the Watter.[5]

Charles II and Catherine de Braganza appear to have enjoyed such entertainments. They are reported as having made much use of the pair of rich gondolas presented to them by the Venetian state in September 1661. The vessels were manned by four Venetian gondoliers. The Dutch travel writer William Schellinks observed in June 1662 that 'King Charles II had a canal dug there, so that one can go by water with barges right up to the gardens.' The King's swans and Spanish geese also added an exotic note to the gardens.[6]

In the late 1660s a variety of repairs and improvements were made to the canal. Purbeck stone pavings and copings were laid by the master mason Joshua Marshall, timber revetments were renewed and landing stages built at both ends of the canal, suggesting that it was increasingly used for pleasure.

Charles II's improvements also extended to the other divisions of the park. Count Lorenzo Magalotti reported in 1669:

The amusements of hunting and fishing are not wanting, those diversions being at hand in the park, which is of considerable size, both in length and breadth, enclosing large meadows, where the preserved deer feed. To vary the delights of these beautiful premises, several canals or ponds are distributed in different parts of the park, in whose transparent water quantities of fish are seen sporting, which are reserved for the diversion of angling.[7]

The Stud – historically the residence of the Master of the Horse and the breeding establishment for the king's horses – also began to take shape in Home Park under Charles II. Stud House, and what is now known as Stud Nursery, lie concealed in a dense plantation half-way down and in the centre of Home Park, between the Long Water and Kingston avenues. Daniel Marot's perspective drawing for the Great Parterre of 1689 supplies us with among the earliest views of the Stud, which is shown encompassed on two sides by banks of tall trees, its long rectangular paddocks disappearing into the distance (fig. 157).

Bushy House is the most outstanding building to have been raised in the parks during the reign of Charles II. It was built between 1664 and 1665 for Edward Progers, Keeper of Middle Park and Hare Warren, to the designs of William Samwell, and replaced an earlier lodge. Although much altered by the 1st and 2nd Earls of Halifax during their respective tenures, the Samwell house forms the nucleus of the present building (fig. 156).

William and Mary

A great many improvements took place in the parks during the reign of William and Mary. New avenues were planted, basins dug, terraces thrown up, a new Bowling Green was laid out, a second wilderness garden was formed and the Stud was improved. Work began in 1689 with the planting of a pair of diagonal avenues across Home Park to form a *patte d'oie* (fig. 158). This trio of radiating avenues at once transformed the park into what Stephen Switzer referred to as a 'Rural Garden', or a garden in which the far-flung corners of the demesne were drawn to the very heart of the stately mansion and its pleasure grounds. Thousands of trees were marshalled to form the stately alleys which proclaimed the new sovereigns' mastery over a landscape which still bore the scars of the Civil War.

The Queen's Apartments once again became the point of convergence of a princely landscape gesture – the new avenues which radiated from the royal apartments framed views beyond the park's boundaries, to the spire of Kingston Church to the north-east and the open fields of Thames Ditton to the south-east. In around 1701 the Cross Avenue was also planted to link the three spokes of the *patte d'oie* to form a triangle, and two short avenues were laid out to the south and west of the Cross Avenue connecting the Pavilion and the Pavilion Terrace.

As the new avenues were being planted in Home Park, proposals were being drawn up by Nicholas Hawksmoor to cast a great avenue across Bushy Park, from the Teddington Gate in the north to Henry VIII's Great Hall in the south. George London planted 1,050 lime trees to form two great avenues – the Great Avenue, the ring around the future round basin, and the Lime Avenue which intersected it at right angles – before work was suspended. It was only resumed in 1699 when Henry Wise supervised the excavation of the basin and the planting of an additional 732 chestnuts and lime trees in the Great Avenue. Water was then drawn from the Longford River through a brick-lined channel to feed the basin, and the whole northern course of the river was cleansed and made wider and deeper, and new drains were dug to obviate flooding.

Meanwhile plans were afoot to raise a long, flat-topped dyke high above the Thames foreshore south-east of the palace to receive a new bowling green and pavilion. The ensemble was proposed to replace an earlier riverside bowling green built in 1670 for Charles II, which, being laid out in the floodplain, was subject to periodic inundations. The architect of the new scheme was Richard Jones, Earl of Ranelagh. The Great Terrace – now known as the Pavilion Terrace – was proposed to extend in a south-easterly direction, parallel to the river, from the south end of the Broad Walk to a new raised oval green. Ranelagh was Paymaster of the Army and an informed amateur in the arts of gardening and architecture; his designs owed a considerable debt to the Duke of Portland's earlier proposals, which had been formulated upon similar compositions at Marly and Versailles. Ranelagh's solution was practical and elegant. The terrace and the green would provide an attractive walk above the Thames; the pavilion would form a handsome terminus to the terrace, and would be a suitable

replacement for the Water Gallery which was scheduled to be demolished to make way for the extension of the Privy Garden; and the extensive earthworks required to raise the 1,900-foot terrace and the large green would absorb the rubbish generated by the demolitions and the spoil created by lowering the ground of the Privy Garden.

The scheme met with the approval of William III and was completed – with modifications by William Talman – within two years. The most significant change was the replacement of the single trianon with a clutch of four, square brick pavilions laid out symmetrically upon the oval green (figs 159, 160). The green itself was enclosed, except at the two ends, by a low brick wall about three feet high with a Portland stone coping. William III did not live long enough to receive the praise heaped upon his riverside improvements. Samuel Molyneux, Secretary to Frederick, Prince of Wales, writing in 1713, was impressed by the new riverside ensemble, remarking:

> The Scituation of Hampton Court is on a dead Flatt and for such a one, I think the Gardens, the great Canall, the Park and the Bowling Green are beautifully dispos'd enough, the Thames which runs at the foot of the Gardens and along the great Terrace going to the Bowling Green makes one of it's greatest beautys.

And Switzer opined in 1715, the 'Great Terrace beside the Thames' was a 'considerable Improvement', and 'the noblest Work of that kind in Europe'.[8]

After the avenue planting was completed in the parks, the King turned his attention to the eastern terminus of the Long Water: the princely piece of ornamental water ended in a large irregular pool known as Rushey Pond which sat in the Little House Park, in the floodplain of the Thames. The King resolved to rectify this deficiency by formalizing the shape of the pond and casting a geometrical plantation around it. This new plantation became known as the Lower Wilderness, or the Lower Plantation. The garden was neither similar in scale nor composition to the earlier Wilderness east of the palace. Henry Wise proposed to extend the Long Water eastwards, ending in a large octagonal basin that was presumably designed to receive a central fountain. This was not built, however, and for three centuries the avenue remained devoid of any terminal feature. Two oblong plantations,

each formed of two symmetrical parts, were to be placed on either side of the new canal.

In 1701–2 Wise's men grubbed up the unwanted vegetation around Rushey Pond and prepared the ground to receive new borders and walks. Roughly eight thousand hornbeams, one thousand yews and four thousand large laurels were deployed to form the structure of the new plantation. The compartments were planted with a great variety of trees and shrubs including horse chestnuts, laburnum, guelder rose, lilacs, bladder sennas, philadelphus, yellow jasmine, amelanchier, spiraea, sweet briars, mezereons, cypresses and cork trees. Some of the hornbeams, cypresses and flowering shrubs used in the new plantation were orphans from the Privy Garden; 'several lines' of firs and yews were also introduced from the seventeenth-century Wilderness.

Being built on low ground in the Thames' floodplain, the Lower Wilderness fared badly: it was washed away by a flood in around 1720 and again in the spring of 1725, shortly after it had been replanted for a second time. Although efforts were made to embank the river, the Lower Wilderness seems to have been dismantled some time before the mid-eighteenth century. The last surviving remnants of this unfortunate feature are a pair of lacklustre oblong ponds, now known collectively as the overflow.

Elsewhere in the parks the Stud was elevated to the status of 'royal', paddocks were formed in Hare Warren and Middle Park, the late seventeenth-century ice-house by Kingston Gate was repaired (fig. 164), and a number of water meadows which lay in the Thames' floodplain, east of Home Park, were taken in for grazing. They were used by the Master of the Horse from the eighteenth century to the early twentieth century for grazing and hay crops.

Queen Anne and George I

Queen Anne took a great interest in the Hampton Court estate and made significant contributions to the parks. Early in her reign she instructed the making of twenty miles of new 'chaise ridings' through Home and Bushy Parks.[9] The Queen, who was fond of hunting *en chaise* (in a light open top carriage drawn by a single horse), and who according to Jonathan Swift drove 'furiously, like Jehu, and is a mighty hunter like Nimrod',[10] commissioned a circuit which resembled one made a few years earlier at Windsor. A plan and estimate of 1710 outline the new scheme: eight miles of shady

walks – some of which already existed but which were in poor condition – were made within the avenues in Home Park; seven miles of ridings traced the bounds of the Home Park; two miles were to cast across 'the most pleasant parts' of Bushy Park and the remainder were set out within the avenues in the same park. The scheme is the first record of a formalized circuit around the parks, and provides a fascinating insight into the way in which the sovereign galloped her way across the estate.

Although the Queen is reputed to have been disinclined to perpetuate the extravagances of her predecessor William III, she put the finishing touches to the Great Avenue in Bushy Park, erecting the Diana Fountain at the centre of the Great Basin in 1714 (fig. 162). The crowning figure – which had been gilded by the Queen – and her retinue of nymphs, little boys and dolphins were perched high on a pedestal of pilasters, basins, fluted scrolls, frost work, rustic work and water leaves – where they remain to this day. The fountain, which had formerly graced the Privy Garden (fig. 28), had lain in store since 1701. It should be noted that the figure atop the fountain is not, in fact, Diana, but Arethusa – one of the goddess Diana's attendants, who was metamorphosed into a spring. The watery nymph has over her long life been known as Diana, Arethusa, Venus and even Proserpina. Recently, some younger visitors have mistakenly assumed that the fountain was named in honour of the late Princess of Wales.

In the last year of her reign the Queen also embarked on building the Lion Gates, which were raised on the site of the Wilderness Gate, on an axis with the Chestnut Avenue. It was left to George I to complete this enormous screen, as the Queen died before the work was finished. The King also oversaw the construction of the gates on the north and south sides of the Great Avenue in Bushy Park.

Upper Lodge in Old Park, Bushy, came to prominence from c.1710. It became the official residence of Charles Montagu, later 1st Earl of Halifax, when he was appointed Chief Steward of the Honour and Manor of Hampton Court. Halifax laid out extensive gardens, diverting water from the Longford River and local springs to form a series of new waterworks. A new octagonal basin – the New Reservoir – was dug south-west of the lodge, whence the water flowed eastwards over cascades and through rockworks into a string of geometrically shaped pools and linear canals. The lodge,

which had been a modest structure built in 1537, was also rebuilt and realigned to sit in the centre of an earlier lime avenue, terraces were thrown up in front of the house and three walled gardens were formed to the north. Samuel Molyneux reported in 1713 that 'there was here little or nothing remarkable but the Cascade which was not very high, but little and yet very beautifully dispos'd so as to fall between two fine pieces of Grotto Work where places are left for Paintings representing two Caves in which the little walks round the Basin of the Cascade end the paintings are moveable so as to be taken away in Winter'. A painting of c.1715 shows Halifax's impressive new cascade sunk in a broad, shallow dish encircled by gravel walks and smooth angular banks (fig. 166). Stephen Switzer later remarked in his *Introduction to Hydrostatics and Hydraulics* (1734) that 'the Canal and Cascade at Bushey Park . . . is, without doubt, one of the best works of that kind in England, and perhaps as good as any else where'. He also illustrated the Upper Basin in his book.[11]

The Eighteenth and Nineteenth Centuries

The taste for grandiose landscape gestures declined in the 1720s and there followed a long period of inactivity, or at best piecemeal improvements in the parks – this in spite of the fact that during much of the eighteenth century they were under the stewardship of two of the greatest landscape improvers of the age, Charles Bridgeman and 'Capability' Brown. From the 1730s there were, however, no royal masters to commission new works. The Board of Works superintended the management of the estate, but it appears to have taken little interest in it.

The pavilions in Home Park were for many years well-inhabited by a range of grandees, each making his mark, and some spending considerable sums of money on a variety of conveniences, additions and embellishments. These adjustments took their toll on the pretty quartet: the two easterly pavilions were linked by a new building in the early 1790s and the two westerly buildings were pulled down in 1811. A third pavilion was demolished in 1855. The grounds were also subject to numerous, less destructive, alterations: the Duke of Gloucester recast the gardens in 1771–2 and made further improvements in 1792. By 1802 the Bowling Green had been severed from the Great Terrace by a fence and the green itself was laid out as a shrubbery.

The Great Terrace was at first planted only with turf and yew sentinels, which caused Batty Langley to remark in *New Principles of Gardening* (1728) that 'being naked of shade, [it] is thereby useless when the Sunshines';[12] it was subsequently embellished with a double line of elms which became known as the 'aisles'. The walk was enclosed in 1729 on the north side by an iron railing inset with panels which had been removed from the Privy Garden. The Tijou panels were removed in 1861 and replaced with the present railings.

Spyers's views of the late 1770s are a remarkable topographical record of the parks during the reign of George III: dozens of sketches document in astonishing detail new and existing buildings, gardens, park furniture, roads and waterworks, and provide insights into the management of the estate (fig. 165). His

watercolours are, for instance, among the earliest known views of the Stud: they depict Stud House and what was then Stud Farm (now part of Home Park) before it was rebuilt in the late eighteenth century, its hovels and the workaday landscape which surrounded it, as well as groups of horses co-mingling with cattle, deer and sheep in large open paddocks. The views also record that small groups of lime trees were felled in the Long Water and Ditton Avenues to open views between Stud House and the Bowling Green Pavilions. It is likely that 'Capability' Brown opened these keyhole vistas to forge links between the park buildings and to give the Stud a glimpse of the distant Surrey hills.

In Bushy Park, Spyers portrayed no less than three waterworks – one of which, the so-called 'Cascade by the Tea Room', dates from the early eighteenth century (fig. 174). The

'Cascade near the Waterhouse' and the 'New Cascade by the Tea Room' appear to be of later origin. He also documents the changes made by Brown to Bushy House when it was occupied by the retired Prime Minister, Lord North. The tall red-brick house and its handsome dependencies are set in a mature garden of towering trees and dense shrubberies; the open parkland sweeps up to the forecourt's velvet lawn, which is grazed by sheep.

Most fascinating of all are the topographer's depiction of dozens of relict features of the medieval landscape at Bushy – towering flat-topped baulks crowned with ancient, collapsing thorns, and giant pollards, coppice stools and hundreds of veteran trees, many of which were felled shortly thereafter by the impecunious Duke of Clarence when he became ranger of Bushy Park in 1797.

From the beginning of the nineteenth century Home Park and Bushy Park began to drift apart: most of Bushy was opened to the public and became a popular tourist attraction; Home Park, on the other hand, remained the private playground of the Royal Household and a handful of retainers until the mid-1890s when it, too, threw open its gates and admitted the public.

Bushy Park

No aspect of Bushy was so admired as the stately aisles of the Chestnut Avenue. Indeed, such was their popularity that by the 1830s 'Chestnut Sunday' – the day in May on which the trees reached their zenith – became an annual event, attracting thousands of visitors from London and the neighbourhood (fig. 169). A range of images from the 1840s onwards shows throngs

167. (left) A stone pine on the Pavilion Terrace.

168. (below) John Spyers's view of the Cascade at Upper Lodge, c.1775–80. Compare with fig. 166 to see how the feature had evolved since c.1715.

of excursionists picnicking under the trees, or school children going to see the chestnuts. These living galleries of ancient trees were not, however, the only arboreal attractions in the parks. Edward Jesse encouraged his readers to observe and study the parks' other avenues, which were, he remarked, the finest in Europe.

Jesse was among the first writers to encourage visitors to the parks to take an interest in their natural ecology. In *Gleanings in Natural History* (1832) he published a selection of observations on natural curiosities in the parks, noting a colony of 3,750 rooks nested in one of the avenues in Home Park, and a species of huge spider which inhabited the palace precincts. Jesse was particularly fascinated by the old thorn trees in Bushy Park and by a number of other veteran trees, including the remains of two giant elms in Home Park known then as the Giants, the ancient and blasted Methuselah Oak – which survives (fig. 1) – a remarkably fine poplar tree in the Stud House grounds and an elm known as King Charles's Swing. He also made special mention of some evergreen oaks of a very large size in Bushy Park – trees which flourish to this day and are among the oldest trees on the royal estate.[13]

Jesse's energetic promotion of the natural ecology and ancient fabric of the parks was doubtless in part galvanized by the damage inflicted to Bushy during the Rangership of the Duke of Clarence – later William IV – from 1797 to the 1830s. The Duke's ambitions to farm the Bushy estate made the greatest change to the landscape since its emparkment in the sixteenth century. As soon as he had settled in Bushy House he harvested the cash crop of timber, felling 758 trees and denuding the park of most of its ancient cover. Brewer remarked in 1816 that the avenues in Bushy were 'of noble growth, and impart much beauty to the park; but with the exception of these stately avenues, the whole domain is deficient in timber, or ornamental umbrage'.[14] The Duke, to his credit, formed several new plantations, mostly in the area now referred to as the Woodland Gardens, but these modest sylvan offerings did little to atone for his earlier vandalism.

The Duke also enclosed large areas of the deer park for arable farming, pasture and plantations, reducing the area of parkland by almost half. Only on his accession to the throne did he loosen his grip on the estate. Before long many arable fields reverted to grassland, barns and other obtrusive farm buildings were

dismantled and the park began once again to function as and resemble parkland.

From the mid-nineteenth century the popular press began to encourage visitors to enjoy Bushy Park from a picturesque point of view, advising them to wander aimlessly through the park in search of its secluded avenues, open lawns and verdant glades. John Fisher Murray remarked in *A Picturesque Tour* (1849):

How soothing the various commingling sounds that, in quiet harmony, blend on the attentive ear: the ceaseless hum, busy yet obscure, of a thousand insects quivering in the sunny beam: the satisfied cluck-cluck of snow-white chanticleer, leading his dame partlets to some favourite food: the tinkling of the distant sheep-fold, and the merry peal of neighbouring church bells swelling the minor sounds, and giving them substance: the cleanliness and comfort that pervade the place: quiet, gentlemanlike dogs – silky-legged spaniels, wagging their fringed tails when you appear; lady-like, thin-waisted greyhounds, approaching, wooingly to make your acquaintance; cleanly, white-bristled terriers, scorning to imitate the vulgar herd of curs by barking at the stranger; and, more domestic and home-like, grimalkin sunning her tortoise-shell coat on the ledge of a projecting casement; such are the home-like pictures one stumbles upon in strolling though Bushey Park.[15]

Towards the end of the nineteenth century more parkland was reinstated, deer grazing was increased and a variety of new woods was formed including Round, Half Moon, Warren, Oval and Canal plantations.

Home Park

The Stud in Home Park reached its apogee in the early nineteenth century under George IV, who revived the breeding of royal bloodstock and, under the direction of his architect John Nash, lavished over £24,000 on the creation of twenty-six brick-walled paddocks in Home and Bushy Parks, the building of new 'hovels' (horse shelters) and the extension and refurbishment of Stud House and its ancillary buildings. Sayer's *Plan of the Royal Park at Hampton Court* (1841) shows how the Stud had become less a house set in a working landscape than a pavilion set in extensive pleasure grounds (fig. 193). The area of the Stud is much reduced, and the kitchen garden and the extensive paddocks, which

occupied several hundred acres of the parks, are also shown in considerable detail.

The revitalization of the Stud and its expansion into large tracts of the parks, coincided with the decline of deer hunting. George Tattersall reports in *Sporting Architecture* (1841) that 'the buildings at Hampton Court [Stud] are excellent, as far as regards the arrangement of the plan; and carrying out the idea is very complete. But I prefer for my own part a smaller building, as being more capable of management, and more generally adapted to any locality. There is a great waste of space at Hampton Court.'[16]

By the mid-nineteenth century the Stud was in decline and the Studmaster's house – once seriously considered as a potential royal residence by George IV – was regarded as little more than an official habitation for social grandees, or the Master of the Horse, the Master of the Buckhounds or the Crown Equerry. Whereas Queen Victoria took little interest in horse breeding and racing, some of her precursors pursued the sport with great enthusiasm.

The pavilions remained in grace-and-favour occupation throughout the nineteenth century. Although they were generally seen as occupying a very desirable location, some tenants expressed distaste for the neighbouring Barge Walk. For instance, in 1884 Mrs Wyatt, then resident of the last remaining pavilion, wrote to the Lord Chamberlain objecting to the bathing 'which takes place daily in front of the Pavilion windows. The scenes are most indecent – so much so that I do not like to describe them'; and in 1887 she again complained that opening a gate between the Barge Walk and the Terrace would render the house 'uninhabitable… from the extra number of tramps who will come into the area'.[17] Ernest Law, who was granted tenancy in January 1895, was equally hostile towards the public and enclosed part of the Barge Walk to extend his garden, as well as upwards of three acres of Home Park for his own use. Whereas the Barge Walk was a public right of way, the Bowling Green was private. The inhabitants of the Pavilion, therefore, perceived the seclusion of their premises to be under threat.

In the late nineteenth century considerable pressure was put to bear on the Crown to open Home Park to the public. Mr Shaw Lefevre – an ardent preservationist of open spaces – wrote in 1892:

… sooner or later the Park must be thrown open – there is a great population growing up on either side of the river from Kingston to Thames Ditton which it will no longer be possible to exclude.

Even now it is found impossible to exclude them when the Long Water and Ponds are frozen. They swarm over the fences in such numbers that it is found necessary to admit them.[18]

By 1893 two thirds of the park was opened and by 1897 the whole extent – with exception of the Stud, the Paddocks and the Pavilion – was opened as well.

Since the late nineteenth century the parks' ponds and canals have served a variety of recreational uses. The scale model boats of the Hampton Court Model Yacht Club have navigated the Rick Pond since 1897, and Ernest Law reported in 1891 that 'in severe winters' enthusiastic athletes 'may enjoy, on the Long Canal in the Home Park, some of the best skating to be had anywhere within twenty miles of London'.[19] The canal seldom freezes nowadays, making ice skating a rare event. The Home Park Golf Club was established in Home Park in 1895 to a design of the Scottish golf course designer, Willy Park. The Victoria County History (1911) notes that the 18-hole course has 'fine turf and was dry, though somewhat flat'.[20]

The Twentieth Century

From the turn of the twentieth century, Home and Bushy Parks supplied an extensive space for public recreation and diversion. Both the practical and symbolic roles of this space were determined by the transformation of the once rural surroundings into populous suburbs; the importance of the parks, as among the largest open spaces in the area, is poignantly accentuated in H.G. Wells's *The War of the Worlds* (1898). The Martians, advancing upon contemporary London, laid waste to great tracts of Surrey: Woking station was wrecked, the woods beyond Ham and Petersham were set on and Richmond town was burning briskly. Miraculously, however, the 'monsters' fail to inflict any damage on Hampton Court:

In Sunbury, and at intervals along the road, were dead bodies lying in contorted attitudes, horses as well as men, overturned carts and luggage, all covered thickly with black dust. That pall of cindery powder made me think of what I had read of the destruction of Pompeii. We got to Hampton Court without misadventure, our minds full of strange and unfamiliar appearances, and at Hampton Court our eyes were relieved to find a patch of green that had escaped the suffocating drift.

171. (right) Victorian
tourists by the Long
Water in Home Park
by David Cox Jr., c.1860.

172. (below) A solitary
Lombardy poplar in
Home Park.

173. The Rick Pond at the eastern end of the Long Water Avenue.

174. (right) Home Park under cultivation in 1947.

175. (far right) H.B. Zielger's view of *The Queen's Lodge, Bushy Park*, c.1830. The building is now known as Bushy House.

We went through Bushey Park, with its deer going to and fro under the chestnuts, and some men and women hurrying in the distance towards Hampton, as so we came to Twickenham. These were the first people we saw.[21]

The Martians showed greater respect for the parks than the British and Allied armed forces. Parts of Bushy Park had occasionally been used for the exercise of troops which were stationed there during the nineteenth century, and both Bushy and Home Parks were pressed into service during the two world wars. During the First World War grassland was put under the plough and land was set aside for allotments and accommodation for troops. A regiment of Canadian troops was stationed at Bushy and temporary buildings were established in the gardens of Upper Lodge, which served as a hospital. The parks were once again pressed into service during the Second World War (fig. 174). More land was given over to food production, a landing strip was formed by Hampton Wick Gate and a considerable area of the open grassland east of the Chestnut Avenue became part of a large American camp. Camp Griffiss, as it was known, became the site of Supreme Headquarters of the Allied Expeditionary Forces in 1944 and it was here, on the site of Wolsey's former Hare Warren, that the initial planning stages of the Normandy invasion were hatched. The last of the camp's buildings was pulled down in 1963 and the area returned to grassland.

The edges of the parks were the most susceptible to encroachments, since they offered immediate access to the residents of the neighbouring communities of Teddington, Kingston, Hampton and Hampton Wick. Allotments were among the earliest licensed enclosures. Several fields in Bushy Park were leased to Teddington Urban District Council for allotments from the early 1910s.

The removal of the Royal Stud to Sandringham in 1894 hastened the decline of the paddocks and of features associated with equestrian pursuits. The paddocks in Home Park became derelict and all but three were demolished between 1931 and 1935; one of these was cultivated as allotments by the palace's grace-and-favour inhabitants until the mid-1990s; another, which lies adjacent to the north side of the Great Fountain Garden, was given over to the palace's garden apprentices in 1974 and is planted with a wide variety of rare ornamental hollies, an unusual Hampton

Court clone of yellow-leaf horse-chestnut, as well as specimens of stone pine. This wedge-shaped garden is also known as the Arboretum or the Twentieth-Century Garden.

After the Second World War a satellite of the palace nursery was established in the former kitchen garden of Stud House. The garden for many years provided flowers and shrubs for many of the royal palaces. Some of Hampton Court's exotic plants are now over-wintered in temporary buildings in the nursery as both of the former orangeries are given over to the display of sculpture and Mantegna's *Triumphs of Caesar*.

Bushy House became the base for the National Physical Laboratory (NPL) in 1900 and remains in its care to this day. The grounds are remarkably intact and remain strewn with the litter of their former use: a seventeenth-century clock-house looms over the walled garden, and various nineteenth-century buildings, including a conservatory and a pair of lodges, can be perceived amid the shrubberies. Several important developments in military technology were made in Bushy in the twentieth century: radar and the prototype of Barnes Wallis's 'bouncing bomb' were tested and developed at the NPL, and in 1952 the Admiralty erected several large research facilities in the pleasure grounds of Upper Lodge to test and develop submarine technology. Lord Halifax's eighteenth-century water gardens were also appropriated for similar purposes. The testing facilities were demolished in the late 1990s.

Joseph Fisher, the Superintendent of Bushy Park, laid out the Woodland Gardens on the site of the former nineteenth-century Pheasantry between the late 1940s and the early 1960s. The Waterhouse Plantation was also recast in the 1950s: new ponds were dug, walks were laid out and great quantities of rhododendrons, cherries, swamp cypress, London planes and conifers were planted.

The Parks Today

In 1982 measures were taken to halt the decline of the fabric of Home Park: a historical survey was undertaken and a draft plan was prepared to guide their future management and use. Tree planting was identified as a priority – especially in respect of the park's historic avenues. The great gale of 1987 served to galvanize these plans: over 500 trees came down in Home Park – primarily

in the Long Water Avenue – and 1,329 were lost in Bushy Park. The great semi-circle of limes in the Great Fountain Garden was replanted in 1987 and the Cross Avenue in Home Park was replanted between 1992 and 1996 (fig. 177). The success of these initiatives prompted the palace to undertake the replanting of the Long Water Avenue between December 2003 and February 2004 (fig. 176). This avenue had become very patchy, having lost most of its original trees to storms and disease, and been inter-planted in a piecemeal manner over the past 150 years. The old avenue was felled and replaced with 544 lime trees of the same variety as the original seventeenth-century trees. The trees were carefully replanted in their original planting positions, which were determined by archaeology. The avenue was officially opened on 26 May 2004 by Prince Charles, who planted the last lime tree at the north-western corner of the avenue.

The British Mistletoe Society has recently identified the parks as possessing the south of England's most vigorous strain of mistletoe. This parasitic plant, which is commonly associated with apple trees, and rarely seen on oaks, has been found in great quantities throughout the royal estate. In Home and Bushy Parks it has colonized poplars, limes and hawthorns – and in numerous instances it has been found on immature trees. The new limes in the Cross Avenue, for instance, are already supporting healthy colonies of mistletoe.

Home Park has been the home of the Royal Horticultural Society's Hampton Court Flower Show since 1990. The show, which takes place at the west end of the park on either side of the canal, is the world's biggest annual gardening event. The exhibition area covers 40 acres and attracts around 190,000 visitors (fig. 178). The income generated by the flower show has represented a significant source of revenue for Historic Royal Palaces and supplied the principal source of funding for the restoration of the King's Privy Garden in the 1990s.

The Royal Household continues to own a number of features in Bushy, including Barton Cottage, Hawthorn Cottage, Upper Lodge Water Garden and the Royal Paddocks. White Lodge – the eighteenth-century lodge at the west end of Lime Avenue – was restored in 2001 and has become the park office. Two elements of Home Park remain in private use: the Stud and the Pavilion. The large immured pleasure ground of the Pavilion still evokes its

former use. In a 1965 auction notice the grounds were described as a 'delightful natural garden in a really peaceful setting'. The garden, which had a formal rose garden, a lily pond and 'some fine specimen trees and shrubs', was said to 'abound with tame wildlife'. Both parks have flourishing deer herds: Home Park has 300 fallow deer, and Bushy 100 red and 200 fallow deer. Bullocks and sheep ceased to graze in the parks in the 1970s. Ponies are still grazed in the paddocks east of Home Park and in the Royal Paddocks in Bushy.

In 2002 a fountain was installed at the easternmost end of the Long Water: it comprises five jets – a single one-hundred-foot-high geyser encompassed by four smaller plumes – to commemorate the fiftieth anniversary of the accession of Elizabeth II (fig. 179). The fountain – which plays regularly on the half hour – resolves what the mid-Victorian topographer John Weale opined was a great deficiency in the design of the canal: it lacked an eye-catcher at the far end. Writing in 1851, Weale remarked that the tower of Kingston Church gave 'an excellent finish' to the Kingston Avenue, but this 'happy circumstance reminds one too strongly of the defectiveness of the terminations of the other avenues, which would acquire much greater dignity by having a tower, pillar, or some object of the kind to stop them.' He recommended – very presciently – that 'a very artistic group of trees, carried up to a point by a large Lombardy poplar, would even be sufficient to finish the central avenue'.

Since 1989 Bushy and Home Parks have been under separate management: the Royal Parks Agency manages Bushy, and Historic Royal Palaces manages Home Park. Visitors nonetheless move freely between the two parks and perceive them as a single royal estate.

176. (far left) The Long
Water Avenue soon
after replanting in
spring 2004.

177. (left) The Cross
Avenue in Home Park.

178. (right) View of the
Hampton Court Flower
Show in Home Park.

179. (below) The Jubilee
Fountain at the eastern
end of the Long Water
in Home Park.

180. (overleaf) Heron
Pond in Bushy Park.

The Barge Walk

The Barge Walk is the name given to the three-mile-long crescent-shaped ribbon of land that extends from Kingston Bridge to Hampton Court Bridge and lies between the royal estate and the River Thames. The westernmost end of the walk was formed during the time of Henry VIII's extensive building works to the palace, at which time the river became a busy commercial waterway. It is, however, no longer a bustling thoroughfare: the barges that once plied its waters have vanished. The Thames here is a shallow, narrow stretch of river lined with trees, shrubs and paths, and studded with occasional low-lying, alluvial and gravelly islands variously known as 'aits' or 'eyots'. Erosion and scouring by current, flood, dredging, gravel extraction, cuts out of the river banks, embanking, weirs, locks, bridge-building and waterworks have all played a part in determining the present profile and character of the strand. These factors have also made the Barge Walk among the most ecologically rich areas of the royal estate.

The Barge Walk is now partitioned into three divisions, each of which has a distinctive character. The first stretches from Kingston Bridge to Raven's Ait – an islet in the middle of the Thames. The broad, hard paved towpath gives on to the Barge Walk Cottages and is skirted by horse chestnuts, limes and oaks set in smooth grassy swards. The second sweeps in a broad arc from Raven's Ait to the Pavilion: here the walk is at its most picturesque – the gravel towpath glides through long grass and past decaying elm stools and gaunt hedgerows. The third division is the most ornamental in character: the towpath widens into a broad dignified stretch, and marches past the Pavilion Terrace, the Privy and Volary Gardens and the Banqueting House, and lastly past the West Front of the palace. Here the foreshore is sprinkled with ash, poplar, elm and lime and bears the scars of the days when the banks were once a lively scene of commercial river traffic. One cannot, however, consider the character of the Barge Walk without casting one's eyes to the opposite bank: whereas the long strip of waste ground once gave extensive views over the open meadows of East Molesey, and the picturesque villages of Ditton and Kingston, it now overlooks rows of dwellings, their gardens and boathouses, as well as a variety of commercial and industrial premises which sit hard on the opposite bank. The area has, therefore, become increasingly seen as an important buffer between the royal estate and the neighbouring development, and its character

and management have become matters of considerable importance to the palace.

Wyngaerde's bird's-eye view of Hampton Court from the south depicts the river's edge in *c*.1555: a pair of islets emerge from the Thames, two landing stages project from the bank and the naked foreshore is littered with men and animals – all of which are dwarfed by the palace's leviathan water gate (fig. 22). Another view, from the early seventeenth century, shows the towpath raised upon a narrow shelf atop the riverbank and also depicts the outfalls of the palace's Tudor sewers, which formerly discharged waste into the Thames until they were made redundant in 1872.

The Barge Walk began to take its present shape as we know it today in about 1701 when the towpath was extended eastwards from the Pavilion – its earlier terminus – to the Kingston Bridge. Treasury Accounts report that in 1702 the entire length was bordered on its landward side by a bank, a pale and a single row of trees to enclose the paddocks at the east end of the park.

The first bridge at Hampton Court was raised at the westernmost end of the Barge Walk in 1753. This toll-bridge, which was designed by Samuel Stevens in the Chinese style and constructed about one hundred feet west of the present bridge, was a jaunty wooden structure formed of a row of humpacked arches arches, raised on wooden pontoons with fretwork balustrades and four pagoda-like pavilions flanking the central arch (fig. 184). The bridge remained a remarkably exotic addition to the Barge Walk until it was replaced by another more prosaic timber structure in 1778. The Hampton Court Bridge was declared 'free of toll forever' in July 1876 when it was purchased by the Metropolitan Board of Works. The brick and stone bridge that now spans the Thames is the fourth in this location and was built in 1933 to the designs of Sir Edwin Lutyens.

Late eighteenth- and early nineteenth-century surveys depict the Barge Walk as lined intermittently with trees, planted in groups or formal rows, and contemporary reports issued by the Office of Works suggest that sawn oak pales were thrown up to protect the hedges on the landward side of the walk from barge horses and grazing cattle. From about 1849 the area had become a favourite recreational walk for persons of the neighbourhood and visitors to the palace – its popularity coinciding with the opening of the South West Railway station opposite the palace. The Barge

181. The Banqueting
House and the Barge
Walk seen from the
Surrey bank.

182. The Barge Walk by the Pavilion. The brick perimeter wall of the Bowling Green is visible to the left.

183. (left) Bernard
Lens's view of the Barge
Walk, c.1730.

184. (below) View
of Hampton Court
Bridge from the Barge
Walk, c.1775.

Walk was a few years later described in the *Telegraph* as a 'public promenade' and a very 'picturesque spot', boasting six benches along its length. This picturesqueness was short-lived, as in the mid-1870s the Office of Works tidied up the area, stripping the margins of the river and the towpath of their trees, shrubs and groundcover. This round of embellishments attracted some criticism in the gardening and local press. Mr E. Lumley of Surbiton reported in the *Gardener's Magazine* (1875):

> The old wall which separates the Hampton Court Palace grounds from the towing-path has been despoiled of its beauty by the destruction of the ivy which covered it. He asks who is responsible for this act of barbarism, and protests against those who, like himself, love to linger by the charming old palace and gardens. We fear, says the *Surrey Comet*, it is now too late to do anything in the matter, as the whole of the ivy and the greater portion of the beautiful bank and brambles and other wild shrubs which made this walk by the river so pleasant, have been chopped up by the roots.[1]

The area, however, continued to be developed for public recreation: further seats were added to the walk in the 1880s and in the 1890s sheds for the storage of boats also started to appear on the riverside. In 1893 the Hampton Wick Local Board resolved to refurbish the Kingston end of the Barge Walk, which was described as 'a receptacle for waste' and a 'rendezvous for all the ruffians in the neighbourhood'. Those sceptical of the proposed

reforms alleged that improving the ground would only make 'accommodation for a pack of prostitutes'.[2] In the event, trees and shrubs were planted, benches were set out and fences were laid out to protect the grass and trees. Such changes led to an increased use of the towpath, and the combination of this factor and the growth of the neighbouring suburbs put an end to horse and cattle grazing on the foreshore by the end of the nineteenth century. The decline of this traditional use of the Barge Walk precipitated its designation as a public highway in 1906 and its closure to motorized traffic the following year. The highway was, however, no ordinary public right of way: the Crown expressed its opinion that it 'especially desires to preserve the rural and distinctive character which the Barge Walk now possesses'. In this respect they were very successful, as the towpath became so badly degraded by lack of proper maintenance that by 1917 it was declared to be 'very dangerous to any cyclist or horse'.

In 1902 the palace began to take a great interest in the riverbank on the Surrey side of the Thames when a thirty-seven-acre piece of land (the estate of the late Lord Hotham) immediately opposite the palace was put on the market. The Board of Works observed that insofar as there was 'nothing at present to prevent the land being let for any purpose' it was very likely – given the suburban expansion of Surbiton – that it would 'be utilized for some purpose involving the erection of unsightly buildings… which would be seriously detrimental to the amenities of the palace'.[3]

In 1909 the Board was successful in acquiring a seven-acre parcel of the Hotham estate – a triangular-shaped ground that lay between the railway station and the riverbank, and which later became known as Cigarette Island on account of a houseboat of that name that was moored on its banks from *c*.1910. The Board's ownership of Cigarette Island did not, however, safeguard the character of the ground; soon after it had been acquired the foreshore was cluttered with unauthorized houseboats that were something of a local eyesore, blighting the Surrey riverbank until they were removed in 1929.

The residue of the Hotham estate that was not purchased by the Board also posed potential threats to the palace's views. In 1921 the *Surrey Comet* announced that developers were poised to build a new 'Garden Suburb Scheme' on the Ditton and Molesey water meadows opposite the palace. The new development proposed by Utopia Garden Estates was described in the local press as 'the very

newest thing in garden cities with a touch of Venice thrown in; a Utopia in verity, not merely in imagination'. The watery paradise was criss-crossed with canals and 'artistic' Venetian bridges and was to be home to over 10,000 people; its promoter, Colonel Harry Day, and 'a number of influential gentlemen in the theatrical profession', suggested that 'those with a bent for Bohemian life, may, especially, find their tastes fully catered for'. This scheme, like the five re-submisisons that succeeded it, was rejected by Esher and Ditton Urban District Councils. The last scheme to be thrown out was, according to the *Daily Chronicle* in 1927, a 'miniature Venice, with canals and a fleet of gondolas for hire on the taxi-meter system' with a 'sort of "Coney Island" amusement park, laid out with golf courses, tennis courts and lawns for open air dancing'.

In 1925 the Barge Walk was described as 'exceedingly picturesque' and it was noted that large numbers of people made

PTON COURT, FROM RAILWAY STATION 6-573.

187. Tourists arriving
at the palace by boat,
1911. Note the boats
moored at Cigarette
Island (right).

188. (left) Photo published in the *Daily News* in May 1926 promoting the new 'Palm Beach' on the Thames, 'London's new up-river resort at Hampton Court'.

189. (below) The riverbank by the West Front of the palace.

use of it for recreation and exercise (fig. 188).[4] Its popularity can be gauged by the proliferation of ferry crossings which sprang up in the 1920s and 1930s: where in the late nineteenth century there had been three regular services, there were upwards of seven by the late 1930s taking local residents to and from the Barge Walk and Home Park.

In 1926 East and West Molesey Council proposed to schedule a portion of the development land on the opposite bank of the river as 'permanent open space', suitable only for a tree-lined river walk and sports pitches. The *Surrey Comet* pronounced that the scheme would 'very materially add to the beauty of this stretch of River … and would enable the Council to get rid of the ever increasing nuisance at present existing on the land in question – the Caravan Dwellers & Occupiers of Sheds, etc. which are anything but desirable and a menace to health.' The scheme was implemented in 1934–5 when the banks were planted with a line of chestnuts – a gesture which referred directly to the Chestnut Avenue in Bushy Park. The palace managed to halt the permanent colonization of Cigarette Island and the adjoining meadows with 'noisy and vulgar casinos, round-abouts, cheap bungalows and other attractions' (as the Office of Works described them), but was unable to staunch the tide of development which swept over much of the Surrey banks from the early 1930s onwards.

A new planting scheme was drawn up in the mid-1930s for the western edge of the walk – from the Privy Garden to the Pavilion – to block views to the new developments on the opposite bank. Sixty-two trees were planted, including black, grey and Berlin poplars, alders, wych elms, hawthorns and Caucasian wingnuts. This in turn prompted the Metropolitan Public Gardens Association to lobby for further improvements to the opposite end of the walk.

Although small pleasure craft had made use of the riverbank below Trophy Gate since the early nineteenth century, commercial passenger traffic on the Thames only began to take off in the 1870s when punts, boats, canoes, steam and electric launches, pleasure steamers and paddleboats began to ply the river, landing passengers by means of portable gangways. From 1890 the Commissioners of Works began issuing licences to control the spread of 'unsightly structures' of 'a more permanent character' that were being thrown up on the beach south of Outer Green

Court for storing boats. These arrangements were formalized in 1903 and again in 1916 when the Commissioners granted Harry Taggs and Joseph Theophilus Mears licences to erect floating landing stages for the use of their steamboats and launches at the western end of the Barge Walk.

River traffic began to decline in the 1940s after the building of the new Hampton Court Bridge and today only one 'local' landing stage remains in operation and a single concession – Turk's Launches – remains on the foreshore. Over the past few decades a variety of piecemeal improvements have taken place along the length of the Barge Walk, including the planting of new trees and the rebuilding of the riverbank. In 1998 the towpath of the Barge Walk was designated as a component of the Thames Cycle Route – part of the national cycle network. The Barge Walk is now regarded as an important ecological corridor and has been identified by the *Thames Landscape Strategy* (1994) – an integrated environmental planning and management document – as among the most outstanding stretches of the River Thames.

The Fame of Hampton Court Palace Gardens

For almost half a millennium the royal landscape at Hampton Court has inspired countless imitations at home and abroad. The objects of admiration have varied over the centuries – from bold and innovative gestures, such as William and Mary's extravagant parterre gardens and vibrant displays of carpet bedding in late-Victorian times, to features of extraordinary pedigree, distinctiveness and longevity such as the seventeenth-century Maze and 'Capability' Brown's Great Vine.

The reputation of the gardens was established in the reign of Henry VIII, when they became 'almost more famous and admired than the palace itself'.[1] No Tudor royal residence, except Richmond Palace, had gardens as magnificent and as extensive as Hampton Court, and no courtier's pleasure ground could vie with its palatial splendours. However, it is known that some features such as the Mount and its menagerie of heraldic beasts, were replicated in the grounds of the royal palaces of Nonsuch and Whitehall and at Lord Burghley's house of Theobalds in Hertfordshire. It is possible, too, that the gardens influenced the design of Philip II's garden at the monastery of San Geronimo (later Buen Retiro) near Madrid, as it is recorded in 1554 that the Spanish King – then husband of Mary I – instructed his architect to build 'galleries, towers, moats and flower-gardens, after the pattern of the country-house in England where he had lived with Queen Mary'.[2]

We know more about the reception and imitation of the palace gardens from the seventeenth century, when they exercised particular influence over the layout of nearby estates in the Thames Valley. These include the grounds of the 1st Duke of Lauderdale at Ham House, which John Evelyn described in 1678 as 'inferior to few of the best Villas in Italy itself', and which were supplied with a range of ornament including 'Parterres, Flower Gardens ... Groves, Avenues, Courts, Statues, Perspectives, Fountains'. Lord Ossulston at Dawley in Middlesex also appears to have borrowed freely from Hampton Court to enhance the setting of his estate, creating in the 1690s a great semi-circle of trees with radiating avenues and cross avenues in his park (fig. 191). And some time before 1740, the grounds at Osterley Park were recast in the Hampton Court taste for a rich banker, Sir Francis Child the Younger (fig. 192). Here a *patte d'oie*, a canal and wilderness were laid out to complement his substantial suburban villa. John Rocque's *Survey of the County of Middlesex* (1754) documents a variety of smaller villa gardens in and around the metropolis – such as Kempton, Hanworth and Moor Parks, Chiswick, Wanstead and Woodcock Lodge – which were also doubtless inspired either by first-hand experience of the Great Fountain Garden and the radiating avenues in Home Park, or by a knowledge of contemporary topographical descriptions and engraved prints.

The influence of Hampton Court's formal gardens also extended further afield – the most notable examples being the Great Canal dug for the 12th Earl of Kent at Wrest Park in Bedfordshire (c.1703) and Sir Thomas Hewett's extensive gardens at Shireoaks, Nottinghamshire (c.1710). The principal ornament of Hewett's ambitious 'watery' garden was a canal that was specifically built to surpass in length and ingenuity of design the Long Water at Hampton Court, where Hewett had been Surveyor-General of Woods and Forests. Hampton Court gardens also indirectly influenced a range of foreign gardens as gardeners came to the palace to train under the Royal Gardeners: in 1738 Matthew Charbonnière – son of Matthias Charbonnière, the court gardener at Herrenhausen – was put under the care and instruction of Charles Bridgeman 'for his Improvement in the Art of Gardening'; and in 1769, when Catherine the Great sent her gardeners Petr Andreev and Trofin Kondrateev to England, the Russian Ambassador in London tried to find them temporary positions at Hampton Court to gain practical working experience under 'Capability' Brown.[3]

From the late eighteenth century, interest in the great but decaying formal gardens of the palace began to wane and it was only the more antiquarian-minded visitors who admired the overgrown topiary of the Privy and the Great Fountain Gardens. What were generally considered outmoded vegetable deformities were, in their eyes, historical and horticultural curiosities. The fanciful gardens of clipped yew and box created by the next generation were inspired by the palace's topiary but were not contrived to be slavish re-creations of those at Hampton Court. These 'pure' topiary gardens – gardens without the complement of late seventeenth-century ornament – were an innovation of early nineteenth-century garden design and were made to stimulate imaginative musings on the remote past and to confer a semblance of antiquity upon the gardens and their proprietors.

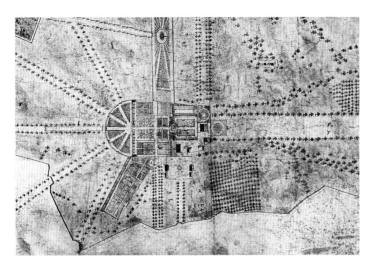

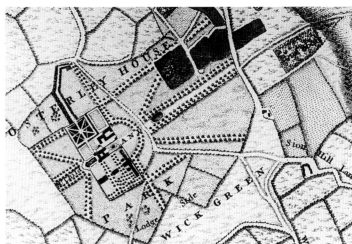

The topiary gardens at Levens Hall in Cumbria (1818) and Packwood in Warwickshire (c.1820) (fig. 194) owe a considerable debt to the decayed grandeur of the palace gardens; and Dorothy Whitmore-Jones's whimsical topiary garden at Chastleton, Oxfordshire (1833) was very possibly inspired by the same. William Barron's gardens created for the Earl of Harrington at Elvaston Castle, near Derby (from 1835) and William Andrews Nesfield's topiary garden formed at Witley Court, Worcestershire for the Countess of Dudley (from c.1864) were, it seems, created in the same antiquarian spirit. Both gardens were, however, planted with mature topiary, for immediate effect. Barron successfully transplanted immense cedars and yews, often hundreds of years old, and introduced a snaking topiary arbour and trees clipped into the form of birds into the gardens at Elvaston.

This interest in evoking the past through striking, large-scale borrowings from Hampton Court also extended abroad. W.H. Matthews reported that in the United States, where 'very few of the embellishments of bygone Europe have failed to achieve reproduction', Miss Cornelia Warren laid out a replica of the Hampton Court Maze in her garden in Waltham, Massachusetts. The labyrinth was planted in 1896 and was formed with native arbor vitae.[4] Further afield, Francisco Adolfo Eastman, whose maternal grandfather had been an under-gardener at Hampton Court in the 1870s, laid out a myrtle variant of the palace's maze at Casa de Los Reyes in the outskirts of Valparaiso in Chile (c.1920). A pair of palms was placed in the centre, in imitation of the horse-chestnuts at Hampton Court.[4] Between 1931 and 1933, the Chief Clerk of the Office of Works received requests for plans of the maze from South Rhodesia (Zimbabwe), Australia and Peru.

From the third quarter of the nineteenth century the palace's high standard of flower gardening and the originality and exuberance of its spring and summer bedding displays made Hampton Court a place of pilgrimage for gardeners everywhere. The 'flowery splendour' of the public gardens was unsurpassed and remained so until the First World War. Public enthusiasm for the palace's gardens reached its apogee in the mid-1920s when it was commonly held that the beauty of the gardens exercised a 'greater attraction to many visitors than the historical interest of the palace itself'.[5] This surge in interest was a direct result of the publication of Ernest Law's popular garden book *Hampton Court Gardens: Old*

and New; A Survey, Historical, Descriptive and Horticultural (1926) and his annual supplements entitled *The Flower-Lover's Guide to Hampton Court*, which supplied detailed descriptions of the famous gardens, plant lists (in English and not in 'absurd, uncouth Latin names'),[6] bedding schemes, as well as photographs, drawings and annotated garden plans. Ernest Law was also responsible for developing the public's appetite for old-fashioned English gardens. Early in the 1920s he developed a knot garden, which approximated Tudor exemplars, for Shakespeare's House in Stratford-upon-Avon. He later transported the idea to Hampton Court where he created the Elizabethan Knot Garden (fig. 55). From 1924, this became the inspiration for further knot gardens, including those at Kensington Palace (known as the Sunken Garden) and at Brompton Hospital Sanatorium in Frimley, Surrey. These gardens copied the planting, building materials and layout of Law's original.

Ernest Law's literary outpourings on the gardens at Hampton Court also served to define them as a storehouse of ideas, to be appropriated on a smaller and more modest scale for humbler settings. Although he remarked in 1891 that no money or art could possibly re-create the Pond Garden at Hampton Court, this small sunken pleasure ground became the palace's most copied garden. It first received lavish praise in Reginald Blomfield and Francis Inigo Thomas's *The Formal Garden in England* (1892), which encouraged its readers to make formal gardens in imitation of it. Rose Standish Nichols, the influential American author and landscape architect, later illustrated and described the Pond Garden in her book *English Pleasure Gardens* (1902), and used it as a basis for the design of a garden at her family estate at Mastlands in Cornish, New Hampshire.[7]

The Berlin architect and author Hermann Muthesius had a special regard for Hampton Court. He was profoundly influenced by Blomfield and Thomas during his stay in England between 1896 and 1903, and through his three-volume book *Das englische Haus* (1904–5) he popularized in Germany the taste for the geometrically arranged gardens of what he called 'the golden age of formal garden design in England'. Muthesius's contemporary, the Dusseldorf landscape architect Reinhold Hoemann, described the Pond Garden in 1909 as 'a remarkable piece of English garden design. It would have been worth travelling to England just to see

191. (far left) Plan
of Dawley Court,
Middlesex, c.1700,
showing radiating
avenues.

192. (left) Detail from
John Rocque's *Survey of
the County of Middlesex*
(1754) showing the
garden plan at Osterley
House.

193. John Sayers's *Plan
of the Royal Park at
Hampton Court* (1841)
clearley shows the
geometrical layout of
Home Park and the
palace gardens.

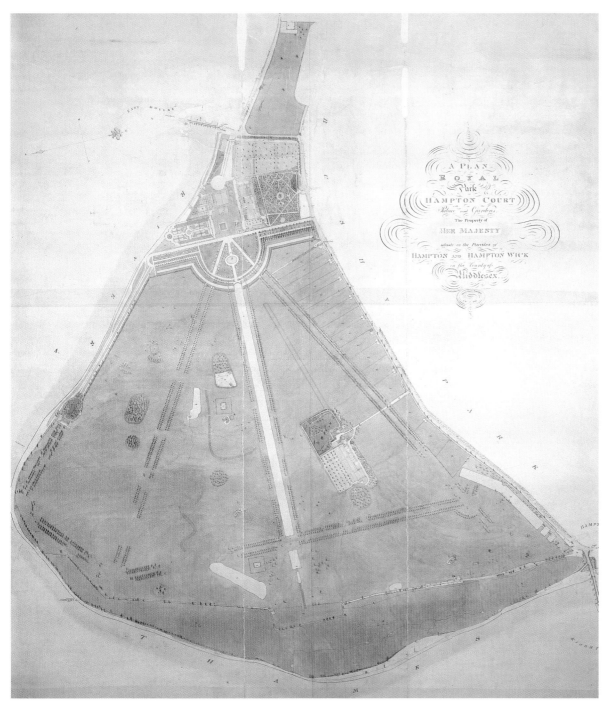

194. Victorian topiary at Packwood, Warwickshire.

195. (right) The heraldic posts in the 'Tudor Garden', St Donats Castle, Wales (2000).

196. (below right) Ceramic heraldic finials at the Somers Town Estate in London, 1934.

197. (overleaf) The Privy Garden at Hampton Court, after a snowfall, 2002.

this garden and, I do not doubt, that the impulses we were offered here, will bear plentiful fruits.' In this respect he was right: by 1913 the garden had been copied at a garden exhibition in Breslau (now Wroclaw, Poland) and within a few years it had also influenced the layout for the corporate gardens of Berndt in Zirlau, Silesia, and the sunken garden in the Vorgebirgspark in Cologne.[8]

A correspondent of *The Garden* remarked in July 1927 that the Pond Garden at Hampton Court was 'not only to be admired' but could actually be 'possessed, on a modified scale, even by a dweller in the suburbs, who has no more than a rectangular plot enclosed by the brick walls which divide him from his neighbours.' The plan could be 'adapted to suit both the individual purse and the size of the plot available'. The writer implored his readers to ' go to Hampton Court, and study the garden there. Note the planting arrangement, and above all try to feel the atmosphere of the garden, so that when it is reproduced, everything will be in harmony.' Readers were, however, advised to 'ponder over the plan' published in *The Garden* and 'after due consideration, decide whether it would be advisable to lay out an exact replica of the garden at Hampton Court, or whether to use only a portion of the plan'.[9] The Pond Garden was replicated by Ernest Law at Kensington Palace, and it was subsequently copied, with modifications, by the 6th Earl of Onslow, at Clandon Park i n Surrey.

Long-lost features of Hampton Court were also occasionally re-created in modern gardens. The sixteenth-century Privy Garden, for instance, inspired a handful of imitations – the most outstanding of which was the Edwardian 'Tudor Garden' at St Donats Castle in Glamorgan, South Wales. St Donats had had ties with Hampton Court from the time of Henry VIII; the royal palace, however, continued to exert influence on the Welsh castle centuries later. Between 1901 and 1909 Morgan Stuart Williams recast a broad south-facing terrace overlooked by the castle in an effort to evoke its Tudor origins: the ground was divided into four grassy plots arranged around a central seat formed from a sixteenth-century well-head formerly in the castle's central court, and a complement of King's Beasts mounted on slender stone piers was erected in the garden (fig. 195).

The fame of the gardens occasionally influenced other aspects of daily life. In the mid-1930s, the sculptor Gilbert Bayes created

a series of brightly coloured ceramic finials to crown washing post lines in housing developments built by the St Pancras Housing Improvement Society (fig. 196). These mock-heraldic embellishments were intended to cheer up the courtyards in these model workers' dwellings and were inspired by the finials that once adorned the Tudor Privy Garden at Hampton Court. More exotic and ephemeral were the 'novel garden table centres' devised by Lady Susan Birch, who in 1926 struck a 'new note in dinner-table decoration' with her 'shell-flower' table centrepiece, which was conceived as a miniature tribute to the gardens at Hampton Court. Her 'exquisite composition' was cunningly made to resemble 'an old-world wall garden, a little bit of Hampton Court – with the red wall covered with peach blossom, and with the flowers of the season in full bloom'.[10]

Since the end of the Second World War, several of the palace's major landscape initiatives have been directed towards the conservation of existing historic fabric and occasionally the restoration of early garden layouts. In the course of this work – and especially after the replanting of the Cross and Long Water Avenues in Home Park (1996 and 2004 respectively) and the reconstruction of the Privy Garden (1995), Hampton Court has become a leader in the field of landscape repair and restoration. These projects and others have contributed to a greater public awareness of the historic development of the estate, which has in turn promoted a greater enthusiasm for practical conservation and an appreciation of garden history.

Today the gardens of Hampton Court Palace continue to exert their influence and fascination far beyond the compass of the park pale. The royal landscape not only provides a magnificent illustration of the accumulated richness of five centuries of gardening, but also serves as a fitting setting for the palace of Hampton Court.[11]

Notes

Legend
BL   British Library
PRO   Public Records Office
WORK   Papers at the National Archives,
         Kew (NA)

Introduction

1 Strong, Sir Roy, *The Renaissance Garden in England*, (London, 1979), p.32.
2 'The King's mistress Barbara Villiers, Countess of Castlemaine and Duchess of Cleveland, had a keen interest in gardening, and may have been responsible for some gardening improvements during her Keepership at Hampton Court.'
3 Switzer, Stephen, *The Nobleman, Gentleman, and Gardener's Recreation* (London, 1715), p.39.
4 *Ibid.*, p.57.
5 *Ibid.*, p.62.
6 Law, Ernest, *The History of Hampton Court Palace*, (London, 1885–91), vol. iii, p.293. Ernest Law (d.1932) was the author of 11 guidebooks on the palace and its gardens.
7 *Penny Magazine*, vol. x, p.378.
8 Law (1885–91), vol. iii, pp.324–5.
9 Stroud, Dorothy, *'Capability' Brown* (London, 1984), p.123.
10 Barrington, Daines, 'On the Progress of Gardening', *Archæologia*, vol. vii (1785), pp.124–5.
11 Loudon, John, *Gardener's Magazine*, vol. ix (1833), p.478.
12 Law (1885–91), vol. iii, p.351.
13 Dickens, Charles, *Little Dorrit* (Harmondsworth, Penguin Classic, 1985) pp.359–60.
14 Law, (1885–91), vol. iii, pp.351–2.
15 Murray, John Fisher, *A Picturesque Tour of the River Thames in its Western Course*, (London, 1849), p.160; Howitt, William, *Howitt's visits to remarkable places* (London, 1840), p.233.
16 Cook, Emily Constance, *London and Environs*, 2nd ed. (London, 1898), p.446.
17 *The Times*, November 1852.
18 Law, (1885–91), vol. iii, p.368.
19 *Ibid.*, pp.410–1.
20 WORK 16 28/10.
21 Law (1885–91), vol. iii, p.371.
22 The first guidebook was George Bickham's book ii of *Deliciæ Britannicæ* (1742).
23 Dickens, Charles Jr., *Dictionary of London, 1879. An Unconventional Handbook* (London, 1879), pp.359–60, 440.
24 Law (1885–91), vol. iii, p.426.
25 Hutton, W.H., *Hampton Court* (London, 1897), pp.232-3.
26 *Journal of Horticulture*, 18 August 1910, p.155.
27 Law, *Hampton Court Gardens: Old and New; A Survey, Historical, Descriptive and Horticultural* (London, 1926), p.70.
28 Sands, Mollie, *The Gardens of Hampton Court: four centuries of English History and Gardening* (London, 1950), p.234.
29 The document was finalized in 2004, and launched in May of the same year.

The Privy Garden

1 Evelyn, John, *Elysium Britannicum, or the Royal Gardens*, ed. John E. Ingram (Philadelphia, 2000), p.123.
2 It is, for instance, clear that there was a knot garden as late as 1535–6 north of the King's gallery, and that the garden extended northwards to the chapel. This would suggest that the King and the Cardinal's knot gardens were possibly one and the same. It is also possible that Wolsey had a privy garden south of his gallery, and a privy garden south of the west range of the palace – south of Base Court.

3 Strong (1979), p.25.
4 Hentzner, Paulus, *A Journey into England in the Year 1598*, trans. R. Bentley, ed. Horace Walpole (Strawberry Hill, 1757), p.82.
5 E36/245 ff.61, 83 (NA); BL Add.MS 8219 f.133v.
6 Platter, Thomas, *Thomas Platter's Travels in England 1599*, ed. Peter Razzell (London, 1995), p.67.
7 *Ibid.*, pp.67–8.
8 Colvin, Sir Howard, ed., *The History of the King's Works*, (London, 1963–82), vol. iv, pp.36, 144; E351/3230 (NA); Colvin, vol. iv, pp. 36, 108, 144.
9 Platter, p.68.
10 Entry of June 1662, in Exwood, Maurice and H.L. Lehmann, trans. and eds., 'The Journal of William Schellinks: Travels in England, 1661– 1663', *Camden Society*, 5th series, 1 (London, 1993), p.87
11 Thurley, Simon, *Hampton Court: A Social and Architectural History* (London, 2003), p.223.
12 Edmund Gunter's *Description and use of his Majesties Dials in Whitehall Garden* (1624) is testimony to the King's infatuation with sundials of the most remarkable kind.
13 Marr subsequently published a 'description and use' of the instrument.
14 See Groom, Susanne, 'The Progression of Statuary in the Privy Garden at Hampton Court Palace', *The London Gardener*, vol. viii (London, 2003), pp. 36–51.
15 *Calendar of State Papers Domestic, Commonwealth*, 1659, p.204; Monconys, Balthasar de, *Journal des Voyages Monsieur de Monconys*, 3 parts (Lyon, 1666), p.78.
16 De Beer, E.S., ed., *The Diary of John Evelyn*, (Oxford, 1959), vol. iii, p.325.
17 Monconys, p.78; Magalotti, Count Lorenzo, *Travels of Cosmo the third, Grand Duke of Tuscany, through England during the reign of King Charles the Second* (London, 1821), pp.330–1.
18 *Ibid.*, p.330.
19 Exwood, Maurice and H.L. Lehmann, p.87.
20 Monconys, p.78.
21 Magalotti, p.331.
22 Lady Castlemaine was appointed chief steward of the Mansion and Honour of Hampton Court in the mid-1660s.
23 Thurley (2003), p.152.
24 The interaction of so many players in the design and layout of the Privy Garden makes it impossible to unravel. See Thurley (2003), pp. 236–7.
25 Switzer, *Ichnographia Rustica: or, the Nobleman, Gentleman, and Gardener's Recreation*, 3 vols (London, 1718), pp.150–1.
26 Switzer (1715), p.57.
27 WORK 5/52, folio 581 (1701–2).
28 Murray (1849), p.180; *Knight's Cyclopædia of London* (London, 1851), p.66; Cole, Sir Henry, *Some Thoughts on Hampton Court Palace* (London, 1859), p. 100.
29 *The Cottage Gardener*, 18 August 1887, p.137.
30 Law (1885–91), vol. iii, p.427.
31 Law (1926), p.60.
32 Unlike previous so-called restorations – particularly the Dutch Garden in the neighbouring Pond Gardens – this initiative broke new ground as it was the first instance which combined an informed archaeological and archival approach to garden reconstruction, displacing the impressionistic revival of English tradition.
33 Thurley (2003), pp.395–6.
34 Simon Thurley, ed., 'The King's Privy Garden at

Hampton Court Palace, 1689–1995', special edition of *Apollo* (1995).
35 The restoration was led by Dr Simon Thurley, then Curator of the Historic Royal Palaces, in collaboration with an in-house team of curators and various external specialist advisory groups; external contractors executed the building works and the palace's garden team carried out the planting and associated garden works.

The Pond Gardens

1 Jacques, David, 'The "Private Gardens" at Hampton Court', unpublished report for HRP (London, December 2003), p.6.
2 Christianson, Paul, 'The Riverside Gardens of Thomas More's London', unpublished manuscript (2003).
3 Switzer (1715), pp.57–8.
4 Gough, Terry, 'The Exotic Garden: restoration of William and Mary's Lower Orangery Garden', *Historic Gardens*, 2nd ed. (London, 2002), p.8.
5 Jacques (2003), p.19.
6 Cox, Thomas, *Magna Britannia et Hibernia Antiqua et Nova*, 1724, vol. iii, p.9.
7 The Trianon was contrived in the late 1660s for Louis XIV. See Thurley (2003), p.193.
8 The terrace was also known as the 'slope bank' in the Glass Case Garden.
9 *Gentleman's Magazine*, 1798, p.885.
10 WORK 16/150, 6 December 1825.
11 Carus, Karl Gustave, *The King of Saxony's Journey through England and Scotland in the year 1844*, trans. by S.C. Davison (London, 1846), p.120.
12 WORK 16/1240.
13 *Gardeners' Chronicle*, 10 June 1899, p.381.
14 Law (1926), p.75.
15 *Gardeners' Chronicle*, 1899, vol. i, p.381.
16 The last remnants of grace-and-favour occupation disappeared in the mid-1990s, when two garden sheds and a kerchief-sized plot were swept away at the south end of the Flower Quarter.
17 *Country Life*, 2 June 1900, p.709.
18 *Gardeners' Chronicle*, 1 March 1919, p.99.
19 *Daily Sketch*, 12 May 1914; Law (1926), pp.65–7.
20 Law (1926), p.68.
21 *The Field*, 27 May 1927.
22 *The Times*, 28 November 1951.

The Great Fountain Garden

1 De Beer, E.S., vol. iv, p.645.
2 Published in Law (1885–91), vol. ii, pp.277–308.
3 The building work was only completed in March 1692 when the plumber was paid for laying a lead roof over the carcass of the new range.
4 WORK 5/51.
5 Defoe, Daniel, *A Tour Thro' the Whole Island of Great Britain*, 3 vols. (London, 1724–7), vol. i, Letter III, p.8.
6 *Calendar of Treasury Books*, vol. xvi (1700–1), p.88; *Calendar*, vol. xvii (1702), p.1073.
7 Switzer (1715), pp.62, 57.
8 Langley, Batty, *New Principles of Gardening* (London, 1728), p.vi.
9 Defoe, vol. i, Letter III, p.9.
10 Defoe (1742 ed.), vol. i, p.239.
11 Boyd, J.P., ed., *The Papers of Thomas Jefferson*, vol. ix (Princeton, 1954), p.369; Simond, Louis, *Journal of a Tour and Residence in Great Britain during the Years 1810 and 1811 by a French Traveller* (Edinburgh, 1815), p.122.

12 Hughson, David, *Walks through London* (London, 1817), p.359
13 *Gardener's Magazine*, vol. ix (1833), p.478.
14 *Ibid.*, vol. xiii, January 1837, p.8.
15 Johnson's achievements were praised as evoking 'a sort of Arabian enchantment to one released from the whir and suffocation of London'. Cole, p.96.
16 *Gardeners' Chronicle*, 4 September 1841, p.584.
17 Quoted in *London Illustrated News*, 8 May 1847.
18 Trotter, William Edward, *Select Illustrated Topography of Thirty Miles round London* (London, 1839), p.61.
19 Knight, Charles, *The Land We Live In: A pictorial and literary sketch-book of the British Empire*, 4 vols (London, 1847–50), vol. i, pp.143–4.
20 *Ibid.*, p.143.
21 Elliot, Brent, *Victorian Gardens* (London, 1986), *Victorian Gardens*, p.14.
22 Beaton, Donald, *The Cottage Gardener*, 6 November 1856, p.84.
23 *Ibid.*
24 'The Gardens at Hampton Court', *Surrey Comet*, 20 August 1921.
25 Cole, Nathan, *The Royal Parks and Gardens of London, their History and Mode of Embellishment* (London, 1876), pp.39–42.
26 Law (1885–91), vol. iii, p.426.
27 *Westminster Gazette*, 14 June 1917.
28 'Hampton Court: A Note of Alarm', *Surrey Comet*, 15 February 1919.
29 *Gardeners' Chronicle*, 1 March 1919, p.98.
30 *Country Life*, 14 June 1919, p.713.
31 *Country Life*, 22 February 1919, pp. 207–8.
32 *Observer*, 24 August 1919.
33 Law, Ernest, *The Flower Lover's Guide to the Gardens of Hampton Court* (London, 1923), p.11.
34 *The Field*, September-October 1926.
35 *Daily Chronicle*, August 1926, p.11.
36 Knight, vol. i, p.142.

The West Front
1 WORK 1980.
2 WORK 1980, memo of 10 December 1890.
3 *Journal of Horticulture*, 4 October 1906, p.321.

The Courts
1 Colvin, Howard and Newman, John, eds, *Of Building: Roger North's writings on architecture*, (Oxford, 1981), p.63.
2 NA, Private Correspondence, 1816.
3 Boyle, Eleanor Vere, *Seven Gardens and a Palace*, 3rd ed. (London and New York, 1900), p.295.
4 The West Front had by this time ceased to be referred to as the 'Outer Green Court' and was sometimes known as the Palace Yard, or the Barrack Yard.
5 Bickham, George, *Deliciæ Britannicæ; or the Curiosities of Hampton Court, Windsor Castle…* (London, 1742), ii, p.58; *Knight's Cyclopædia*, vol. iii, p.61.
6 *Gardener's Magazine*, 23 January 1892, p.44.
7 White, Adam, 'A Biographical Dictionary of London Tomb Sculptors *c.*1560–*c.*1660', *Walpole Society*, vol. lxi (London, 1999), p.40.
8 Colvin, Sir Howard, ed., *The History of the King's Works*, (London, 1963–82), vol iv, pp.143–4.
9 Hentzner, p.80.
10 WORK 5/51, folio 537.
11 Macky, John, *A Journey through England in Familiar Letters*, (London, 1732), vol. i, p.71; Bickham, p.111

12 Murray, p.161; *Knight's Cyclopædia*, p.141.
13 *The Cottage Gardener*, 6 November 1856, p.84.
14 Law, *New Historical Guide*, p.175.
15 Boyle, pp.292–3.
16 *Parliamentary Survey* (1653) published in Law (1885–91), vol. ii, pp.258–71.
17 WORK 5/52 (February 1702).
18 WORK 19/1222.
19 Law (1885–91), vol. iii, p.328.

The Wilderness
1 E36/241, p.109 (NA).
2 Evelyn, 'Groves, Labyrinths, Dædales, Cabinets, Cradles, Pavilions, Galleries, Close-Walkes and other Relievo's', *Elysium Britannicum*, pp.139–60.
3 Sir John Soane's Museum, MS Court Orders Sir Christopher Wren, 1671 ff. 97r-99r; Wren Society, xviii, p.62.
4 Richardson also lamented the fact that the 'grand Entrance' [the Lion Gates] that led to the Wilderness from Bushy Park had 'pitiful low gates, which by no means correspond with the pillars'. *Tour* (1742 ed.), vol. 1, p.240.
5 Defoe, vol. i, Letter III, p.9.
6 *Ibid.*, pp.239–40.
7 British Library, Add.MSS 41135, f39, Sir William Chambers to Thomas Worsley, 13 September 1774.
8 *Journal of Horticulture*, vol. lvii, 5 November 1908, p.450.
9 *Morning Post*, 8 May 1913.
10 *Gardeners' Chronicle*, 1 March 1919, p.99.
11 Yates, Edward, *Hampton Court* (London, 1935), p.171.
12 *London in 1710. From the travels of Zacharias Conrad von Uffenbach*, ed. and trans. W.H. Quarrell and Margaret Mare (London, 1934), pp.153–4.
13 Evelyn, *Elysium Britannicum*, p.142.
14 Jacques, 'The Grand Manner', pp.129–31.
15 Anon., published in *The British Magazine*, 'Reflections on Walking in the Maze at Hampton Court'. *Archæologia: or miscellaneous tracts relating to Antiquity* (1785), vol. vii, p.125.
16 *The Mirror*, 6 August 1825.
17 Murray, p. 182.
18 Hutton, p.128.
19 Cook, p.446; *Journal of Horticulture*, vol. LVII, 5 November 1908, pp. 450–1.

The Tiltyard
1 PRO T1/81.37.
2 WORK 19/25/4; WORK 16/152.
3 *The Cottage Gardener*, 6 November 1856, pp.83–4.
4 *Ibid.*, 29 September 1881, p.286.
5 WORK 16/1086.
6 WORK 16/1086.
7 *Surrey Comet*, 3 April 1926.
8 Yates, p.172.
9 WORK 16/1087.

The Glasshouse Nursery and Tennis Court Lane
1 Switzer (1718), vol.ii, pp.234–5.

The Parks
1 Coursing means the hunting of hares with greyhounds; shooting is the killing of game with guns; hunting is the pursuit of game with hounds.
2 The last significant extension to the park was made in 1620, when Court Field was added to the south-west side of Bushy.

3 See Woodbridge, *Princely Gardens*, p.179, for this translation of Mollet's text.
4 De Beer, E.S. ed., *The Diary of John Evelyn*, (Oxford, 1959), vol. iii, p.324.
5 *Ibid.*, p.182.
6 Exwood, Maurice and H.L. Lehmann, p.87.
7 Magalotti, p.331
8 Switzer (1715), p.57.
9 PRO, T/1/126.
10 Swift, Jonathan, *Journal to Stella*, 31 July and 7 August 1711.
11 Switzer, Stephen *An Introduction to a General System of Hydrostatics and Hydraulics*, (London, 1734), vol. i, p.403, and plate xxxiv.
12 Langley, p.x
13 Jesse, Edward, *Gleanings in Natural History* (London, 1832), pp.60, 105, 152–5.
14 Brewer, J. Norris, *London and Middlesex; or, an historical, commercial, & descriptive survey of the Metropolis of Great-Britain*, vol. iv (1816), p.483.
15 Murray, p.185.
16 Tattersall, George, *Sporting Architecture* (London, 1841), p.9.
17 WORK 19/67.
18 Quoted in Thurley (2003), p.355.
19 Law (1885–91), vol. iii, p.421.
20 Cockburn, J.S., ed., *A History of the County of Middlesex*, Victoria County History of the Counties of England, (Oxford, 1911), vol. ii, p.387.
21 Wells, H.G., *The War of the Worlds* (London, 1898), p.191.

The Barge Walk
1 *Gardener's Magazine*, 27 February 1875, p. 98.
2 WORK 16/165.
3 WORK 19/84, 207 & 219.
4 WORK 16/1827.

The Fame of Hampton Court Gardens
1 Thurley (2003), p.89.
2 Sands, p.70. It is not known whether anything came of these proposals.
3 The Russian gardeners, in fact, ended working under Thomas Cloase – a collaborator of Brown. I am grateful to Dr Marcus Köhler for these references.
4 Matthews, W.H., *Mazes and Labyrinths: Their History and Development* (London, 1922), p.142.
5 *Acton Gazette*, 23 May 1924.
6 *Morning Post*, 22 July 1926; *Daily Express*, 22 July, 1926; *Daily Graphic*, 24 July 1926; etc. Law had earlier protested in a letter to the *Daily Chronicle*, and in his book *Hampton Court Gardens: Old and New* (1926) that 'horrible botanical names' disfigured gardens.
7 Birnbaum, Charles A. and Karson, R., eds, *Pioneers of American Landscape Design* (New York and London, 2000), pp.262–3.
8 Schneider, pp. 57–72.
9 'Making a formal Sunk Garden', *The Garden*, 16 July 1927, pp.460–1.
10 *Sunday Express*, 14 March 1926.
11 Law (1885–91), vol. iii, p.432.

Bibliography

Alan Baxter & Associates, 'Hampton Court Palace Barge Walk (Hampton Court Bridge to Home Park)', for HRP (London, March 1996)

Barker, Rosalin, *Hampton Court Palace Maze and Garden Trails* (London, 1991)

Batey, Mavis and Woudstra, Jan, *The Story of the Privy Garden at Hampton Court* (London, 1995)

Bezemer Sellers, Vanessa, *Courtly Gardens in Holland 1600–1650* (Amsterdam & Woodbridge, 2001)

Bickham, George, *Deliciæ Britannicæ; or the Curiosities of Hampton Court, Windsor Castle . . .*, 2 vols (London, 1742)

Birnbaum, Charles A. and Karson, R., eds, *Pioneers of American Landscape Design* (New York and London, 2000)

Bonner, G.W., *The Picturesque Pocket Companion to Richmond and its Vicinity, Hampton Court, etc.* (London, 1832)

Boulding, Anthony, *The History of Hampton Court Palace Gardens* (London, 1994)

Boyd, J.P., ed., *The Papers of Thomas Jefferson*, vol. 9 (Princeton, 1954)

Boyle, Eleanor Vere, *Seven Gardens and a Palace*, 3rd ed. (London and New York, 1900)

Brewer, J. Norris, *London and Middlesex; or, an historical, commercial, & descriptive survey of the Metropolis of Great-Britain*, vol. iv (1816)

Bushy Park at War: D-Day, Royal Parks Agency, 2nd ed. (London, 1995)

Carus, Karl Gustave, *The King of Saxony's Journey through England and Scotland in the year 1844*, S.C. Davison trans. (London, 1846)

Chettle, George Herbert, *Hampton Court Palace* (London, 1943)

Cockburn, J.S., ed., *A History of the County of Middlesex*, Victoria County History of the Counties of England, vol. ii, 2 vols. (Oxford, 1911)

Cole, Sir Henry, *Some Thoughts on Hampton Court Palace* (London, 1859)

Cole, Nathan, *The Royal Parks and Gardens of London, their History and Mode of Embellishment* (London, 1876)

Colvin, Sir Howard, ed., *The History of the King's Works*, 6 vols (London, 1963–82)

____, *A Biographical Dictionary of British Architects, 1600–1840*, second ed. (London, 1978)

Colvin, Howard and Newman John, eds, *Of Building: Roger North's writings on architecture* (Oxford, 1981)

Cook, Emily Constance, *London and Environs*, 2nd ed. (London, 1898)

Daniels, Harold Griffith, *East and West Molesey and their surroundings, together with an account of Hampton Court* (London, 1907)

De Beer, E.S., ed., *The Diary of John Evelyn*, 3 vols (Oxford, 1959)

Dedinkin, Mikhail, 'Hampton Court Rediscovered', *Hermitage Magazine*, vol. 1 (summer 2003), pp. 48–52

Defoe, Daniel, *A Tour Thro' the Whole Island of Great Britain*, ed. Samuel Richardson, 3 vols (London, 1724–7)

Dépret, Louis, *Windsor . . . le Château et son histoire, la forêt, Richmond et Hampton-court, récits et souvenirs* (Paris, 1863)

The Diary of Ralph Thoresby, F.R.S. . . . (1674–1724). Now first published from the original manuscript by the Rev. Joseph Hunter, 2 vols (London, 1830)

Dickens, Charles, *Little Dorrit* (London, 1855–7) (Harmondsworth, Penguin Classic, 1985)

Dickens, Charles Jr., *Dictionary of London, 1879. An Unconventional Handbook* (London, 1879)

Elliot, Brent, *Victorian Gardens* (London, 1986)

Ernest Law Collection of cuttings and photographs (c.1899–1926), Historic Royal Palaces Archive, Hampton Court Palace

Evans, J., *An Excursion to Windsor in July 1810 through Battersea, Putney, Kew, Richmond . . . and Hampton Court* (London, 1817)

Evelyn, John, *Elysium Britannicum, or the Royal Gardens*, ed. John E. Ingram (Philadelphia, 2000)

Exwood, Maurice and H.L. Lehmann, trans. and eds, 'The Journal of William Schellinks: Travels in England, 1661–1663', *Camden Society*, 5th series, 1 (London, 1993)

Gough, Terry, 'A Restoration Plan for the Long Water Avenue, Hampton Court Palace', unpublished report for HRP (London, April 2000)

____, 'The Exotic Garden: restoration of William and Mary's Lower Orangery Garden', *Historic Gardens*, 2nd ed. (London, 2002), pp. 7–11

Green, David, *The Gardens and Parks at Hampton Court and Bushy Parks* (London, 1974)

Groom, Susanne, 'Inventory of Statuary at Hampton Court Palace', unpublished report for HRP (London, 1996)

____, 'The Progression of Statuary in the Privy Garden at Hampton Court Palace', *The London Gardener*, vol. viii (London, 2003), pp. 36–51

Groos, G.W., *The Diary of Baron Waldstein* (London, 1891)

Grundy, John, *The Stranger's Guide to Hampton-Court Palace and Gardens* (London, 1843)

'Hampton Court Palace: Gardens Strategy Report and Recommendations', Historic Royal Palaces (London, June 1997)

'Hampton Court Palace Gardens, Estate & Landscape Conservation Management Plan', *Historic Royal Palaces* (London, February 2004)

Harris, John, 'Water Glittered Everywhere,' *Country Life* (6 January 2000), pp. 44–7

Hawthorne, Nathaniel, *The English Notebooks*, ed. Randall Stewart (London, 1941)

Heath, G.D., 'The Pheasant Court – The Confectionary – 'The Lyons' – Round Kitchen Court', unpublished paper, Heath Archive, Hampton Court Palace (London, November 1977)

____, 'The Bowling-Green Pavilions at Hampton Court', unpublished paper, Heath Archive, Hampton Court Palace (London, March 1985)

____, 'Guards at Hampton Court Palace', unpublished paper, Heath Archive, Hampton Court Palace (London, April 1985)

____, *Hampton in the nineteenth century* (London, 1993)

____, *Hampton Court: The Story of a Village*, eds Kathy White and Joan Heath (London, 2000)

Hentzner, Paulus, *A Journey into England in the Year 1598*, trans. R. Bentley, ed. Horace Walpole (Strawberry Hill, 1757)

Howitt, William, *Howitt's visits to remarkable places* (London, 1840)

Hughson, David, pseud. [i.e. David Pugh], *Walks through London* (London, 1817)

Hunt, John Dixon, 'The Anglo-Dutch Garden in the Age of William and Mary', *Journal of Garden History*, vol. viii, nos. 2 & 3 (London, 1988)

Hunt, John Dixon and Willis, Peter, eds, *The Genius of the Place: the English Landscape Garden 1620–1820* (London, 1975)

Hunt, Marylla, 'Hampton Court Palace – the Maze; a paper on the practical and technical issues', unpublished report for HRP (London, 1999)

Hutton, W.H., *Hampton Court* (London, 1897)

Jacques, David, 'Hampton Court Gardens: Archive relating to changes 1699–1713 at the PRO [Public Record Office]', unpublished document (London, 1994)

____, 'Hampton Court Gardens Strategy: A History of the West Front and Associated Barge Walk', unpublished report for HRP (London, December 1998)

____, '"Capability" Brown at Hampton Court', *Hermitage Magazine*, vol. 1 (summer 2003), pp.52–5

____, 'The "Private Gardens" at Hampton Court', unpublished report for HRP (London, December 2003)

Jerrold, Walter, *Hampton Court* (London, n.d.)

Jesse, Edward, *Gleanings in Natural History* (London, 1832)

____, *A Summer's Day at Hampton Court* (London, 1839)

Jordan de Colombier, Claude, *Les Delices d'Angleterre. Voyages historique de l'Europe*, vol. iv (Le Hay, 1706)

Keate, E.M., *Hampton Court Palace. A short popular guide to the palace and gardens* (London, 1932)

Knight, Charles, *Cyclopædia of London* (London, 1851)

____, *The Land We Live In: A pictorial and literary sketch-book of the British Empire*, 4 vols (London, 1847–50)

Knox, Tim, 'Hampton Court Railway Station Environs: Topographical Study', for HRP (London, November 1998)

Lambert, David, 'Notes on the history and character of the Barge Walk, Hampton Court', unpublished report for HRP (London, October 2000)

____, 'Notes on the history and character of the Tilt Yard Gardens', unpublished report for HRP (London, October 2000)

Land Use Consultants, 'Hampton Court Palace: Landscape Strategy and Resource Plan', unpublished report for Department of the Environment, Parks, Palaces Presentation and Central Services Division, London (London, September 1989)

_____, 'Longford River Strategic Management Plan', unpublished report for the Royal Parks Agency (London, May 2001)

_____, 'Bushy Park: Historic Survey and Landscape Management Plan', unpublished report for the Royal Parks Agency (London, July 2002)

Langley, Batty, *New Principles of Gardening* (London, 1728)

Law, Ernest, *The History of Hampton Court Palace*, 3 vols (London, 1885–91)

_____, *Hampton Court…a popular guide to the Palace and gardens* (London, 1921)

_____, *The Flower Lover's Guide to the Gardens of Hampton Court* (London, 1923)

_____, *A Short History of Hampton Court* (London, 1924)

_____, *Hampton Court Gardens: Old and New; A Survey, Historical, Descriptive and Horticultural* (London, 1926)

Longstaffe-Gowan, Todd, 'At play in the field of the Lords', *Antiquarian Book Review* (London, May 2003), pp.36–9

Macky, John, *A Journey through England in Familiar Letters*, 3 vols (London, 1732)

Magalotti, Count Lorenzo, *Travels of Cosmo the third, Grand Duke of Tuscany, through England during the reign of King Charles the Second* (London, 1821)

Mason, G.B., *The Stranger's Guide to Hampton Court Palace and Gardens* (London, 1825)

Monconys, Balthasar de, *Journal des Voyages Monsieur de Monconys*, 3 parts (Lyon, 1666)

Morris, C., ed., *The Journeys of Celia Fiennes* (London, 1947)

Murray, John Fisher, *A Picturesque Tour of the River Thames in its Western Course; including particular descriptions of Richmond, Windsor, and Hampton Court* (London, 1849)

Norden, John the Elder, *Speculum Britanniae, the first parte: An historicall, & chorographicall discription of Middlesex* (London, 1593)

Le Palais de Hampton Court; les tableaux, les tapisseries, et les jardins (London, 1862)

Peers, C.R., 'On the Stone Bridge at Hampton Court' *Archæologia*, LXII (1910), pp.309–17

Platter, Thomas, *Thomas Platter's Travels in England 1599*, ed. Peter Razzell (London, 1995)

Popular Guide up the Thames to Kew, Richmond, Twickenham and Hampton Court (London, 1879)

Quarrell, W.H. and Mare, Margaret, *London in 1710. From the travels of Zacharias Conrad von Uffenbach* (London, 1934)

Richardson, Samuel, ed., *A Tour Thro' the Whole Island of Great Britain* (London, 1742)

Ryan, Ernest, *The Thames from the Towpath* (London, 1938)

Sands, Mollie, *The Gardens of Hampton Court: four centuries of English History and Gardening* (London, 1950)

Saussure, César de, *A Foreign View of England in the Reigns of George I. & George II., the Letters of Monsieur César de Saussure to His Family*, trans. and ed. Madame van Myden [*c*.1725] (London, 1902)

Simond, Louis, *Journal of a Tour and Residence in Great Britain during the Years 1810 and 1811 by a French Traveller*. (Edinburgh, 1815)

Strong, Sir Roy, *The Renaissance Garden in England* (London, 1979)

_____, 'How did his Garden Grow', *Country Life* (17 February 1994), pp.46–8

Stroud, Dorothy, '*Capability' Brown* (London, 1975)

Summerly, Felix, pseud. [i.e. Sir Henry Cole], *A Hand-book to the Architecture, tapestries, paintings, gardens, and grounds, of Hampton Court*, (London, 1841; 2nd ed. 1843)

Switzer, Stephen, *The Nobleman, Gentleman, and Gardener's Recreation* (London, 1715)

_____, *Ichnographia Rustica: or, the Nobleman, Gentleman, and Gardener's Recreation*, 3 vols (London, 1718)

_____, *An Introduction to a General System of Hydrostatics and Hydraulics*, 2 vols (London, 1734)

Tattersall, George, *Sporting Architecture* (London, 1841)

'Thames Landscape Strategy: Hampton to Kew' (London, 1992)

Thurley, Simon, ed., 'The Privy Garden, Hampton Court Palace 1689–1995,' *Apollo* (London, 1995)

_____, 'Hampton Court, Middlesex: The Palace in the 19th century', *Country Life* (1 June 1995), pp.80–5

_____, *Hampton Court Palace: The Official Guidebook*, Historic Royal Palaces Agency (London, 1996)

_____, *Hampton Court: A Social and Architectural History* (London, 2003)

Travers Morgan Planning, 'Royal Parks Historical Survey: Hampton Court and Bushy Park', produced for the Department of the Environment, Directorate of Ancient Monuments and Historic Buildings (London, August 1982)

Trotter, William Edward, *Select Illustrated Topography of Thirty Miles round London* (London, 1839)

Up and Down the Thames, from London Bridge to Hampton Court…by the Victoria Steamboat Association's Steamers (London, 1893)

Views of Hampton Court Palace [with a description from Lysons' Middlesex Parishes] (London, 1800)

The Visitor's Handbook to Richmond, Kew Gardens, and Hampton Court, etc. (London, 1849)

Wells, H.G., *The War of the Worlds* (London, 1898)

Wey, Francis Alphonse, *A Frenchman sees the English in the 50s* (London, 1935)

White, Adam, 'A Biographical Dictionary of London Tomb Sculptors *c*.1560–*c*.1660', *Walpole Society*, vol. lxi (London, 1999)

Willshire, William, *The Stranger's Guide to Hampton Court Palace and Gardens* (London, 1866)

Woodbridge, Kenneth, *Princely Gardens: the origins and development of the French formal style* (London, 1986)

Woudstra, Jan, 'The Display of Exotic Plants at Hampton Court Palace', draft research paper prepared for HRP (London, September 2000)

Yates, Edward, *Hampton Court* (London, 1935)

Index

Page numbers in *italics* refer to the captions to the illustrations. The initials HC refer to Hampton Court.

Acknowledgments

The Publishers have made every effort to contact holders of copyright works. Any copyright holders we have been unable to reach are invited to contact the Publishers so that a full acknowledgment may be given in subsequent editions. For permission to reproduce the archive images on the following pages, the Publishers thank those listed below.

Ashmolean Museum, University of
    Oxford/www.bridgeman.co.uk:
    34–5 above, 105 below, 112, 138 above
Courtesy of the Austrian National Library,
    Vienna: 81
© The Trustees of The British Museum:
    12 (1961-4-8-1), 172 (1951-10-9-1)
© English Heritage. NMR: 90, 107, 142 above
Getty Images: 189
Courtesy of The Illustrated London News
    Picture Library: 19 left, 19 right, 140

Museum Boijmans Van Beuningen,
    Rotterdam: 84, 167 left
The National Archives of the UK:
    87 (TNA: PRO ref. WORK 32/311),
    195 (TNA: PRO ref. WORK 32/1349).
By kind permission of Orleans House Gallery,
    Twickenham, London Borough of
    Richmond upon Thames: 126 right
Pepys Library, Magdalene College,
    Cambridge: 42
Private collection: 174 below, 194
London Borough of Richmond upon Thames,
    Local Studies Library: 128
The Royal Collection © 2005, Her Majesty
    Queen Elizabeth II:
    11, 14–15, 83, 165, 173
© Vivian Russell: 196, 197 above
Reproduced with permission of St Pancras and
    Humanist Housing Association: 197 below

Courtesy of Sir John Soane's Museum,
    London/www.bridgeman.co.uk: 124, 163
© The State Hermitage Museum,
    St Petersburg: 48 below, 114, 118,
    120 below, 127
© The Collection of L.W. Strudwick: 190
© TfL Reproduced courtesy of
    London's Transport Museum:
    96 left, 120 above right, 133
University Library, Utrecht:
    138–9 centre (MS 1198, f.143v)
Christopher Wood Gallery,
    London/www.bridgeman.co.uk: 95 left
Yale Center for British Art, Paul Mellon
    Collection, USA/www.bridgeman.co.uk:
    155, 157 below, 168 left, 187 above

All other images are © Historic Royal Palaces